Mussolini and Italy

Edward Townley

Series Editor
Martin Collier

Heinemann

HEINEMANN ADVANCED HISTORY

H E I N E M A N N   A D V A N C E D   H I S T O R Y

Heinemann Educational Publishers
Halley Court, Jordan Hill, Oxford OX2 8EJ
A Part of Harcourt Education Limited

Heinemann is the registered trademark of
Harcourt Education Limited

© Edward Townley 2002

First published 2002

ISBN 0 435 32725 9

04 03
10 9 8 7 6 5 4 3 2

Designed and typeset by Wyvern 21 Ltd, Bristol

Printed and bound in the UK by Bath Press

Index compiled by Ian D. Crane

Picture research by Liz Moore

Photographic acknowledgements
The author and publisher would like to thank the following for permission to
reproduce photographs:

AKG London: 64, 130
Associated Press: 115
Corbis/Hulton-Deutsch Collection: 43, 122
Corbis: 92
Hulton Archive: 8, 15, 19, 32, 37, 53, 110, 135, 192 (top left, bottom left)
Popperfoto: 14, 20, 80, 192 (top right), 194
Topham Picturepoint: 38, 46, 54, 89, 192 (centre, bottom right)

Cover photograph: © Hulton Getty

CONTENTS

HOW TO USE THIS BOOK

This book is divided into two parts. The AS part attempts to explain what happened in Italy in the period from the end of the First World War in 1918 through to the end of the Second World War in 1945. It gives the student in-depth information and some analysis. The questions at the end of each chapter will challenge the student to use the information in the chapter to analyse, prioritise and explain the important aspects of the subject. In this way students will acquire a clear understanding of the key features of each topic. The topics selected and the depth of treatment have been based on the AS syllabuses of the major examination bodies.

The A2 part is more analytical in style and is related to major themes in the study of fascist Italy. Students who are intending to use an A2 section should read the relevant chapter in the AS part of the book. For example, those studying how far Italy was a totalitarian state should read AS Chapter 3 on the creation of Mussolini's dictatorship and A2 Section 4. The A2 part is written in such a way that it is also useful for AS students who wish to extend their understanding of the subject.

At the end of the AS and A2 parts there are Assessment sections. These have been based on the requirements of the new AS and A2 specifications provided by the awarding bodies. Exam-style questions are provided along with detailed guidance on how students might answer them.

AS SECTION: NARRATIVE AND EXPLANATION

Piedmont In the 1850s, Piedmont had expanded its economy to the point that it was the wealthiest state in Italy. Its prime minister in the 1850s, Count Camillo Cavour, had attracted French support to help remove Austria from Lombardy. This encouraged other states to vote for political union. By 1861 the union had expanded to include the south. Italy was complete with the inclusion of Venice in 1866 and Rome in 1870.

INTRODUCTION

Italy became a unified kingdom with Rome as its capital in 1870. The country had been unified under the leadership of the northern kingdom of **Piedmont** and unification had depended on foreign assistance rather than being the result of a great national movement. The inhabitants of the other Italian regions regarded unification with deep suspicion as a piece of Piedmontese expansionism and this survival of local rather than national loyalties was to prove a major weakness of the new state.

- Loyalty was hindered by the very high property qualification required before men obtained the right to vote so that even in 1900 only one man in fifteen had the vote.
- Internal cohesion was hampered by the refusal of the Catholic Church to recognise the new state and its forbidding Catholics to take any part in Italian political life. This was because unification of the country had taken Church lands in central Italy. The Catholic Church's stance was particularly serious for the new state because the vast majority of Italians were practising Catholics.
- The north and south were divided economically and culturally.

The south of the country, totally dependent on agriculture in a period of falling food prices across Europe, was backward and poor. Industrial growth from 1871 to 1919 took place in the north. There was much social unrest in the 1890s. Poverty led to outbreaks of civil unrest accompanied by violence. Forty thousand troops had to be used to restore order in Sicily in 1893 and in 1898 nearly

Italy in 1870. The dates of annexation to the Kingdom of Italy are shown.

100 people lost their lives in violent outbreaks in the industrial city of Milan alone.

Foreign policy

Italy was one of the lesser European powers. It established settlements in Eritrea and Somaliland in north-east Africa, but in 1896 suffered a humiliating defeat at **Adowa** when it attempted to expand its control into Ethiopia (Abyssinia). In 1912 it gained the colony of Libya. In 1882, it joined the Triple Alliance with Austria-Hungary and Germany. This gave the country diplomatic security. Unification had left many hundreds of thousands of Italians still under foreign rule in Austria, Switzerland and France. Many Italians hoped for the return of these so-called **irredentist lands**. Despite its membership of the Triple Alliance Italy remained neutral when the First World War broke out in 1914 and, in 1915, in the hope of gaining territory on its frontier with Austria, it entered the war on the Franco-British side.

Post-war instability

From 1919 to 1922, the country suffered from political instability and growing social and economic unrest, and it was in this period that the fascist movement, led by Benito Mussolini, emerged and established a small parliamentary presence. It soon abandoned most of its socialist ideas and became a right-wing protest movement, gaining support from those disillusioned by the aftermath of the war and fearful of revolutionary communism. By 1922, Mussolini had become prime minister in a coalition government and, in 1925, imposed himself as dictator.

The fascist state

The fascist state was dominated by Mussolini, first referred to only as the *Duce* (leader) of the fascist movement but, after 1925, as the *Duce* of the Italian state. Mussolini dominated political decision-making and also became the object of a vast propaganda campaign which presented him to the Italian people as an infallible leader. He became increasingly obsessed with international affairs and, in the 1930s, led Italy to create an empire in Africa, with the conquest of Ethiopia, and then into military alliance with Germany, where Hitler had seized power in 1933.

KEY TERMS

Adowa, 1896 This was a massive humiliation. In 1935 Mussolini invaded Abyssinia, partly to avenge the humiliation by an inferior Ethiopian force (see pages 105–12).

Irredentist lands These were lands predominantly in Austria–Hungary. They included Trentino, Trieste, Istria, South Tyrol, Fiume and North Dalmatia. All bar the last two were gained by Italy in 1919 under the terms of the Treaty of Versailles. To nationalists, the failure to get Fiume and North Dalmatia made Versailles a 'mutilated victory'.

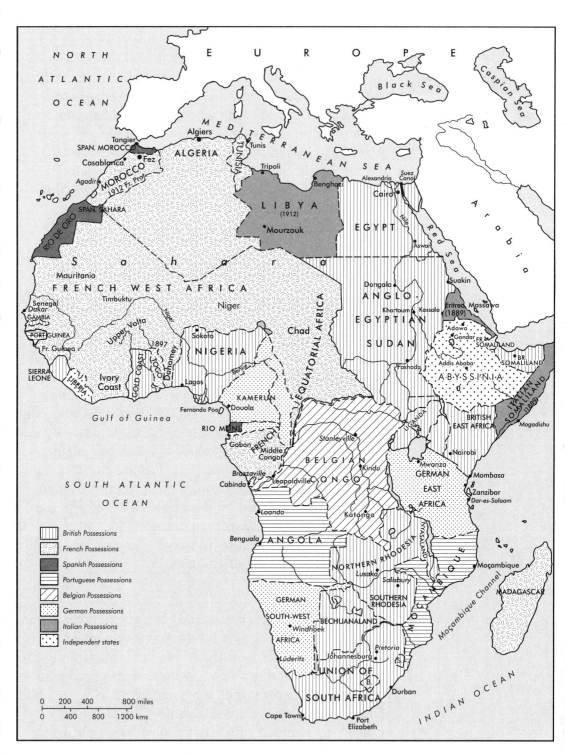

European possessions in Africa by 1914.

Mussolini and Italy

The collapse of fascism

The Second World War broke out in 1939: Italy joined on the German side in 1940, when it looked as though total victory was only a matter of days away. The Italian military proved generally ineffective as Italy was drawn into Hitler's extending war, first against the Soviet Union and then against the United States of America. By 1943, Italy itself had been invaded and Mussolini was deposed. The fascist dictatorship was at an end at that point, but Mussolini had a brief resurrection as a German puppet-leader in northern Italy. In 1945, he was captured and killed by Italian anti-fascist forces as he tried to escape into Switzerland.

CHAPTER 1

The weaknesses of Liberal Italy

INTRODUCTION

In 1919, **Benito Mussolini** led a loose organisation of mainly discontented ex-soldiers, known as the *fasci di combattiment* – the **fascists**. Despite the post-war turmoil afflicting Italian politics, in the 1919 elections the fascists failed to win a single parliamentary seat. Yet, in 1922, Mussolini became prime minister. His fascist movement still had only 35 seats out of the 508 in the Chamber of Deputies, the elected house of parliament. Mussolini was in fact put into office by a handful of prominent non-fascist politicians while those who might have stopped this happening remained largely inactive. There were both long- and short-term reasons why Liberal Italy turned to the fascists.

ITALIAN POLITICAL WEAKNESSES BEFORE 1914

Coalition politics

Italy had finally been united as one kingdom in 1870, with a constitution based on the model of a **parliamentary monarchy**.

- Its parliamentary constitution was similar to the British Westminster system with an upper house, the Senate, and an elected lower house, the Chamber of Deputies.
- The Senate, which had its members appointed on a lifetime basis by the king, was usually the less active, if only because of the advanced age of most of its members. The Chamber, elected every five years, was the more powerful of the two houses for, although government ministers were appointed and could be dismissed by the king, they were usually drawn from the Chamber.

KEY PERSON

Benito Mussolini 1883–1945 Prime minister of Italy and dictator 1922–43. He trained as a teacher and in 1902, while living in Switzerland, he became a socialist. He was expelled from Switzerland for revolutionary activity. After military service in 1910 he founded a weekly socialist paper and began a career as one of Italy's most notable jounalists. By 1911 Benito Mussolini was editor of the socialist paper *Avanti*. He was expelled from the Socialist Party when he abandoned the pacifist line and advocated joining the First World War against Austria. In 1914, he founded the important paper *Il Popolo d'Italia*, which after the end of the war became the main single source for spreading the fascist message. In 1915, when Italy entered the war, he joined the army and was wounded. He returned to journalism in 1917 where he took a fiercely anti-pacifist and anti-socialist line.

KEY TERMS

Fascists Groups founded in 1917–18 to fight those they felt were unpatriotic. After 1919, they built up a strong-arm presence in several of the northern cities but were still not in any position to seize power by force.

Parliamentary monarchy The king was head of the state but political power rested in parliament.

Political instability

By 1914, it might seem likely that Italians, after over 40 years, should have got used to the practice of parliamentary politics and for this reason alone that the political system should have acquired some stability. However, the system had many weaknesses and, in the years immediately before 1914, became more difficult to manage. Since the creation of the Italian state, political life had been the monopoly of a small social elite: the **franchise** was, prior to 1912, extended to only 2 million men. An element of stability was, however, provided by the monarchy, with Victor Emmanuel III becoming king in 1900, a post he held until 1946.

Trasformismo

In parliament, political parties were weak. Political principles or philosophy played little part in the government of the state. The groupings of middle-class **liberal** politicians moved in and out of office as the result of deals among themselves that involved the creation of large political coalitions. Politicians were encouraged to join these coalitions by being bribed with favours. This was known as *trasformismo*. The politician most closely associated with *trasformismo* was **Giovanni Giolitti**, who was prime minister on five separate occasions between 1892 and 1922. The dominant political group, the liberals, was made up of a series of informal personal groupings. It was not a structured party, and had no need to organise itself or to develop formal links with the parliamentary constituencies in a period when few had the vote. Alongside the liberals was a small group of radicals, often divided among themselves but generally in favour of more economic freedom, lower taxes and reform of the monarchy and the military. In 1895, a Republican Party was created with a political agenda not unlike that of the radicals; but, for personal reasons, they were generally unable to work together.

The *trasformismo* system did little to solve Italy's pressing social and economic problems. By 1914, Italy still faced the problems of illiteracy, sanitary squalor, excessive rates of emigration, regional differences and the economic backwardness of many of the rural areas.

ECONOMIC AND SOCIAL PROBLEMS

Italy was plagued by a range of difficult economic problems arising from limited industrial development and an inefficient agrarian economy. Central to these was what is still commonly referred to as the problem of **the south**, where a primitive peasant agriculture supported a social and political order dominated by a few great landowning families. The south formed one of the most backward regions of Europe and the north–south divide was to be one of Italy's most enduring problems.

Agrarian society
The north
- On the north Italian plains, agriculture underwent revolutionary changes in the period 1890–1910 with new crops like sugar beet alongside the traditional production of wheat, production of which nevertheless improved sharply.
- It was an area of diverse and profitable agriculture with crops such as grapes, rice, olives and maize alongside dairy farming.
- Mechanisation, fertilisers and irrigation schemes made farming more efficient.
- In this region the days of the subsistence peasant farmer, growing food largely to feed the family, were over. Larger farms run by **capitalist** tenant farmers employing landless farm labourers on short contracts became the norm. The result was **social division**.

The south
In more remote hill areas and, above all, in the southern mainland and in Sicily and Sardinia there was little change in agriculture between 1871 and 1919.

- Here agriculture was still desperately backward, poverty widespread and society and the land despotically controlled by small numbers of landowners.
- Incomes in the south were perhaps half what they were in the economically advanced northern region.
- Government schemes to improve the southern economy – transport improvements and industrial subsidies – had

Giovanni Giolitti in 1910.

KEY TERM

Malaria Before 1900, more than 15,000 people died of malaria in the south every year. The disease comes from swamps, which are home to the malaria-carrying mosquitoes. Between 20 per cent and 30 per cent of all deaths in the south were malaria related.

KEY STATISTICS

Steel production This increased from 140,000 tonnes (each 1000 kilograms) in 1900 to 930,000 in 1913. Iron production rose from 20,000 tonnes to 430,000 tonnes in the same period.

KEY TERM

Nationalised Owned by the state.

little effect and socially and economically the south remained a different, backward world.

- Most damaging to the south was **malaria**.

INDUSTRY

The 20 years before the First World War saw impressive industrial growth, based on a dramatic expansion in hydroelectric power and with new engineering industries developing rapidly in the northern towns. **Steel production** increased and yet, such was the general economic expansion, great quantities of iron, steel and coal still had to be imported. The state played a much greater part in industrial development than was the case in Britain and France.

- Government pressure was put on the banks to provide money for hydroelectricity schemes and for setting up electricity companies.
- State subsidies were provided for industries regarded as politically important, notably shipbuilding.
- Other industries were protected by tariffs on competing foreign imports.
- In 1905, the financially fragile railway system was **nationalised**.

A pattern of state intervention in the industrial and financial economy was well established before 1914, and new political ideas began to pave the way for fascism.

Compared with other European industrial nations, however, Italy was still an industrial infant and, even in 1914, is best seen as still a largely agrarian country. One noteworthy consequence of the industrial acceleration was the emergence, in north and central Italy, of a significant urban working class that was to add a potentially troublesome political element to Italian society.

REVOLUTIONARY NATIONAL IDEAS

In the last years before the First World War Italian

The weaknesses of Liberal Italy   9

intellectual life was confronted with a range of radical new ideas that, by challenging the liberal consensus, had a great impact on the course of Italian history. Among the most influential figures propounding these ideas were Gabriele D'Annunzio (see page 20) and **Filippo Marinetti**. The new climate of ideas was hostile to the Liberal State. The leading intellectual of the time, Benedetto Croce, systematically attacked the corruption and the drift in Italian society, and helped to create a climate where intelligent people came to despise the state they lived in and began to look for cleaner, more vigorous, models of how society should be organised.

INCREASED POLITICAL INSTABILITY, 1900–14

New political movements
None of the social and economic changes need have led to imminent political breakdown but, even before 1914, the political system was also becoming increasingly difficult for the liberal politicians to manage. The most obvious threat to a political system with a narrow base of support was the emergence of parties with mass support.

The Socialist Party
In the 1890s, the Socialist Party (the PSI), founded in Genoa in 1892, had built a base in the northern industrial towns and, by 1900, had 32 seats in the Chamber of Deputies and was producing its own daily newspaper *Avanti*. The **socialist** deputies were mainly middle-class intellectuals. In 1904, 22 out of 28 PSI deputies were university graduates. Giolitti found it difficult to absorb the socialist deputies into a coalition. The leading socialist was Filippo Turati who, in 1903, declined to join Giolitti's government because of the bitter feelings among the working class about government suppression of union activity. However, some socialists were prepared to be bribed although this divided the PSI (see **Socialist division** opposite).

Catholic involvement
After 1904, there was growing political activity and organisation among Catholics. In that year the papacy,

KEY PERSON

Filippo Marinetti 1876–1944 A poet and masterly publicist who, in 1909, founded the important artistic movement, the Futurists, which set out to challenge the cultural torpor of Italian society. In his writings he welcomed the new industrial age dominated by machinery, embraced the idea of speed and glorified the nobility of war. He had great influence over other writers and artists on a European-wide basis and attracted a large and excited following among educated Italians. He played a significant part in preparing Italian society first for entry into the First World War and later for the tempting vigour of fascism. As an active artistic movement, Futurism failed to survive the horrors of the war but Marinetti went on to become a fascist in March 1919, attending the inaugural meeting in Milan and playing an important role in the early development of fascist radical ideas that, by 1922, had been discarded.

KEY TERM

Socialism A political and economic theory that advocates that the community as a whole should own and control the economy (the means of production, distribution and exchange).

frightened by the growth of socialism, had relaxed the prohibition on Catholic participation in Italian politics known as 'non-expedit' that had been issued in 1881 by Pope Leo XIII. In the 1909 election, seventeen Catholic deputies were elected to the Chamber. In 1913, the Catholic Electoral Union sought guarantees on educational issues and attitudes to divorce before it recommended Catholics to vote for individual liberal candidates – the so-called **Gentiloni Pact.**

The main issue that divided Church and state was the 'Roman Question' – that is, who controlled Rome. The papacy felt that Rome had been illegally taken from them in 1871; the state denied the Church's right to control Rome. Until the Roman Question was resolved, the Church refused to recognise the state.

Like the socialists, individual Catholic politicians remained outsiders to government and yet, by 1914, the mass voting power they commanded made them indispensable partners in *trasformismo* politics; they often voted with the liberals in the Chamber and shared power with them in the local government of cities like Turin and Florence. The most influential of the Catholic political leaders was the priest **Luigi Sturzo.**

The Nationalist Party

A right-wing Nationalist Party emerged as a political force in the years immediately before 1914. It had its origins in the fact that many Italians felt that the Liberal State had failed to build a proper Italian nation.

The nationalists were also affected by feelings of inferiority because Italy had been left behind in the race to build an overseas empire: in 1881, for example, the French had occupied Tunis and, in 1896, an Ethiopian force had inflicted a humiliating defeat on the Italian army at Adowa. The nationalists became politically more significant as a result of the imperial excitement sparked off in 1911 by the start of a war to seize Libya from the collapsing Turkish Empire.

Nationalist newspapers and journals flourished, calling for a more active foreign and imperial policy and demanding increased military spending. They were clearly a party of the right, embracing conservative social values; fiercely anti-socialist, they wanted strong laws to curb trade union activity. The nationalists could not be absorbed by a Liberal State which they saw as weak.

The emergence of these new political groups, all appealing in different ways to a new mass electorate, meant that the liberal system of coalition politics, based on narrow class interests and revolving around a few well-known individuals, would be very much more difficult to sustain in the future.

Italian gains at Versailles Treaty, 1919

Italy, 1919–22.

A wider franchise

In 1912, the need to ensure continued support for the difficult Libyan war led politicians to extend the vote to all men once they reached 30 years of age. This new electorate, increased in 1912 from 3 million to over 8 million male voters, could no longer be as easily manipulated or bribed as the nineteenth-century electorates had been. The middle classes were appalled at the ignorance of the new electors, 70 per cent of whom, it was estimated, could neither read nor write. Italy was entering a new age of mass politics that would pose unknown dangers for the survival of *trasformismo* politics practised by the narrowly based elite of liberal politicians. Italian political life was already becoming more turbulent before Italy entered the **First World War**. Then, in 1915, Italy's entry into the First World War bitterly divided the liberal politicians.

THE PRESSURE OF THE FIRST WORLD WAR ON ITALIAN POLITICAL LIFE

Introduction

Rather than unifying the Italian people, the experiences of war created deep divisions among them, most notably between the war's supporters and those who opposed it or saw it as a mistake. These divisions were still there at the war's end and proved fatal to the continuation of the traditional Liberal State. By creating serious new social and economic problems, by sowing discord among Italy's political leaders and by creating a volatile electorate in the country, the war greatly intensified the danger of political breakdown.

Intervention in the war: Italy's problem

The outbreak of the European war in July–August 1914 created grave problems for Italy's leaders.

- On the one hand, since 1882 the country had been committed by the defensive alliance with both Germany and the Austrian Empire. To abandon the alliance with such powerful countries could expose Italy to many dangers.

Impact of the First World War The importance of the war in destabilising Italian society should not be underestimated. High inflation between 1914 and 1918 devastated the savings held by the middle classes. Increasing worker militancy and occupation of the land by the landless labourers increased the feelings of insecurity among the middle classes. To this sector of Italian society, the threat of revolution seemed very real.

- On the other hand, Italy had serious territorial ambitions on its northern frontier that could only be achieved at the expense of Austria and, therefore, the obligations to the Triple Alliance.

Fortunately, in 1914 Italy was able to treat Austria as being the wartime aggressor against its small Balkan neighbour Serbia so that the defensive nature of the Alliance allowed Italy to remain neutral in the early months of the war.

The prime minister, **Antonio Salandra**, and his foreign minister Sidney Sonnino felt emotionally committed to wresting as much 'Italian' land from Austria as they could and there was no doubting the strength of public feeling on the issue. Negotiations with the Austrians produced minimal concessions of territory so that the Italian government opened negotiations with France and Britain and, in April 1915, signed the **Treaty of London**.

Intervention in the war, 1915

In May, Salandra denounced the Austro-German alliance and entered the war on the Franco-British side. The risks were enormous, for the Austro-German alliance might well emerge victorious from the war and would then wreak a terrible revenge on Italy. Continuing neutrality was an equally uncertain option: it would avoid the hardships of war but, almost certainly, would bring no territorial gains regardless of which side was victorious.

Political divisions over intervention

Joining the war immediately imposed enormous strains on the country's political system; it deeply divided Italy's leading liberal politicians. Salandra used the king's executive power and took the country into the war almost secretively, without consulting parliament. This was not unconstitutional, for matters of peace and war were the responsibility of the king and his government. However, most Italians were opposed to entering the war and even some members of the government were unconvinced. Giolitti, the most experienced politician of the pre-war period, was outraged. The majority of members of parliament – deputies and senators – were opposed to entering the war.

Antonio Salandra.

Mussolini in 1921, aged 39.

- The nationalists strongly favoured intervention, as did many leading radicals and republicans. Marinetti and the other Futurists along with the warlike D'Annunzio used their popularity and considerable intellectual stature to promote Italian intervention. With war fever so strong, patriotism became the best available card for right-wing leaders to play.
- The leaders of the Catholic Church were often against intervention but tended to keep diplomatically quiet and co-operated with the war effort. The socialists were more openly critical of the conduct of the war but avoided opposing it in principle. Socialist leaders, often middle-class intellectuals, tended to be more anti-war than the rank and file of the party.
- The outstanding exception was the gifted journalist and orator, Benito Mussolini (see page 6), who abandoned his socialist **pacifist** stand and wrote and spoke passionately in favour of intervention. He was sacked from his post as editor of the official socialist paper *Avanti* and expelled from membership of the Socialist Party, but went on to found the strongly pro-war paper *Popolo d'Italia*.
- The right-wing Salandra hoped for a short war to strengthen the Liberal State. His hopes were dashed. His government fell in June 1916.
- Other 'democratic interventionists' like the radical Francesco Nitti favoured intervention but wanted a national war, harnessing public opinion to a great struggle to liberate Italians under Austrian rule. This never happened.

Wartime politics

The majority in the Chamber of Deputies had been opposed to intervention in the war and were never reconciled to its conduct. Neither the Catholics nor the socialists took any part in government and even the various liberal leaders remained divided over its conduct. **Wartime governments** were therefore politically weak and failed totally to rally national enthusiasm for the war:

- Giolitti, with a following of 100 deputies, had been against intervention and wanted peace negotiations. He was accused of defeatism and was politically isolated outside his own group. He had been the best known of the pre-war liberal leadership and his new isolation was probably the single most unfortunate domestic political consequence of Italy's intervention in the war.

The difficulties that political leaders had in working together to provide wartime Italy with effective government reflected the deep divisions brought about by the manner of its entry into the war and remained unresolved at its end.

The impact of war: military events

The Italian forces became bogged down in a war of attrition conducted over months of trench warfare and artillery bombardments along the foothills of the Alps. Five million men, mainly conscripts, fought bravely in appalling conditions suffering around 1.3 million casualties between 1915 and 1918.

In October 1917, the Austrian forces, stiffened by the presence of German troops, ended the stalemate by breaking through the Italian lines at the Battle of **Caporetto**, throwing the Italian army back in complete chaos over 160 kilometres and taking over 300,000 prisoners. The initial enemy penetration had turned into a rout when the Italian command structure had collapsed and reserve troops were not brought into the line. **General Luigi Cadorna** blamed defeat on the cowardice of the troops and had several hundred of them shot.

After Caporetto, the Italian army was fighting on Italian soil to prevent further enemy advances into the heart of the country. Grimly they held on under a new and more competent commander, General Armando Diaz. Rations and facilities improved and discipline became less arbitrary. Special groups of commandoes – the *Arditi* – were formed and carried out daring raids on and behind enemy lines. It was only when Austria itself was on the point of political collapse in 1918 that the Italian army mounted a full-scale assault on its lines. This in turn led to a collapse in Austrian morale and, in the very last days of the war, the Italians could claim a major victory as their armies swept on unopposed. This was the much publicised **victory of Vittorio Veneto.**

The impact of war: the economy

The war imposed great strains on the Italian economy and Italian society. The country made immense strides in developing its wartime armaments production and ended the war with more artillery than the British army and by building, in 1918 alone, over 6500 aircraft. The First World War is commonly described as a **total war**. The term can justly be applied to the Italian effort for, in addition to the large conscript army, the philosophy adopted for war supplies was one of production at any cost. Companies such as **Fiat** received cheap loans to re-equip factories and military contracts on favourable terms. Inevitably, it was the industrialised north that benefited most from war finances and the gap with the still poverty-stricken south grew ever wider. A few firms made huge profits – Fiat grew fivefold on the strength of demand for army vehicles – but industry generally became too dependent on wartime demand and faced problems when war ended abruptly in 1919.

To achieve maximum war production the government ran up large budget deficits and borrowed heavily abroad, especially from Britain. As a result, the post-war **national debt** stood at 85 billion lira, a fivefold increase on the 1914 figure. This disturbing increase must, however, be set against the fact that, owing to the government also financing war production by printing money, the value of the lira at the end of the war was only a quarter of what it had been in 1914. The vast size of the national debt might have seemed a crippling burden to politicians faced with the urgent problems of post-war reconstruction but it was the consequences of **inflation**, with prices four times higher in 1918 than they had been before the war, that were to prove the more potent source of social and political turbulence.

The impact of war: the society
Town

* The most immediate and dramatic impact of the war on the 'home front' was that industrial workers and the factories were placed under military discipline with men no longer free to move jobs or to strike.

KEY TERMS

Total war One in which all of the nation's human and economic resources are committed to securing victory.

Fiat A car manufacturing company founded in 1899 by a number of cavalry officers, including Giovanni Agnelli. Fiat stands for *Fabbrica Italiano Automobile Torino* – Italian cars made in Turin.

National debt The total debt owed by the state to its own citizens and to foreign creditors.

Inflation A general rise in prices leading to a fall in the purchasing power of money.

- This, coupled with price inflation running 25 per cent ahead of wage increases and food shortages, built up great resentment among the urban workforce.
- In 1917, food riots in Turin had to be put down by the military whose actions led to some 50 deaths.
- The wartime discontent among industrial workers led to a great increase in the membership of socialist trades unions and the Socialist Party, and was to encourage further **direct action** after the war was over.

Country

- In the countryside the most immediate impact of the war arose from the fact that half of the 5 million strong conscript army had been peasants or rural labourers. That food production was not more seriously interrupted by this exodus was a result of more women working on the land but it also indicates the extent of over-population in the countryside.
- Wartime inflation was the main engine of social change in the countryside. Peasant debt, which had often been crippling, was paid off and traditional rent payments became less of a burden so that the peasants, unlike the urban workforce, enjoyed a new prosperity at the expense of their landlords (see **Land redistribution**).

Demobilisation

The end of the war with the apparently overwhelming victory of Vittorio Veneto was followed by the swift **demobilisation** of 5 million conscripts and 160,000 junior officers.

- Many of these men, embittered by the experience of fighting a drawn-out war of attrition, now saw themselves as the saviours of the nation in war and expected suitable recognition in peace.
- Disdainful of the politicians, so many of whom had opposed the war, they proved a major cause of political turmoil and became useful fodder for political extremism. As they returned home, they fuelled both the unrest in the industrial towns and the land hunger in the countryside.

Italy's northern frontier, 1915–24.

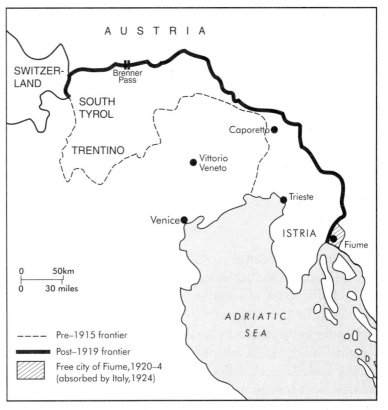

Vittorio Orlando at the 1919 Paris Peace Conference.

THE 'MUTILATED VICTORY'

If the Battle of Vittorio Veneto provided patriots with their glorious victory in war, the allegedly unsatisfactory peace terms that Italy's political leaders secured at the Paris Peace Conference in 1919 were easily seen as the betrayal of that victory and those whose blood had secured it. The legend of the army betrayed was to form a large and enduring part of the fascist appeal. In part the liberal leaders were responsible for this misrepresentation. Italy in fact made solid territorial gains by the **Treaty of Versailles**, more land (14,500 square kilometres) than any of the other victorious nations and in line with what it had been promised at the 1915 Treaty of London. Nationalists, who had tended to exaggerate the scale and the significance of the Italian military victory, but who had been key political supporters of the war, felt that this was not enough and demanded that Italy should be more fully rewarded for its considerable efforts in the war.

In response to feelings like this, in 1919 Prime Minister **Vittorio Orlando** made the mistake of raising Italian demands beyond what the other Allied leaders thought reasonable. They allowed some minor advances on Italy's north-eastern frontier over what had been agreed in 1915 but refused to go beyond this. In particular, the Italian government publicly demanded control of the Adriatic port of Fiume and, when this was denied them, it became a potent symbol among Italians of their victorious army betrayed both by the Allies and by the weakness of the liberal government that had failed to stand up for Italian interests.

D'Annunzio at Fiume

This widespread feeling was exploited in September 1919 by the Italian poet and war hero, **Gabriele D'Annunzio**, who captured the imagination of the Italian people when, with some 2000 armed followers, he seized Fiume and occupied it for fifteen months. He demonstrated that actions could be more effective than the words of politicians. Adventurers of every kind – students, ex-servicemen, followers of the pre-war Futurists – all flocked

Gabriele D'Annunzio.

to the city and, while the occupation lasted, D'Annunzio was never out of the eye of the Italian public.

Nitti

Chronic government instability hindered any solution to the crisis, which first became the responsibility of Francesco Nitti, who was prime minister of three separate governments from June 1919 to June 1920. Nitti, who had already infuriated army leaders and right-wing politicians by cutting military spending and pardoning army deserters, was afraid to take military action against the occupiers in case the army refused to obey the government's orders. He therefore did nothing to counter D'Annunzio's illegal **paramilitary** occupation.

Giolitti

In June 1920, the aged and experienced Giovanni Giolitti became prime minister and acted more decisively, seeking a way out of the crisis by negotiating with the newly formed state of Yugoslavia, the rival claimant to Fiume. In November 1920, a compromise was reached at the **Treaty of Rapallo.** Opponents of the Italian government were easily able to exploit the arrangement over Fiume as a cowardly compromise and the loss of Dalmatia as a denial of Italy's just claims. On Christmas Day 1920, the occupation of Fiume was ended by Italian military action against its Italian occupiers, which simply added further to popular anger against Giolitti's government.

D'Annunzio's daring example of direct political action challenged the weakened Liberal State and, by appealing directly to mass public opinion, provided a powerful example for the fascists. Indeed the fascists later directly copied his use of both black shirts as paramilitary uniform and of speeches relayed by loudspeakers from public balconies.

Results of the Fiume crisis
* The Fiume crisis added to the general dissatisfaction with the parliamentary political leaders like the 'cowardly' Nitti and the 'unpatriotic' Giolitti.

KEY TERMS

Paramilitary Organised on military lines but not part of the regular armed forces.

Treaty of Rapallo By this treaty Fiume became an independent state. As part of the deal the Italians had to abandon their claim to the bulk of Dalmatia, on the eastern coast of the Adriatic Sea, which had been promised to them by the Allies at the 1915 Treaty of London.

- It encouraged Italians to turn to one or other of the extremist parties for a solution to other pressing problems.
- D'Annunzio remained an inspiration to Mussolini with whom he continued to keep in touch. In 1922, he welcomed Mussolini coming to power.

THE POST-WAR POLITICAL CRISIS, 1919–22

Electoral changes

After the war the old liberal leaders struggled vainly to maintain the already creaking pre-war *trasformismo* game of coalition governments. Electoral changes that they themselves introduced after the war encouraged further political instability:

- In December 1918, Vittorio Orlando (prime minister, 1917–19), prompted by the many sacrifices brought about by the war and anxious to win the support of those who had fought in it, introduced **universal male suffrage**. This extension of the franchise was particularly helpful to the socialists.
- In 1919, Francesco Nitti, seeking to block the extremist parties, fundamentally altered the arrangements for electing the Chamber of Deputies to one using **proportional representation** based on party lists of candidates in 54 giant constituencies.

The Popular Party

The other immediate post-war change that was equally unhelpful to the liberals came when the Catholics, much strengthened by their constructive role during the war, founded in 1919 a political party, the Popular Party (the *Popolari*). This was not just a party of the Church; it embraced Catholics of different political views and was more an uneasy alliance than a formal party. It was, however, likely to command mass voting support in a Catholic country with a powerful Church hierarchy. The new party at least ensured that the Catholics would extract a much higher price before co-operating in future with the liberals.

Results of the 1919 election

Liberals supporting Giolitti	91
Right-wing liberals	23
Radicals	67
Reformist Socialists	21
Socialists	156
Popolari (Catholics)	100
Others	50

(Based on M. Clark, *Modern Italy*, 1996)

The 1919 election

The results of the 1919 election, held under Nitti's new arrangements, were a disaster for the liberals.

- The Socialist Party and its bitter enemy, the Catholic Popular Party, both capable of capturing the votes of large numbers of the recently enfranchised, became the two dominant parties in the Chamber. Neither on its own was strong enough to form a government and there was no prospect of the two parties working together.
- The **liberal groups**, on whom any hope of stable **coalition government** therefore rested, had been much reduced in size in the election and were increasingly fragmented, largely as a result of their wartime differences.
- Liberals like Giolitti found it difficult to find allies, for the socialists had emerged from the war as a more extreme party, inspired by the **political changes in Russia** and committed to radical political and economic change. The *Popolari* would extract a high price for their co-operation and were unlikely to be reliable allies, while the Roman Question remained unresolved. Given the breakdown of deputies in the Chamber it is not surprising that, after the 1919 election, there was considerable government instability as prime minister after prime minister strove to construct and maintain parliamentary coalitions.

Giolitti made a series of deals with the *Popolari* and formed a coalition government in June 1920 with them but his **anti-clerical** past made relations with their leader, Sturzo (see page 11), very fraught. And yet, when he sought a deal with the socialists instead, he antagonised both his own liberal deputies and leading Catholics. His problems were compounded by the firmer discipline of the bigger parties: individual deputies could no longer afford to break ranks and join Giolitti in return for liberal bribes. The days of freewheeling *trasformismo* political deals were coming to an end. Ominously, in the 1921 local government elections, both the *Popolari* and the socialists continued their electoral advance at the expense of the parties supporting the government. Giolitti was for many a controversial figure, marred even for some fellow liberals by his ferocious opposition to Italy joining the First World War and by his authorising the military action that ousted the heroic D'Annunzio from Fiume. Hemmed into a corner and with no clear plan in mind, in May 1921 the **unpopular Giolitti** called a general election and hoped for the best.

The 1921 election

The **electoral system** required combined party lists of candidates to be formed before the election. The most significant of these was the government list, which in 1921 was in Giolitti's gift. He had to produce a list of candidates attractive to the voters but from which he could then go on to construct a government that would be able to work together. The skill was in attaching enough other groups to the liberals to ensure that a liberal-led coalition could survive any vote of confidence in the Chamber. He had a great belief that men drawn in from the fringes of politics, even known troublemakers, could be turned into constructive parliamentarians – they could be tamed. And so in the changed circumstances of the 1921 election, in an effort to maintain the liberal role of constructing coalition governments in the *trasformismo* tradition, the aged Giolitti allowed himself to be lured into an **electoral pact with Mussolini** (see page 32).

The election failed to break the political deadlock in the Chamber of Deputies.

- The voting strength of the socialists and the *Popolari* was virtually unchanged with 123 and 107 deputies respectively.
- Significantly, having entered parliament thanks to being on Giolitti's list, the fascists then declined to give his government parliamentary support.
- In these circumstances, and with too many different groups represented on the government list for any hope of stability, Giolitti resigned as prime minister.
- In the next sixteen months, leading up to Mussolini himself becoming prime minister in October 1922, there were three different coalition governments, all of which inevitably lacked a secure parliamentary majority (see page 34).

Giolitti's unpopularity In the post-war period (1918–22) Giolitti was Italy's foremost politician. However, his opposition to the war had made him deeply unpopular with a number of politicians. This made successful coalitions led by Giolitti far more unlikely.

The electoral system At the time of the 1921 election, the electoral system was still based on the 54 giant constituencies and proportional representation.

Electoral pact with Mussolini Fascist candidates were included in Giolitti's list of election candidates.

The last liberal governments

PM	Dates
Nitti	June 1919–June 1920
Giolitti	June 1920–May 1921
Bonomi	June 1921–February 1922
Facta	Feb 1922–July 1922
Facta	July 1922–October 1922

Results of the 1921 election

Pro-government candidates	
Fascists	35
Nationalists	10
Liberals	103
Centre groups (radicals and reform socialists)	108
Others	2
Total	**258**

Opposition parties	
Republicans	22
Popolari	107
Socialists	123
Communists	15
Others	10
Total	**277**

<hr>

KEY TERM

Biennio Rosso Meaning Two Red Years: in 1919 and 1920, as trade union activity revived, there was a series of strikes, often marked by violence, and a breakdown of law and order, with accompanying food riots in which shop supplies were plundered. The war had greatly increased the size of the urban workforce and post-war experience encouraged workers to tougher direct action. The 1917 communist revolution in Russia inspired some to dream of a new political order as a solution to their economic grievances.

The 1921 election changed the political scene dramatically. As a result of Nitti's system of proportional representation and of Giolitti's incautious invitation to Mussolini, the fascists came out of the election with 35 seats in the Chamber of Deputies. This handful of seats was, in 1922, to prove the springboard to government and in this respect the election was a significant turning-point for the Liberal State.

GROWING CHAOS, 1919–22

The economic crisis
The governments from 1919 to 1922 proved incapable of tackling the growing economic crisis facing post-war Italy. The main elements in the crisis were:

- the government's abrupt switch from war production to meet state military orders, ending war loans and wartime controls, in order to return to free-market peacetime production, which resulted in several large firms going bankrupt as military orders collapsed;
- the existence of 2 million unemployed workers by the end of 1919, partly a result of the rapid demobilisation of 5 million soldiers;
- the galloping post-war inflation: in 1919 the lira lost almost half its value, with devastating consequences for the savings of the middle classes.

Social dislocation
The war and the economic crisis that followed encouraged labour militancy in industry and in agriculture.

Town
- By 1920, almost 3.5 million workers were organised in trades unions, 2 million of them in the increasingly extreme socialist General Confederation of Labour (CGL). Widespread unrest including strikes resulted in these years being nicknamed the **Biennio Rosso**.
- There was a clear revolutionary feel to some of the incidents. A localised general strike in the north in April 1920 and an army mutiny in Ancona in June 1920 threatened more instability. In a revolutionary move

unions in Turin set up factory committees in 1920 that asserted their right to control production.

- The most important example of labour unrest was the **Occupation of the Factories** in September 1920. The result was a deep distrust of Giolitti's government on behalf of the industrialists.

With hindsight it seems likely that the majority of the strikers, far from being revolutionaries, were probably people simply trying to defend their wartime standard of living in the troubled post-war economic climate. This is not, however, how they were seen at the time by the middle classes and by the Italian political establishment.

Country

- In the countryside returning soldiers forcibly occupied many of the lands of the great estates, particularly in the south, much of which was uncultivated or previously common land. The number of peasant owners of land doubled to 3.5 million. Their long-standing ambition achieved, the peasants ceased to be a revolutionary force but settled down to the tasks of subsistence agriculture.
- Agricultural labourers came under the control of **Labour Leagues** that fought a series of bitter disputes with farmers over wage rates. In some areas such as Emilia and Tuscany, rural local government fell under socialist control. They then lent support to the labourers, laying down local wage rates and conditions of work.

Throughout Italy the countryside was in turmoil. Landlords and the larger tenant farmers, plagued in 1919 and 1920 by bad harvests, felt threatened by either peasant occupiers or by militant socialist trades unionists. Local government was slipping out of their control, their right to own property was being challenged and the government seemed indifferent to all that was happening, indeed appeared to support their enemies.

CONCLUSION

The consequence of the social and economic crisis was a collapse in confidence in the political system. Labour

Occupation of the Factories Began as a dispute over wages but ended up with 400,000 workers taking over their factories. The industrialists thought a revolution had started. Giolitti intervened to end the occupation, which he managed to do but only after he had given the unions a promise of influence in industry.

Labour League A rural trade union. For many Labour Leagues the hope was that the land would be nationalised and turned into labourer-owned collective farms. This was never to happen but, in 1919 and 1920, Giolitti's liberal–*Popolari* coalition government did tend to support peasant aspirations and instructed the prefects (the senior local government officers in each province, appointed by central government) to legalise land confiscations. By October 1922, such confiscations were being confirmed on a permanent basis.

unrest, food riots and perceived government leniency with the unions upset the middle classes and the establishment. Violence gave the impression that Italian society was on the edge of breakdown. Faced by the rioters but fearful of public opinion, Nitti's government failed to back the police and assert the rule of law; and so the crisis became one of public order, with law and the institutions of the state directly challenged and failing to respond.

In practice, much of the violence came from the right, especially from the counter-revolutionary, strike-breaking tactics of Mussolini's fascist street fighters, but this was largely ignored by the authorities and by all those who feared the 'Red menace' with its alleged new support from communist Russia. It became increasingly clear that, if the government could not protect middle-class Italy from the dangers of a left-wing *coup* like the 1917 Bolshevik Revolution in Russia, then wealthier citizens would have to look elsewhere for help.

SUMMARY QUESTIONS

1 Why, even before 1914, was it becoming more difficult to form stable governments?

2 In what ways did Italy's part in the First World War make Italian politics more turbulent?

3 What were the main problems facing Italy at the end of 1918?

4 What electoral changes after 1918 made the construction of stable governments almost impossible?

5 Why did control of the port of Fiume become a major issue and how did what happened there encourage political extremism?

6 Why in 1920–1 did 'respectable' Italians increasingly fear a left-wing revolution?

CHAPTER 2

Fascism's appeal, 1919–22

THE ORIGINS OF FASCISM

Meeting, March 1919

Italian **fascism** has been dated from 23 March 1919 when 100 or so ex-servicemen and left-wing revolutionaries attended a meeting in Milan advertised in *Popolo D'Italia*, the newspaper founded and edited by Mussolini (see page 6).

To distinguish themselves from the political parties they so despised, those present at the meeting in Milan took the full title of *Fascio Italiano di Combattimento* (Italian Combat Group). Among those present was Filippo Marinetti, leader of the pre-war Futurists (see page 10) and Feruccio Vecchi, a leading member of the *Arditi*. Mussolini was the main speaker and his proposals set the tone of the meeting. Early fascist ideas came from the Futurists and were very radical, though few survived through to 1922. They included:

- replacing the monarchy with a republic;
- confiscating the property of the Catholic Church;
- peasant ownership of the land and worker management of industry;
- steeply rising taxation of the rich, especially war profiteers;
- a national minimum wage;
- votes for women.

Within a few days Marinetti and Vecchi organised an attack on the socialist newspaper *Avanti*, totally destroying its offices. Mussolini quickly defended this action but took no part in it. He was ready to take advantage of the violence of his followers and later praised the destruction as the first act of fascist violence. However, he was also anxious not to take unnecessary risks personally and keen

KEY TERM

Fascism The term fascio simply means 'a group' and has ancient Roman origins coming from the bundle of twigs that were a symbol of the authority of the magistrates of the Roman Empire. There had been earlier fascio but the term 'fascism' was first used at this time and was soon used only to identify the group around Mussolini, probably because of his frequent use of it in his newspaper.

to show his own respectability. Nevertheless, at this point he organised a private army of several hundred *Arditi* for whom he provided arms. It was the beginning of a pattern of behaviour – the alternating use of force and respectability coupled with political manoeuvring – that persisted until at least 1926.

In its early days, fascism was an urban-based movement that developed particular support from ex-servicemen and students discontented with their own lot and with the state of post-war Italy. From Milan it spread first to the other towns of northern and central Italy. But numbers were small and Mussolini's followers were merely one of several right-wing groups demanding radical political change and opposed to the traditional political parties and leaders, especially those like Giolitti who had been against entry into the war. The fascists were, at first, overshadowed by the much larger numbers supporting D'Annunzio whose patriotic zeal and paramilitary organisation they copied.

The fascist appeal

Social confusion and the political drift in post-war Italy gave Mussolini and his fascists their chance.

- Their appeal rested on the ideas of the movement, which appeared to offer direct solutions to the complex social, economic and political grievances of many in the Italian state.
- From the outset fascism stressed national identity and the desirability of national strength and glory, and this appealed to many of those who had fought in the war, who despised the numerous politicians who had opposed the war and who also felt betrayed by the 'mutilated victory'.
- In 1919, fascism also presented a **left-wing political programme** with quite revolutionary social and economic changes intended to appeal to disillusioned socialists.

Rural fascism

Fascism's first important advance came in 1920 when it managed to move out from the northern towns to establish its presence in the surrounding countryside. It was socialist activity there that gave the fascists their opportunity. In the economic turmoil affecting post-war Italy, socialist Labour Leagues had managed to organise the landless labourers of the region and challenge the power of the large tenant farmers and landlords by threatening to seize control of farms (see page 26). Young fascists, organised into *squadristi*, went out from the towns and violently attacked the socialist Leagues. The traditional leaders of rural society – landowners and large farmers – were happy to encourage their new allies, and the local police took their lead from them and did not interfere.

These early 'victories', trading on fear of socialism and appealing to right-wing elements, not only gave the fascists a much higher profile across northern and central Italy but also began to change the nature of fascism. The gangs of ex-soldiers who went out on lorries to terrorise the rural trades unions became a major and enduring feature of fascism across the country and one that was copied in the towns to oppose union attempts to browbeat employers by occupying factories.

The *squadristi* had no difficulty in obtaining arms and, with their anti-socialist commitment, often received help, or at least helpful indifference, from the army and the police. By late 1920, they had proved so effective that many rural landlords and urban industrialists in northern and central Italy, tired of government indifference to their plight, were willing to pay generously for their help against the threat from socialists and trades unionists. A pattern of tolerated right-wing violence became established and important economic groups were drawn into supporting the fascists, morally and financially. Many liberals applauded the violence that the fascists handed out, seeing them as defenders of the country against the threat of a left-wing takeover.

Mussolini stood apart from the early activity of the *squadristi* but, when they began to attract not just financial contributions but also a steady flow of new **rural recruits** for the movement, he was quick to take credit for their role as protectors of society.

KEY TERMS

Squadristi Members of the fascist paramilitary movement run by ex-army officers. The movement's title was *squadrismo*. Often they were simply thugs in black shirts. The *squadristi* leaders were known as *ras*. Their main enemy were socialists. On some occasions, such as in Parma in 1922, they fought pitched battles against their enemies.

Rural recruits The membership of the *squadristi* came from those who feared the rise of socialism: the labourers, small tenant farmers, farm managers, better-off peasants – and their growing strength enabled the fascist *squadristi* to challenge the socialist hold on the countryside in northern and central Italy.

There were major confrontations, which, during 1920 alone, led to over 200 people being killed. By mid-1921, the rural socialists had been beaten and the fascist *squadristi* were in control of large areas of the countryside.

The Pact of Pacification, 1921

The emergence of the *squadristi* as the result of a series of independent local initiatives did, however, present Mussolini with a number of problems that were not really resolved until the late 1920s.

Pact of Pacification This was part of Musslini's attempt to make the fascist movement more respectable and committed to a legal path to power and directly challenged those *squadristi* leaders who saw fascism as a revolutionary movement and were committed to destroying its enemies by violent confrontation. Mussolini probably also hoped to woo members of the other unions away from their support of the Socialist Party.

Mussolini's relationship with the *ras* Several of the *ras* were to be bitterly disappointed with Mussolini's cautious constitutional behaviour after he became prime minister in October 1922. They had assumed that there would be a revolutionary takeover of the state from which they and their *squadristi* members would be the chief beneficiaries. Mussolini, however, still had to devote much time and thought to retaining their support while not alienating important respectable opinion.

- The *squadristi* leaders (the *ras*) each had their own local power base through the control of *their* men and the position they had created in their own locality.
- The *ras* were usually more radical – politically and socially – than Mussolini himself and their views could not just be ignored.

The *Duce* (see page 33) was given a sharp reminder of the influence of the *ras* in August 1921 when, fearful that the growing violence between left and right would lead the government to take action, he signed a deal, the **Pact of Pacification**, between the fascist and socialist trades unions. However, Mussolin's deal was rejected by several of the leading *ras*, some of whom went so far as to urge D'Annunzio to replace Mussolini as fascist leader. A split was avoided only when Mussolini abandoned the pact. The episode illustrates the difficulties he had at this stage in keeping control of the movement he had done so much to create and his deteriorating **relationship** with it.

FASCISM'S CHANGING PROGRAMME, 1919–22

Appeal to vested interests

By 1921 the fascist programme became more conservative. Fascism's strident, often violent, opposition to communism and socialism had from the start appealed to the prosperous middle classes and to the better-off peasantry, to anyone who owned a little property or had a job that earned a wage slightly above that of the urban worker. By late 1921, fascism meant *squadrismo*, anti-communism, patriotism and strike-breaking. In different

Benito and Rachele Mussolini with their five children, 1930.

areas it had different meaning. However, it became attractive to those who felt the Liberal State no longer protected their interests.

The fascist direction appealed to conservatives through attempts to calm the fears of the Catholic Church by making clear the movement's strong commitment to family values, particularly in opposing divorce. There were hints in 1921 that the fascists would be prepared to negotiate sensible terms to resolve the Roman Question. The strength of fascism was that it remained a diverse ideology, the early fascists retained their radical idealism, the *squadristi* continued to emphasise their virility and, frequently, their violent disposition but undoubtedly, during 1920 and 1921, there was a move to the right that helped to attract more conservative support.

1921 election

Mussolini's opportunity to place candidates on Giolitti's government list in the 1921 election made fascism more respectable. Mussolini took a detailed interest in the selection of the candidates, ensuring their respectability and, by fascist standards, their moderation. He had been quick to recognise the progress fascism had been able to make as a result of the violent threat coming from the *squadristi* but, by 1921, he was aware that violence alone did not provide a **route to government**.

Mussolini's family Rachele Mussolini kept out of the limelight and seemed to prefer the private life of an ordinary housewife. Benito Mussolini had several mistresses but only in 2001 did it become public that the long-suffering Rachele also had a secret lover for many years. Their daughter Edda, widow of the executed fascist foreign minister, Ciano, revealed this in a taped deathbed interview given in 1995. She claimed that her mother told Benito of the affair but that he took no steps to end it and that it was Edda's own adolescent outrage that brought it to an end.

Mussolini and the route to government The more success *squadristi* violence achieved the more likely it was to provoke a powerful reaction, either galvanising the liberal leaders or provoking action from the army. Mussolini therefore had to hold his more radical followers in check in order to convince the other political leaders and the electorate that he was willing to work within the parliamentary constitution.

Foundation of the Fascist Party

A key step in keeping control over the *squadristi* came in
October 1921 when **the Fascist Party** was formally
established on a national basis (*Partito Nazionale Fascista*
or PNF). By 1922, the main elements in fascism's appeal
were:

- its vigorous and apparently effective anti-socialism;
- its stress on patriotism as contrasted to the liberal
  failures to protect Italian interests;
- its emphasis on Mussolini's leadership and the
  beginning of the cult of the *Duce* (Mussolini as the great
  leader of fascism and, potentially, of the nation).

The radical political agenda of the first meeting in Milan
in 1919 had, however, disappeared.

THE MARCH ON ROME, OCTOBER 1922

The fascist advance, January–September 1922

The political weaknesses that plagued Italy after the First
World War reached their climax in the summer and
autumn of 1922. From the beginning of the year, fascist
violence had increased in intensity and scope throughout
northern and central Italy. It was no longer a question of
picking off the enemies of fascism; the fascists were now
deliberately geared to seizing control of both towns and
entire provinces.

- In May, the leading *ras*, **Italo Balbo,** used 50,000
  unemployed men to occupy Ferrara and forced the
  council there to set up public works schemes to provide
  them with work. In June, he led his *squadristi* in force
  to Bologna and evicted **Cesare Mori.**
- In July, the extremist *ras* Roberto Farinacci of Cremona,
  launched a savage attack on the lives and the property of
  non-fascist leaders in the town.
- In September, *squadristi* moved out from Venice to seize
  the main towns in the German-speaking area of South
  Tyrol and drove out the legal administration.

Fascist successes in gaining local control almost everywhere except in Rome and in the south were greatly helped by the active support, or at least helpful indifference, of many of the police and local government officials, vast numbers of whom thoroughly approved of the fascist stand against the socialists. The outcome of the fascist March on Rome (see page 37) only makes sense in the context of this series of earlier fascist coups in the provinces. This left the central government powerless in these areas, its decrees unenforceable. Here the fascist *squadristi*, not the government in Rome, were the rulers.

Failure on the left

The **natural enemies of the fascists** did remarkably little to prevent the fascists entering government. Indeed, the few things that were done by the left were actually helpful to the fascist cause.

- The socialist movement had split in two in January 1921 and a small **Communist Party** emerged from the split, linked to and partly financed by the Bolshevik government in Russia.
- In late July 1922, the socialist-dominated trades unions formed an **Alliance of Labour** to resist the fascists and called a 24-hour general strike. This received little support, even in the big industrial centres like Milan and Turin, and the Catholic and communist unions did not participate. The weakly supported strike provided an opportunity for the fascists to attack the strikers and to make a show of providing voluntary services before posing as the saviours of the country.

Government weakness

By summer 1922, it was clear that the maintenance of law and order required the liberal ruling elite to strike some sort of deal with Mussolini – either that or take decisive, presumably military, action against him and his violent followers. Throughout the previous three years a series of weak governments had consistently failed to confront the country's internal problems (see pages 22–6) and this would not change in 1922. From February, **Luigi Facta** was prime minister, a post he accepted reluctantly only because the *Popolari* refused to co-operate with Giolitti.

KEY THEMES

The Communist Party
However feeble the threat this party posed, its mere existence was a propaganda goldmine to the fascists. More seriously, even after the communists had broken away the socialists were unable to agree to work with the liberals so long as they in turn were associated with the Catholic *Popolari*.

Alliance of Labour strike
Support was weak, which can be seen in the fact that only 800 out of 10,000 Fiat workers went on strike.

KEY PERSON

Luigi Facta 1861–1930
Was twice appointed prime minister in 1922, leading weak, divided governments for a few weeks on each occasion. He sought compromise with fascist violence but finally decided to make a stand against Mussolini's threats only for the king to refuse to back him. Facta's government was narrowly based and many of its supporters were more fearful of a socialist *coup* than of the fascists. They believed that the fascists could be brought into government and would then be useful allies against the left.

Facta saw himself simply as a caretaker until Giolitti could yet again manufacture a coalition.

For his part, Mussolini was content through the summer of 1922 to continue negotiating quietly with the parliamentary leaders. He created an impression that he would be only too happy to co-operate in maintaining the normal political processes, but first asked for four government posts for his handful of parliamentary followers and then went on to demand that he be made prime minister.

Mussolini threatens the March

It was Mussolini's threat to organise a fascist march on Rome to take control there, and so, he claimed, to save Italy from anarchy and from communism, that provoked the final crisis that, in turn, led to his becoming prime minister. The threat was issued at a fascist rally in Naples on 24 October which was attended by over 40,000 supporters. Facta's government was so nervous that the military garrison in Rome was increased in the face of the fascist threat.

In pursuing his twin strategy, of allowing fascist violence to intimidate opponents while at the same time conducting political negotiations with them, Mussolini faced two grave dangers.

- Despite all the obstacles, an anti-fascist coalition could be made, led by a politician such as Giolitti that would block his rise to power.
- His own followers, led by the more excitable of the *ras*, and emboldened by their recent successes in taking over the government of so many provincial towns, would reject his frustrating political manoeuvres and seek someone else to lead them towards a revolutionary seizure of power.

Calling the March on Rome was his way of averting both these dangers.

The more immediate danger was that the anti-fascists would agree to work together. In **Mussolini's speech on**

KEY SPEECH

Mussolini's speech on fascist intentions *Our programme is simple. We want to govern Italy ... It is not programmes of salvation that are missing in Italy. It is the men and the determination ... we must tackle the problem of how to replace this political class which has always, in the last few years, pursued a policy of abdication when confronted by that wind-filled puppet which is called Italian socialism. I believe this replacement is urgent and the more radical it is the better it will be ... I believe that the monarchy has no reason to oppose what we must now call the fascist revolution. It is not in its interests because if it did it would immediately become an adversary, and if it became an opponent it is clear we could not save it because for us it is a matter of life and death ... We must have the courage to become monarchists.*

fascist intentions given on 20 September 1922 at Udine, Mussolini went out of his way to limit this danger by trying to reassure both the king and the army that, whatever fascism's other objectives, it did not seek to challenge *their* role in the state. However, the underlying menace was scarcely hidden. Mussolini was particularly concerned that Giolitti, the most experienced and resolute of the liberal leaders, who had ended the Fiume occupation in 1920 by using the armed forces, would be persuaded by Facta to end his differences with D'Annunzio. This would be a first step towards forming a new and stronger coalition government that would apply pressure on the king to use the army to end the violence in 1922. Mussolini opened separate negotiations with D'Annunzio and also swiftly prepared his plans for the March on Rome. At the same time, he used the public platform provided by the party conference in Naples to demand that Facta took leading fascists into his cabinet or face the consequences. He played heavily in his conference speech of 24 October on the alternatives before fascism – whether it would come to power legally or violently – because its coming to power was inevitable. The fascist delegates were swept into a frenzy. This political blackmail – 'Let us into government legally now or we let loose a revolution against the state' – produced panic among some, but not all liberal politicians.

Immediately after he left the Naples conference Mussolini returned to Milan to set the much-publicised **March on Rome** on its way and at the same time continue his negotiations with leading liberals. Such moves succeeded in giving the impression to those in Rome that a successful revolution of national proportions was underway.

Nevertheless, Prime Minister Facta, having first hesitated, then kept his nerve and, at 5 am on 28 October, resolved at last to resist the insurrection. He had already reinforced Rome's military and checked on the loyalty of the troops there and had then established that the king as head of state and therefore commander of Italy's armed forces would issue a royal decree establishing **martial law**. The initiative had already slipped to the fascists. Now they would have to be forcibly turned out of the public buildings that they had just occupied rather than simply being prevented from entering them.

KEY THEME

March on Rome There were to be four columns of marchers starting from different points, each led by a prominent fascist and under the overall direction of Balbo, the *ras* from Ferrara.

In order to heighten tension the arrangements were deliberately given the appearance of military operation.

The first step, late at night on 27 October, was to demoralise the government and its supporters by seizing police stations and other government buildings in the towns that the fascists already controlled.

KEY TERM

Martial law Comes about when military government is imposed and ordinary law suspended. However, the king feared martial law.

Victor Emmanuel III King of Italy 1900–46. In 1922, he allowed Mussolini to become prime minister rather than impose martial law. Having again failed to stand up to Mussolini in 1925, as the *Duce* assumed dictatorial powers, he was politically powerless until, in 1943, he summoned the courage to dismiss him. He abdicated in 1946 and died in 1947.

The marchers They came to Rome in buses, lorries and cars, not on foot.

However, when Facta went to obtain the king's signature on the decree at 9 am, he found that **Victor Emmanuel** had changed his mind and now declined to sign it. A stunned Facta offered his resignation as prime minister and the king immediately accepted it.

Royal dilemma

The various factors that might account for the king's change of heart are examined in A2 Section 1 of this book, but it would pay ambitious AS students to spend a few minutes considering them here, for the significance of his action is difficult to overestimate.

- Having failed to back Facta, Victor Emmanuel had to find a new prime minister. Facta had been a follower of Giolitti, who was unlikely to be willing to succeed him in these fraught circumstances and who had indeed deliberately stayed away from Rome as the crisis deepened.
- It was therefore logical for the king to approach Salandra, Giolitti's great enemy among the liberals. Salandra accepted the king's request to form a government, but insisted that any viable coalition would have to include fascists in the cabinet. He offered them four places, which gave Mussolini what he had demanded less than a week earlier at the Naples conference.
- Safely back in Milan, Mussolini was by now prepared to play for higher stakes and, ignoring contrary advice from leading fascists, he rejected the offer. Salandra then informed the king that without fascist co-operation he could not form a government, and that Mussolini would have to be invited to see if he could do so.
- The king was therefore driven to telephone Mussolini, who first established that he was being invited to Rome to be offered the post of prime minister, and not some lesser role, before setting out by train from Milan.

Mussolini becomes prime minister

On 30 October, Victor Emmanuel formally asked Mussolini to form a government and, on 31 October, a victory parade of 70,000 fascists marched through the streets of Rome to be saluted by the king. **The marchers**

Victor Emmanuel III in 1930.

The fascist leaders in Rome after the March on Rome. (They were, from left to right: leading syndicalist Michele Bianchi; Emilio de Bono who became the first leader of the Fascist Militia; Cesare de Vecchi, *ras* in Turin; Mussolini and Italo Balbo, *ras* in Ferrara.)

had only set out for Rome after the king had made his offer to Mussolini and when all prospect of opposition from the police and army had vanished. For those *squadristi* members who had dreamed of a revolutionary conquest of Rome and the forcible seizure of the state, it was an anti-climax but for Mussolini it was a great political and personal triumph. He was prime minister, appointed by the king and he now insisted that the king allow his 'fascist legions' a victory march through Rome.

CONCLUSIONS

Political breakdown?
By 1922, Italian political life had reached a point of breakdown.

- The origins of the breakdown lay in the weaknesses of the Liberal State and were made more acute by the changes in the franchise and the growth of new political parties before 1914. This in turn helped to undermine the coalition politics that made the system function.
- The war and its aftermath created new problems. Most dangerous was the division among the ruling elite between those who had supported it and those who had

been adamantly opposed to it, making co-operation against a common enemy virtually impossible.

- The war raised expectations of land and social reform, especially among the demobbed soldiers.
- Post-war extremist parties flourished and political violence became the norm. The infant fascist movement, vigorous in defending the urban streets against left-wing extremism, was seen by influential sections of Italian society including the king as the best hope to end the political crisis of the Liberal State and to safeguard Italy, and their own vested interests, from a communist revolution.

Political miscalculation?

There was no 'fascist seizure of power', no 'fascist revolution' and it could be argued that Mussolini became prime minister by entirely constitutional means. Victor Emmanuel appointed Mussolini as prime minister in a coalition government as the best hope for preserving law and order. Others must share the blame for this outcome. In a catalogue of mistakes:

- Facta had called for martial law too late to make an effective stand;
- Salandra, the right-wing liberal leader, declined to form a government that did not include fascists in it;
- Giolitti, the grand old man of Italian politics, stayed away from Rome at the critical moment.

Most of the old political class chose to ignore the daily acts of fascist violence and saw Mussolini's appointment as just another turn in the game of *trasformismo* politics. They comforted themselves with the thought that experience of office and its rewards would calm the fascists who were, after all, in a minority within the government. Few politically experienced onlookers expected the Mussolini government to last any longer than its short-lived immediate predecessors.

Even in the last few days of October 1922 fascism's success was not inevitable. If the king or any one of a handful of liberal politicians had acted differently towards the fascist threat, even at the last minute, then in all probability

Mussolini could have been stopped. As it was, the calculation that the most sensible course was to tame fascism by bringing it into the political system and requiring it to assume the burden of government in coalition with other political parties, seemed at the time an entirely rational one. In practice, it proved a gigantic miscalculation.

SUMMARY QUESTIONS

1 How did the policies of the fascists change between 1919 and 1921? How did this affect the nature of their support?

2 Describe how important decisions by Giolitti, in 1921, and Victor Emmanuel, in 1922, helped the political fortunes of the fascists.

3 'The March on Rome never took place.' Why then was Mussolini able to bluff the king into appointing him prime minister?

CHAPTER 3

Consolidating the fascist regime, 1922–5

INTRODUCTION

- In 1922, Mussolini was in office as yet another coalition prime minister, dependent on the support of political rivals, and apparently no more likely to provide long-term stability than earlier post-war governments.
- By the end of 1925, he had formed a stable and subservient government, having bluffed his way through a major political crisis provoked by the murder of the socialist politician Giacomo Matteotti. He had defeated his opponents, freed himself from the constraints imposed by his own followers and made himself indispensable to the conservative elements in the state, including the monarchy and the Catholic Church.
- From 1926 to 1929, a series of institutional changes and deals with conservative groups secured his rule on a permanent basis and, in 1929, an extraordinary agreement with the Catholic Church ensured acceptance of his regime for much of the 1930s.

ESTABLISHING GOVERNMENT: FIRST STEPS

Having accepted the king's summons to form a government Mussolini faced urgent problems for which he had no readily prepared solutions and, indeed, no set programme of reforms to enact. In the first instance he wanted above all to convince non-fascist politicians that nothing had really changed and that, once law and order had been restored, politics would soon be **normalised.**

There were only 32 fascist deputies in a Chamber of 535 and Mussolini therefore had no choice but to form a government largely of non-fascists. Therefore, he proceeded to create a coalition of right-wing elements, which he called a **National Government.**

Emergency powers

This coalition achieved its first objective, for the new government was generally welcomed by liberal and right-wing politicians and, indeed, by some trade union and left-wing leaders. This acceptance, following Mussolini's unconventional route to office, also speaks volumes for the general disgust felt with the impotence and the antics of previous parliamentary politics. When parliament met in November 1922, in a remarkably provocative **speech to the Chamber**, which included a colourful threat that the fascists might choose to close parliament down, Mussolini demanded that he be given full powers to govern alone. The speech included a tribute to Victor Emmanuel for his refusal to impose martial law, which had prevented civil war and 'allowed the fresh and ardent *fascisti* to pour itself into the sluggish mainstream of the state', and acknowledged the important role the Catholic Church had played in Italian history.

The deputies were still deeply divided but, with only the socialists and communists dissenting, Mussolini was given the sweeping powers that he demanded within three weeks of his becoming prime minister.

- Despite Mussolini's crude intimidation of the deputies, several leading liberal politicians were among the majority who voted to give him the emergency powers; they included Giolitti, Orlando and Salandra.
- It is clear, however, that they and many lesser figures of the political centre and right welcomed the opportunity for a new start – to sweep away the corruption of the old *trasformismo* system and provide a more effective defence against left-wing anarchy.
- The general feeling among the Chamber of Deputies, that Mussolini should be given the chance to provide the country with a more effective government than it had recently enjoyed, was reflected in the Senate where his new powers were again approved by a majority of 196 to 16.

KEY SPEECH

Mussolini's speech to the Chamber of Deputies as prime minister *I am here to defend and give the greatest value to the revolution of the blackshirts … I could have carried our victory much further and I refused to do so. I imposed limits upon my action. With 300,000 young men, fully armed, ready for anything and almost religiously prompt to obey any command of mine. I could have punished all those who have slandered the* fascisti *and thrown mud at them. I could have made a bivouac of this gloomy hall. I could have shut up Parliament and formed a government of* fascisti *exclusively. I could have done so but I did not wish to do so, at any rate for the moment … .*

CONTROLLING THE FASCIST SQUADS, 1922–3

Parliament had easily been persuaded to accept Mussolini's new powers but establishing fascist control over the country was a longer and less tidy process. The first major problem confronting Mussolini was the need to keep the *squadristi* under control.

Some of the *ras* had extreme aims. Men like **Farinacci**, the *ras* of Cremona, wished to seize control of the state, by closing down all other political parties and parliament. This would mean a series of illegal actions amounting to a revolution, the precise opposite of Mussolini's apparent aim of working within the established political structures and pursuing a policy of normalisation.

Other fascist leaders, like **de Vecchi** in Turin, continued to pursue local vendettas against old political opponents and sought the material rewards of victory in their own localities, by violent means whenever necessary. Unless they were held in check they too would make a mockery of normalisation. If their violence went too far or went on too long it might well provoke a backlash against fascism, uniting its divided opponents or causing the army to act to restore order.

Fascist Militia

Mussolini realised that he owed his position as prime minister to his followers' potential for violence and to his own reputation as the only man who could prevent such violence getting out of hand. Nor could the *squadristi* go without reward, for then they might turn against him.

His solution was to create the Fascist Militia (MSVN) in January 1923.

- Its membership was made up of the 300,000 blackshirts who were paid out of state funds and were directly answerable to Mussolini.
- From its inception ex-army officers were put in charge of the local units to undermine the power of the unruly *ras*, a process helped by over 200 of the most quarrelsome of the *ras* being expelled from the fascist movement.
- The Militia provided jobs to keep provincial fascists busy.

Roberto Farinacci in 1939.

- They were all put into uniform and encouraged to have a high public profile, mounting ceremonial guard on public buildings and on public occasions.
- Initially their oath of loyalty was to the *Duce* not to the king, though this changed later (in August 1924 as Mussolini struggled to survive the Matteotti crisis).

The Fascist Militia, often **compared with the German SA/SS**, was the outward sign that Italy was indeed a fascist state but the Militia had no real political power. Its foundation was one of Mussolini's most creative political moves. It reassured non-fascists and strengthened his control of the fascist movement, all at the expense of Italian taxpayers.

The cheka
At the same time Mussolini took the precaution of creating a secret personal bodyguard of fascist thugs, referred to as the cheka, who terrorised opponents of Mussolini whether fascist or non-fascist. The leader of this sinister group, Ameriqo Dumini, was one of Mussolini's closest advisers. He played the central role in the sensational murder of the socialist Matteotti, which led to the most serious crisis Mussolini had to face in these years (see pages 53–7).

Fascist Grand Council
In December 1922, leading fascists were also reassured about their own importance by the very public establishment of the Fascist Grand Council. This was an important consultative committee on which most of them were invited to sit. From the start this body was dominated by Mussolini. It provided him with a valuable means of controlling the leading members of the PNF and through them asserting his authority over the party, if necessary by employing the services of the cheka.

Growth of the Fascist Party
The danger that fascist extremism would undermine Mussolini's apparent strategy of disarming opponents by normalising politics was also reduced by the dramatic growth in the membership of the PNF in the months after Mussolini became prime minister.

HEINEMANN ADVANCED HISTORY

- Some 300,000 strong in October 1922, membership totalled almost 800,000 by the end of 1923.
- These newcomers were inspired largely by the prospect of the economic advantages to be derived from joining the Fascist Party.
- The biggest single addition to the fascist ranks came in February 1923 when the **nationalists** closed down their own organisation and joined the PNF, with their paramilitary organisation, the 'Blueshirts', merging into the Fascist Militia.

ESTABLISHING A WIDER CONSENSUS, 1922–3

In his first year in office, Mussolini had to devote much attention to his fascist followers. The growth of the Fascist Party and the activities of the Fascist Militia helped to create a wider base of support. Acceptance of the new regime was made easier by the economic boom that Italy enjoyed in the years 1922–5 as world trade recovered from the dislocations of the First World War (see pages 73–83).

News manipulation

Mussolini himself, described by the historian Denis Mack-Smith (*Mussolini*, 1982) as the best **popular journalist** of the period, paid particular attention to publicity.

- In these early days in office he was always available and welcoming to journalists, and devoted a great deal of time to checking what they wrote about him, even writing to editors to suggest how their treatment of important topics could be improved.
- In June 1923, he wisely obtained for himself power to control the work of the press by decree, and was then able to use this to good effect in the Matteotti crisis of 1924 (see pages 53–7).
- In July 1923, his ill-advised seizure of the Greek island of Corfu (see pages 100–1) and the subsequent enforced withdrawal were presented to the people as a great Italian victory, thus setting a pattern for the exploitation of foreign policy 'triumphs' in order to promote the regime's popularity at home.

Mussolini's manipulation of the press was, even at this

KEY THEMES

The nationalists They included many landowners, senior members of the civil service and the upper middle class generally. Their strong support for the monarchy and their conservatism on most political and social issues, especially those relating to the ownership of land, further diluted fascist revolutionary zeal.

Mussolini: the popular journalist Even in power, Mussolini continued to edit the newspaper *Popolo d'Italia*. Its circulation was widespread and it became the best organ of publicity for the regime.

HEINEMANN ADVANCED HISTORY

early stage, masterly and this alone gives him some claim to be the first modern dictator. Mack-Smith has commented: 'His sort of fascism could never have appeared before the days of popular journalism.'

Dealing with dissidents

Both the law and violence were used to harass opposition to the regime.

- The **freemasons** were treated with deep suspicion as a secret society and, in February 1923, fascists were forbidden to be members, though many fascists ignored the instruction.

KEY TERM

Freemasonry An international male secret society organised in 'lodges' to provide mutual help for its members.

After the March on Rome in 1922, fascists destroy the Rome office of the socialist paper *Avanti.*

The mafia A secret criminal society that had its origins in medieval Sicily but which had spread through Italy.

Aurelio Padovani Idealist fascist leader in Naples. He was dismissed in 1923, then partially reinstated. He met a dramatic end in 1926 when the balcony from which he was speaking collapsed.

- From June 1924, the **mafia** was pursued by legal and illegal means, even in its heartland of Sicily. The drama of this 'war' against organised crime appealed to Mussolini and provided favourable publicity in the newspapers.
- In an attempt to strike a deal in November 1922 with the socialist trade union movement, the General Confederation of Labour (CGL), Mussolini had offered its leaders a place in his government and had proposed the amalgamation of socialist trades unions and fascist labour syndicates. This offer was renewed in July 1923, but it so outraged some of the *ras* that Mussolini had to abandon the idea. After that, left-wing political and union leaders were harassed by the Fascist Militia and were systematically spied on by the state police acting under Mussolini's personal control.
- Violence was used to intimidate possible opponents among the urban working class. In the most notorious incidents fascist *squadristi*, now part of the Fascist Militia, stormed the working-class districts of Parma and Turin in late 1922, inflicting injuries on the inhabitants and damage on houses and shops. The fascists now controlled the police so there was neither protection nor redress for their victims.

THE PROBLEM OF THE SOUTH

Fascism emerged as an essentially urban movement based in the towns of central and northern Italy. However, even when Mussolini became prime minister fascism had still made little mark on the south of the country with its backward rural economy. This created particular problems for Mussolini after 1922. On his first day as prime minister he publicly pledged that the economic and social problems of the south would soon be solved by his government and, in 1923, during a typically spectacular visit by battleship to Sicily, he promised to bring to an end the island's poverty, squalor and crime.

The fascists of the south were few in number and drawn from outside the traditional hierarchies of the region. They were usually young men, like **Aurelio Padovani**, the fascist militia commander in Naples, opposed to the corruption of *trasformismo*. Many were still revolutionaries and this did not fit well with the political compromises Mussolini had made with right-wing interests in Rome.

The attachment of the nationalists to the fascist cause in March 1923 gave fascism more of a presence in the south but political control still rested with the old liberal and conservative families who had controlled the region for decades. Short of promoting a political revolution, fascist control of the south of the country depended on striking a deal with this group.

- Fortunately the fascists now commanded the full resources of the Italian state and, as the actions of the prefects made clear, were the sole dispensers of government money and government contracts to the region.
- The liberal leaders in the south were quick to realise that continued access to state funds now involved working with Mussolini's government. The government-appointed prefects in the region reinforced this message through their control of state contracts and their powers to control local councils.
- Those local dignitaries who continued to take an independent line found that they and their localities were simply starved of funds and, inevitably, all but a tiny minority soon came into line.
- Reward came in the 1924 election when the more acceptable leaders were included on the list of government candidates, in itself a powerful inducement to conform. Fascism's progress in the south since 1922 is illustrated by the fact that the government list in that election received over two-thirds of the votes cast there.

Fascism was no longer a radical movement but had embraced the traditional conservatism and corruption of the region. The radical young fascists of the region, like Padovani in Naples, were no longer needed and, by May 1923, he had been dismissed. Inevitably, but with the important exception of the pursuit of the mafia, the region's pressing social and economic problems received little attention.

EARLY RELATIONS WITH THE CATHOLIC CHURCH

The Catholic Church hierarchy was greatly alarmed by the left-wing threat evident in the disturbances of 1920–1 and had much to gain from the establishment of a right-wing government able to guarantee stability. Mussolini recognised the enormous influence that the Church exerted in Italy and saw how valuable its endorsement of his regime would be. From the start he worked hard to reassure Church leaders that they had nothing to fear from fascism. He was helped in this by his **attack on the freemasons**.

Mussolini was not an enthusiastic churchgoer. However, he tried to bury his atheist past and now attempted, though only intermittently, to present himself as a devout Catholic, having his grown-up children baptised and going through a Church wedding service. In 1923, he introduced a series of **measures that pleased the Church**.

The Church at first responded cautiously but the longer Mussolini stayed in power the more likely it was that a mutually advantageous deal could be done between the Church and the fascist regime. Mussolini also hoped to weaken Church support for the *Popolari* (Catholic Party) and he had some measure of success when the papacy ordered the left-wing priest, Luigi Sturzo (see page 11), first to resign from the leadership of the *Popolari* (July 1923) and then to leave the country (October 1923).

In 1922, the *Popolari* were partners in Mussolini's coalition government, with two leaders in the cabinet. The party was, however, deeply divided over such co-operation with the fascists and the issue dominated its 1923 conference, attracting great publicity, which irritated Mussolini immensely. He therefore dismissed the two *Popolari* ministers and so inevitably weakened his parliamentary position. However, Mussolini had already prepared for this event.

KEY THEMES

Attack on the freemasons
The Catholic authorities had always been hostile to freemasonry as a secret society tinged with pagan rituals, a rival source of authority to the Church. They therefore welcomed Mussolini's attempt to discourage fascists from becoming masons.

Measures that pleased the Church Mussolini's measures included:

- a state grant to improve clergy salaries;
- the introduction of religious education in schools and universities;
- making the distribution of contraceptives and the promotion of birth control a criminal offence;
- a ban on a number of anti-clerical journals;
- dropping liberal proposals to tax Church property.

REVISED ELECTORAL SYSTEM

The Acerbo Law
The 1921 election to the Chamber of Deputies was based on **proportional representation** through 54 constituencies. The subsequent political instability had made proportional representation very unpopular with all except the Socialist Party and the *Popolari* who were generally held to have benefited from it. Ironically it was the unwillingness of these two parties to join in any coalition government in which the other was represented that had done most to undermine the *trasformismo* system of coalitions, so helping to let the fascists take power.

Rather than abolish the system fascists proposed modifications. The new arrangements were introduced by a fascist deputy, **Giacomo Acerbo**. Under his proposals:

- an election would be conducted under the existing arrangements and so contested by single parties or groups of parties each with their lists of constituency candidates;
- the votes across the constituencies would be totalled and the party list that had gained most votes would receive two-thirds of the seats in the chamber, provided that it had obtained at least 25 per cent of the total votes cast;
- the remaining third of the seats would then be allocated to the other lists in proportion to the votes each had gained.

Support for and opposition to Acerbo's proposals
- The fascists alone could not have carried through Acerbo's proposals but they were supported by many prominent liberals, who believed that the Acerbo Law would end the chronic political instability.
- Many liberals also felt that the new arrangements would damage the electoral prospects of the left-wing parties, including the radical liberals and the socialists, both of whom would have difficulty in attaching themselves to wider party groupings.
- Deputies were subjected to the fascist threat that, if the measure were not carried, it was very likely that parliament itself would be abolished and that Mussolini

Proportional representation When seats are distributed to each party depending on the number of votes by each party.

The Acerbo Law The passing of the Acerbo Law transformed the electoral system and the 1924 election secured Mussolini's parliamentary position.

Giacomo Acerbo 1888–1969 A fascist member of the Chamber of Deputies whose only importance was that he gave his name to the Acerbo Law.

would then rule the country through **emergency powers**. This threat was made all the more potent by the sight of armed fascist blackshirts patrolling the Chamber during the debate.

- The *Popolari*, who seemed likely to lose from the new arrangements, were stranded, for they had nothing in common with the non-religious left but their radical social agenda would deny them allies on the right. They should have opposed Acerbo's proposals but were divided about what to do. They were also under pressure from the papacy not to oppose the fascist proposals. Mussolini's attack on the freemasons and his proposals on religious education had paid off in this valuable support from the Church. It was at this point that pressure from the Vatican forced Sturzo to resign his post as leader of the *Popolari*, thus undermining their will to resist.

In the Acerbo vote in the Chamber the three best-known liberals – Giolitti, Salandra and Orlando – voted in favour and were followed by almost all their supporters along with the fascist and nationalist deputies. The *Popolari* abstained and only the socialists and communists opposed the measure, which was carried by 235 votes to 139.

The 1924 election

The way in which the Acerbo electoral system worked to Mussolini's advantage was shown in the election that soon followed.

- For electoral purposes the fascists formed a party grouping with leading liberals, former nationalists and a few *Popolari* members.
- Those selected (Mussolini took a close personal interest in their names and in their backgrounds) were placed on a common list of government-sponsored candidates.
- This list, representing the centre and the right of Italian politics, enjoyed a sweeping electoral success in 1924, obtaining exactly two-thirds of the votes cast and, of course, under the Acerbo system of 'corrected' proportional representation they were entitled to two-thirds of the seats.
- Fewer than two-thirds of the government's electoral bloc members could truly be described as fascists but the

existence of the Acerbo Law had drawn the other candidates into an alliance with them and these deputies were now committed to supporting Mussolini's government.
- Their opponents, socialists, communists, Catholics and unreconciled liberals, divided in the election and afterwards between several small and mutually hostile parties, could provide only token opposition.

Election results

The parliamentary politicians had been outmanoeuvred at their own traditional game of *trasformismo* coalition politics by the man who had until 1922 often preferred direct action as the way to deal with political problems. To argue that Mussolini had not needed the Acerbo Law, because his coalition followers already had two-thirds of the votes, is a mistake, because it was the existence of the law that had enabled him to construct his vote-winning coalition. After the 1924 election to the Chamber of Deputies the seats held by each party were:

- 374 government supporters;
- 39 *Popolari*;
- 46 socialists (but split between two rival socialist parties);
- 19 communists.

The south

The fascists did particularly well in the south of the country, including Sicily, but they did so as a result of the old political leaders of the region, seeing where power and so state patronage were going to lie, joining the government list of candidates. Fascism did not take over the south; rather the old southern elites took over fascism for their own purposes. This meant that the old social and economic patterns of the region were safe from any fascist desire to introduce radical reforms.

Violence

However, Mussolini had not entirely abandoned direct action, for the election had been marked by systematic violence and intimidation of opponents. Terror remained a favoured fascist weapon and, as the historian John Whittam has commented in *Fascist Italy* (1995), given the violent circumstances, the really surprising feature of the

Giacomo Matteotti.

KEY PERSON

**Giacomo Matteotti
1885–1924** A socialist
member of the Chamber of
Deputies. He accused
Mussolini and the fascist
squadristi of winning the 1924
election by use of terror.
Within days he was
murdered, provoking a major
crisis for Mussolini. In 1943,
the Italian anti-fascist
partisans named their groups
'Matteotti Brigades'.

KEY THEMES

Threats to Mussolini
Following the murder of
Matteotti:

- It was generally assumed
  that fascists close to him
  were responsible for
  Matteotti's disappearance,
  with the thugs of his
  personal bodyguard, the
  cheka, blamed.
- Many liberals who had
  failed to oppose Mussolini
  were outraged at what had
  happened. Some of the
  most eminent, who in the
  1924 election had appeared
  on the fascist list of
  approved candidates, now

election was that 2.5 million people voted for opposition
candidates, denying the fascists a majority of the vote in
Milan and Turin, the two great cities of northern Italy.

THE MATTEOTTI CRISIS, 1924

Murder of Matteotti

When parliament reassembled on 30 May 1924 the
socialist leader, **Giacomo Matteotti** spoke passionately and
effectively about the way in which the election had been
conducted, giving examples of intimidation of candidates
and voters. He denounced the tactics employed by the
fascists and claimed that, because of them, the election
results had no validity. Matteotti's speech infuriated
Mussolini who accused his closest followers of cowardice
for allowing such an attack on his integrity to take place.
On 10 June 1924, Matteotti was kidnapped in broad
daylight while on his way to parliament and then beaten
to death. His battered body was not found until August
and, in the meantime, rumours about his fate swept
through political circles. This resulted in **threats to
Mussolini** himself.

Throughout the summer and autumn of 1924,
Mussolini's political future was in the balance. If it could
be proved that he was implicated in the attack on
Matteotti, the criminal courts could be involved and
Mussolini, or others in his government, could be put on
trial. There were also serious political implications for
parliament. Mussolini had been trusted by those non-
fascists who had joined his list of candidates to curb and
to end fascist violence. If that violence was now being
sanctioned right at the top of the government then
something had to be done to prevent total anarchy.

In late December 1924 Mussolini's involvement seemed to
be clearly confirmed by the written evidence of **Angelo
Rossi**. The crisis deepened when his claims were published
in the anti-fascist periodical *Il Mondo*.

Compromise and normality

Before the publication of Rossi's allegations, Mussolini
tried to placate at least some of his critics.

Mussolini's guilt in the Matteotti murder is implied in a cartoon published in an underground Italian newspaper.

- The men most frequently named as the plotters, including Rossi, lost their government posts.
- Mussolini gave up his post as interior minister, which had given him control of the police force searching for Matteotti's killers.
- He issued a decree to have the Fascist Militia amalgamated with the army, army officers replacing *squadristi* leaders. Militia members would now have to swear an oath of allegiance to the king, not to Mussolini.
- Mussolini shrewdly promised to introduce new electoral arrangements that would be based on single-member constituencies, which the liberals were pressing for. As late as December 1924, he was hinting that another general election would be held in the near future and this too pleased moderate government supporters.
- He continued to 'normalise' the conduct of politics – giving nationalists key security posts, with **Alfredo Rocco** becoming Minister of Justice, and bringing liberals into his government.

By these measures Mussolini sought to reassure respectable opinion in Italy that fascist illegality was at an end.

Confrontation with extremists

Many, perhaps the majority, of the *ras* had been bitterly disappointed with the compromises made in 1922 and still wanted a truly fascist state to be established. They may have had no clear plan as to what this meant, but they were quite clear that it did not involve sacrificing

became openly critical, including Orlando, Salandra and Giolitti.
- Reports holding Mussolini responsible for what had happened appeared in opposition newspapers such as the Popolari Party's *Il Popolo* and the socialist periodical *Il Mondo*.
- Public opinion seemed to be swinging against him.
- In disgust the opposition deputies walked out of the Chamber in protest at the disappearance of Matteotti. This is known as the Aventine Secession (see below).

Aventine Secession A reference to political events in the ancient Roman Empire when men withdrawing from political life were said to have gone 'to the Aventine Hill' – one of the hills outside Rome. About 150 of the opposition deputies – mainly communists, socialists and individual *Popolari* – walked out of parliament. They hoped that their dramatic gesture and the suspicions surrounding Mussolini would influence King Victor Emmanuel III to dismiss his prime minister. But their departure meant they lost their voice in parliament and could no longer attack Mussolini there.

themselves in order to please non-fascist politicians. The *ras* were deeply alarmed at the **dismissal of senior fascists** implicated in the attack on Matteotti and saw that the proposal to place their *squadristi* under army control was striking directly at their power base, removing from fascist control the force best able to defend their movement. For extreme fascists the Matteotti affair was an opportunity not for compromise with liberal politics but the moment to press on with creating a truly fascist state. In August 1924, the Fascist Grand Council, at a meeting also attended by many of the provincial *squadristi* leaders, set up a committee to draw up a fascist constitution and plans on how it would be set up.

From the start of fascism Mussolini had faced the problem of holding together the extremists and the moderates in his movement, but he was now finding this increasingly difficult. Even in 1924 he hesitated to provoke a break with the constitution and attempted compromise once more, actually publishing the plans to control the Fascist Militia after the Grand Council meeting that had seemed to set the fascists on a very different course.

Action

Following the publication on 28 December of Rossi's allegations against Mussolini:

- on 30 December, liberals in the government seemed to be on the point of resigning;
- on 31 December, 33 of the *ras*, frustrated by all the talk of compromise and furious at the threat to the Fascist Militia, visited Mussolini. They demanded an end to the attempts to buy peace with the discredited parliamentarians and the creation instead of a fully fascist regime. Ominously on the same day there were fascist riots in Florence.

Mussolini now had to choose between continuing to placate the non-fascists and satisfying the demands of his leading fascist followers.

Mussolini's speech

On 3 January 1925, his decision made, Mussolini **addressed the Chamber** (as reported in the fascist paper *Il Popolo d'Italia*).

- He immediately went on the attack, arguing that he had always sought constitutional paths and that it was those who had walked out of parliament who had behaved unconstitutionally.
- He listed all the conciliatory steps that he had taken and which his opponents had spurned.
- Now these attempts at compromise would be at an end; in future he would provide Italy with strong government, one that would not tolerate slanderous attacks from disloyal politicians, who had abandoned their constitutional duty and walked out of parliament and encouraged newspaper libels about his own conduct.
- He reminded the deputies of the existence of the Fascist Militia but pledged that, thanks to the stern measures he would introduce, he would be able to hold them back.
- He therefore promised to continue working through normal institutions like the police and the local prefects.

The Chamber, dominated still by those elected on the fascist list of 1924, continued to back him, as did the king.

One brief passage in the address to the Chamber has been much debated. Mussolini stated that he accepted sole responsibility for what had happened and this, it has sometimes been assumed, meant that he accepted responsibility for the Matteotti murder. This he did not do. Earlier he had quite clearly denied any part in the crime; in this passage he was accepting responsibility for fascism itself. This declaration, and the references to taking stern measures, in turn reassured the *ras* that Mussolini did not intend to abandon them in pursuit of an agreement with parliamentary politicians.

Enough liberals returned to support the government to undermine any further attempts by their leaders to continue to challenge Mussolini about the murder; an attempt to pass a **vote of censure** on him on 16 January 1925 was howled down by his supporters.

Mussolini survives the crisis

The crisis lasted from June 1924 until at least Mussolini's decisive speech of 3 January 1925. In that period many factors aided his **survival**.

all that has happened [very vigorous and repeated applause; many voices shouting, 'We are with you! All with you!'] … *If Fascism has been nothing more than castor oil and the truncheon, instead of being a proud passion of the best part of Italian youth, then I am to blame* [applause]. *If Fascism has been a criminal association, then I am the chief of the criminal association!* [vigorous applause] … *If all the violence has been the result of a particular historical, political and moral climate, then responsibility for this is mine, because I have created this climate with a propaganda that has lasted from the Intervention Crisis until today.*

Gentlemen, Italy wants peace, tranquillity, calm in which to work. We shall give her this tranquillity by means of love if possible but by force if necessary [lively applause]. *You may be sure that within twenty-four hours after this speech the situation will be clarified in its every aspect.*

KEY THEME

Mussolini's survival In explaining Mussolini's survival a balance has to be struck between the importance of the king's failure to act, the power of the fascist *squadristi* across Italy, and the mistakes and weaknesses of the parliamentary politicians and those who might have been expected to support them.

- The initial walkout from the Chamber of Deputies of 150 of his opponents robbed them of the most effective means of publicising the issue. The Senate failed to condemn the government and urged conciliation.
- Those who left had gambled on causing such a scandal that the king, who as head of state was the only person who could remove Mussolini, would dismiss the government. This he did not do. Perhaps, as in 1922, he feared civil war if he challenged the fascists. Now their numbers were much larger and the *squadristi* were organised into the Fascist Militia, some detachments of which had been issued arms by the government. Fascist power in the provinces was formidable. In any case, the government had a large parliamentary majority, including a number of prominent non-fascists, so on what grounds could he dismiss it?
- Many conservative Italians, including the king, still feared a *coup* by either the socialists or the communists more than they did the continuance of fascist rule.
- Thanks to the 1924 election the government bloc in the Chamber far outnumbered the combined opposition, which was in any case fragmented and unable to work together. Crucially, key non-fascist members of the government – nationalists and the distinguished military ministers – did not resign and this provided a sound reason for the king not to dismiss the government.
- The public was not much interested in this scandal among politicians. There were only a few public meetings and poorly supported strikes in protest against the government. The socialists and the communists made no effort to mobilise their considerable support among the urban working class.
- The owners of the press were easily browbeaten into silence.
- Mussolini made enough concessions (see page 54) to quieten the opposition and then, when this failed to end the affair, he acted decisively on 3 January 1925.

THE INTRODUCTION OF AUTHORITARIAN GOVERNMENT, 1925

Within months of his January 1925 speech, Mussolini had begun to dismantle the institutions of the Liberal State.

The press

Persistent newspaper criticism of his conduct had been perhaps the greatest danger faced by Mussolini during the Matteotti crisis and the press soon paid the price for this.

- Censorship was tightened, copies of newspapers were confiscated and pressure was put on the owners to dismiss 'unsatisfactory' editors.
- In December 1925, the Press Law required that journalists had to be on an official register before they were allowed to work. The fascists controlled the register and by this time the press was effectively muzzled.
- The radio had, since 1922, been an instrument of state propaganda.

These new measures gave the fascists a virtual monopoly in the dissemination of information.

Opposition parties

- Those deputies who had walked out of the Chamber in 1924 were physically prevented from returning because, it was claimed, they had behaved unconstitutionally.
- Denied any support by the Vatican, the *Popolari* disintegrated early in 1925 and many right-wing deputies, ex-nationalists and liberals came to terms with the victorious government.
- The other parties, notably the various socialist groups, struggled on for the moment but provided no effective challenge to Mussolini.

The *Legge Fascistissime*

Passed in December 1925, the *Legge Fascistissime* greatly strengthened central government political control. It:

- banned all opposition political parties and non-fascist trades unions;
- created the new post of head of government specifically for Mussolini;
- strengthened control over the press;
- set up a new secret police service and special courts to try political offences;
- in local government replaced elected mayors and councils with government-appointed officials, the

podestà, thus silencing another potentially independent voice.

In January 1926, Mussolini was given the power to issue laws by personal decree.

Police powers

The pressure on potential troublemakers (that is, opponents of the government) was, as Mussolini had promised in January, organised by the police, supervised by the central-government appointed local prefects. In 1925, there was intense police activity against suspected opponents of the regime and this pattern was to continue and be refined in subsequent years, becoming a normal feature of life in the fascist state.

The armed forces

Changes in the control of the armed forces in 1925 were largely symbolic: the minister of war was dismissed and replaced by Mussolini and plans to reduce the size of the army were dropped. The army approved of the regime's attacks on left-wing dissident elements and its strong line on law and order. It also welcomed the talk of national greatness and an active foreign policy. The military's future was secure under fascism but Mussolini found it prudent also to take on the roles of political head of each of the armed forces – army, navy and air force. In view of all his other commitments he could scarcely wield actual control over any one of them, which, to their delight, left the admirals and the generals free to make the policy decisions in their own interests and often to the great detriment of fighting efficiency.

The civil service

Like many new governments the fascists had been determined to weed out unnecessary bureaucracy in government. They had failed to do so since 1922 and failed again in 1925. Under fascism the state bureaucracy continued to grow. However, as part of his determined efforts in 1925 to introduce strong government Mussolini continued to pursue civil servants who were freemasons; perhaps this was intended as the first stage of a total fascist purge of the service. Fascism would tolerate no rival source of loyalty, and Mussolini asserted his control over the fascist movement.

Taming the fascists

As their impatience with Mussolini in the 1924 crisis had shown, the provincial *ras* could still be a considerable disruptive influence, even with their *squadristi* incorporated into the Fascist Militia. And yet, if Mussolini was to retain the tolerance of powerful sections of Italian society, he had to hold them in check. This had been a problem since 1922 and, with outbreaks of fascist violence continuing in the summer of 1925, it was one that Mussolini's 'strong state' simply had to resolve.

In these circumstances it was strange that, in February 1925, Mussolini appointed Roberto Farinacci, the most extreme of the *squadristi ras*, to be secretary of the Fascist Party. He did this in order to emphasise his own moderation and also in the hope that Farinacci's extremism would so alarm other fascists that Mussolini could take action against the *ras*. Simultaneously, Mussolini could have intended Farinacci, an ambitious and energetic man, to attack and undermine the other *ras*, and this is certainly what he did, imposing strict **discipline on them** and on the party. Unfortunately, Farinacci failed to check, indeed encouraged, *squadristi* violence including the public killing in **Florence** in October 1925 of eight members of other parties. At the same time his speeches became more intemperate, attacking both the monarchy and the Church, until Mussolini was either forced to act or perhaps took the opportunity to act, for he must have realised that one day the restless Farinacci could become a real threat to his own position. This was still the case at the end of 1925 for the Fascist Grand Council did not dismiss the party secretary until March 1926 amid many violent protests from the *squadristi*. His fall and banishment to the insignificant town of Cremona marked an end to the power and illegal activities of the *squadristi*.

CONCLUSIONS

The crisis of 1924 and the measures taken to resolve it in 1925 marked a significant turning point in the development of the fascist state. The events of 1925 marked the end of any pretence at normal parliamentary politics and the preservation of the civil liberties of the Liberal State, and their replacement by a new authoritarianism based on Mussolini's personal dictatorship. Historians studying this period of Italian history have debated at some length what Mussolini's intentions were. Two propositions have emerged.

- He sought to end the chaos and drift of Italian politics and establish a strong government but largely within the normal workings of the Italian parliamentary constitution. He was blown off course, in 1924–5, by the seriousness of the Matteotti crisis and the intense pressure of his more extreme followers. He then moved to more radical solutions.
- From the start, he intended to create a fascist state with himself as dictator and with all the state's citizens and material resources committed totally to fascist objectives of totalitarianism and national greatness.

These issues are discussed in A2 Section 2 (pages 159–68) and you may wish to look at this now, while the topic is still fresh in your mind. Remember to separate your ideas on what Mussolini intended in the period 1922–6 from your assessment of what he actually achieved in the years to 1945.

SUMMARY QUESTIONS

1 What were the main threats to the survival of Mussolini's government in 1922–3?

2 How did the operation of the Acerbo Law in the 1924 election secure Mussolini's parliamentary position?

3 What problems did Mussolini face as a result of the murder of Matteotti?

4 Why was Mussolini able to survive the Matteotti crisis?

5 What steps were taken by Mussolini in 1925 to establish dictatorial rule?

CHAPTER 4

Fascist political life, 1925–43

INTRODUCTION

Four features of Italian government in this period are particularly noteworthy:

- the central role played, at many levels, by Mussolini personally;
- the survival and adaptation of much of the political structure of the Liberal State;
- the very limited political role of the Fascist Party and its individual members;
- the creation of the corporate state.

Each of these features affected the way the country was governed.

CONSOLIDATING THE AUTHORITARIAN STATE, 1926–9

At the height of the Matteotti crisis in January 1925 (see pages 53–7), Mussolini promised the Italian people that in future he would provide them with strong government and end the violence and anarchy of the post-war period. By the end of 1925, the formal apparatus for a personal dictatorship backed by extraordinary authoritarian powers was virtually complete.

Removal of institutions of the democratic state
Central institutions
- **Assassination attempts** in 1925 and 1926 provided the excuse for even sterner measures and, again under the terms of the *Legge Fascistissime*, all opposition parties and non-fascist trades unions were banned and individual opposition deputies in the Chamber were declared to have forfeited their seats.

KEY THEME

Assassination attempts In 1925 Major Zaniboni attempted to kill Mussolini. This assassination attempt was followed by one undertaken by an Irish woman, Violet Gibson.

The Special Tribunal for the Defence of the State
This tribunal was run by members of the militia. The judges were from the military who tried political offences. In seventeen years the Tribunal sentenced 26 people who were subsequently executed.

Fascist Grand Council In the 1930s, Mussolini called the Council less and less frequently and it played no part in the great decisions of the decade, even issues of peace and war. Simply by existing it was able to play a decisive role in the fall of Mussolini in 1943 (see pages 135–7) but, before that, other than being a useful reminder to the king as to where power really rested under fascism, it was of little consequence.

- In 1926 the **Special Tribunal for the Defence of the State** was set up to try cases involving anti-fascist activity.
- The government withdrew all passports, reissuing them only to suitable applicants.
- To accompany his new constitutional powers, Mussolini used the police and the courts of law to round up known opponents of the regime, many of whom were then banished to remote parts of the country. This was known as *Confino*.

Yet there was almost no public reaction to the measures, which were generally accepted as necessary to preserve law and order. Police numbers and activity increased sharply and the Special Tribunal was active in dealing with political undesirables and the great loss of personal freedom that these measures brought about needs to be recognised. Italians could survive under fascism but it was already clear by 1926 that they would be wise not to challenge or obstruct the regime, even in trivial ways.

Control of the economy

- In April, the minister of justice, Alfredo Rocco, pushed through laws (the Rocco Laws) that gave the fascist syndicates of workers a legally recognised basis (see page 73). They became the only bodies entitled to negotiate on behalf of workers but in return had to give up all power to strike.
- In July, the Ministry of Corporations was set up to supervise the workers' syndicates and to draw in corporations of employers before becoming a central economic planning ministry.
- In 1927, Rocco produced a Charter of Labour, heavily biased to protect the interests of employers but lacking the force of law.

By these means the government became much more active and had much more control in economic matters. They formed part of the policy to establish the corporate state.

Fascist Grand Council as state institution

In December 1928, the **Fascist Grand Council**, created by the *Duce* in 1923, was formally made a state rather than a party institution. In an encroachment on royal power it was given the right to advise on all constitutional issues, including the succession to the throne and the post of head of government (but only when this post became vacant!) as well as the membership and duties of parliament.

Lateran Pact

In February 1929, the Lateran Pact restored relations between the Catholic Church and the Italian state, doing much to secure wider acceptance of Mussolini's rule (see pages 90–1). By 1929, Mussolini's dictatorship was in place and buttressed by supporting repressive legislation. In purely political terms it did not progress far after that date, and the main interest switches to fascist social and economic achievements and, above all, to Mussolini's excitable and ambitious conduct of foreign policy.

MUSSOLINI'S CENTRAL ROLE

Power in the new authoritarian state stemmed from Mussolini.

* He could make laws by personal decree.
* There was no parliamentary scrutiny of legislation because, from 1926, only fascists and their sympathisers sat in the Chamber of Deputies, though a few, largely impotent, independent members sat in the Senate,

Mussolini, as prime minister, at his desk in 1930.

tolerated because they were ineffective in important matters.

- Victor Emmanuel III was still king and was theoretically still able to dismiss Mussolini but, having failed to take a stand against him in both 1922 and 1925, could easily be bullied into accepting whatever Mussolini decreed.
- Mussolini kept in close touch with the king, for his continued unquestioning support at least ensured that the armed forces would create no trouble for the regime.
- He made a practice of addressing both houses of parliament on important issues, particularly related to his vision of foreign affairs.

Control of policy

- For long periods **Mussolini** personally headed most of the important ministries – particularly those responsible for foreign affairs, internal security and order – and each of the three armed forces.
- Equally important was his habit of interfering in policy issues across the range of government business, often in a quite detailed way. Without Mussolini's support, other ministers had little chance of promoting policy within their own area of responsibility. But once Mussolini's initials had been secured, the minister had a powerful weapon with which to browbeat opponents and ensure that his particular version of government policy triumphed.

Propaganda

Above all, Mussolini's powerful position in the state was buttressed by relentless **state propaganda**.

This publicity harnessed the support of the masses to the regime in ways that had not been necessary in the pre-1914 era and helped change political life forever. It also created a personality cult that silenced opposition and criticism alike.

Mussolini's weaknesses

Mussolini proved an unsatisfactory leader in many respects.

- He was not able to rise above petty detail – for example, he involved himself in the design of police uniforms.

- He did not delegate effectively or choose efficient subordinates.
- In the 1930s, foreign affairs became increasingly important to him and, as a result, there was no force driving Italy on towards fascism's high-sounding *domestic* goals, so that the Italian economy and society were both characterised by drift and complacency.

Other fascist ministers

Under Mussolini there was no idea of cabinet government:

- Each minister took his authority from the *Duce*.
- Each had to follow Mussolini's instructions without question.
- The able fascists of the early days were gradually removed. Edmondo Rossoni, the leader of the fascist unions and an ardent syndicalist was dismissed in 1928; **Augusto Turati**, the colourless but competent party secretary, in 1930; Alfredo Rocco, the hard-working minister for justice, along with the ambitious ex-*ras* Dino Grandi in 1932; and Italo Balbo, the air minister, in 1934.

The able ministers were replaced by lesser men like Achille Starace as party secretary and Guido Buffarini-Guidi as minister of the interior.

- Starace greatly enlarged the size of the Fascist Party but was much ridiculed for his excessive promotion of the cult of the *Duce*, and for his fanatical pursuit of physical fitness and the cult of youth far into middle age.
- Another of the second-rate survivors was Mussolini's son-in-law, **Galeazzo Ciano**, foreign minister from 1936 to 1943, who remained in office simply to carry out Mussolini's orders.
- One able, energetic survivor was Arturo Bocchini, the long-serving head of the state police from 1926 to 1940; another was Giuseppe Bottai, who was removed from the Ministry of Corporations in 1932 but continued in a secondary role as an effective minister of education.

THE CONSERVATIVE STRUCTURE OF GOVERNMENT

The military

Mussolini's assumption of dictatorial powers had been greatly helped by the lack of opposition from the king and from the old political classes in the state. This meant that, once in power and short of instigating a real political revolution, he had to work with and protect the position of these elements within the state or risk his own position.

Italy remained a monarchy and the military certainly saw its first loyalty as being to the king, accepting Mussolini's dictatorship so long as nothing went seriously wrong and so long as its own interests within the state were safeguarded. The sensitivity of this issue was illustrated by Mussolini personally becoming minister responsible for each of the armed forces in 1925, which in practice meant that the decisive voices were those of admirals and generals, most of whom were interested in their own positions and privileges. In consequence, and despite all the lip service paid to **military needs**, Italy was not ready for war in 1939 and functioned remarkably badly when it entered the war in 1940.

Law and order

In other areas of life the survival of the old institutions of Liberal Italy at first provided useful continuity. The police force and the courts continued to provide law and order and did much to bring the era of political violence, including fascist-promoted violence, to an end. They also either destroyed or drove **the mafia** underground, a result of a great increase in their political activity pursuing possible opponents of the regime. The secret police, the OVRA, had a similar reputation, which was deliberately embroidered by the regime. It spied on both opponents and fascists alike but was not particularly efficient and remained under the control of the Ministry of the Interior.

The civil service

The traditional civil service, employing too many staff and lethargic, also survived fascist plans to trim it and make it more efficient The plans were never implemented because

KEY THEMES

Military needs Judged by its own criterion of the central importance of military strength, fascist Italy was not efficiently governed.

Battle against the Mafia. Waged in the 1920s by prefect Cesare Mari, the Battle against the Mafia led to mafia leaders emigrating or being driven underground. The battle was brutal and effective. In 1928, the number of murders in Palermo fell to 25 from 278 in 1924.

thousands of civil servants took the obvious precaution of joining the Fascist Party to protect their jobs. By the mid-1930s, the number of bureaucrats was on the increase again, helped by the need to enforce endless new fascist regulations of everyday life and the economy.

THE ROLE OF THE FASCIST PARTY

Mussolini's assumption of dictatorial powers included marginalising radical fascists, for he took steps in 1925 to bring the fascist *squadristi* under control and to purge the membership of the party.

Leaders
With Farinacci's dismissal in 1926 (see page 60) went the last hope of a radical fascist political revolution and the last chance for an independent party leader capable of standing up to Mussolini. His successor as party secretary, Augusto Turati, carried out Mussolini's programme of centralising power within the party and destroying the power bases of the local fascist leaders until he in turn was dismissed.

Party members
New members usually joined in order to protect their jobs in local government and the civil service. Henceforward, party officers were appointed from above, not elected. The party ceased to be a radical force and, indeed, became a largely non-political institution. It had no share of power in the state or influence on central government policy. An indication of the party's political impotence is that no party congress was held after 1925. Its central executive, the Fascist Grand Council (see page 63), with theoretically vast powers, met only rarely, when summoned by Mussolini. It did not meet once in the eventful years from 1939 to 1942. All this was a major disappointment for those early rank-and-file fascists, who had expected some form of fascist revolution to transform the state rather than the continuation of the old ways and the old forms.

Impact on everyday lives of the people
Despite all this, the party remained important in the provinces:

- as a distributor of endless propaganda;
- as a source of jobs and patronage that soon shaded into corruption;
- in the social sphere as organiser of the leisure activities promoted by the *Dopolavoro*.

The party was the fascist agency closest to the people and the one that had the greatest impact on their everyday lives. In the 1920s, it had been an elite group and, even in the 1930s, its leadership remained a close-knit body drawn from early fascists but the number of **party members** increased rapidly in the 1930s. The party leaders remained active, if powerless, but the bulk of the membership was there in a sleeping role.

THE CORPORATE STATE

This was, in theory at least, Fascist Italy's most interesting and revolutionary contribution to government: an attempt to incorporate all the organised economic interests under the direct control of the state.

- The corporate state was first promulgated in the Rocco Law on trade union activity but then developed very slowly so that it was 1934 before the full system of corporations was in place.
- It appeared to be a decentralised system but this was deceptive for within the corporations the key roles were filled by government appointees.
- The system is best judged in relation to its economic achievements. Unfortunately, corruption and muddle in the eventual 22 corporations often prevented them from promoting any great improvements in economic efficiency (see pages 73–4).

It was only in 1939 that the corporations were made the basis of national political life, replacing parliament. The new structure was soon overtaken by the demands of war, but the mixed economic record of the corporations does not suggest that, even in more normal circumstances, it would have been particularly effective or more than a façade for Mussolini's continuing personal rule.

OPPOSITION TO FASCISM

There was very little political opposition to the regime after 1926.

- Only a few thousand communists managed to keep in contact with each other and produce occasional anti-fascist leaflets.
- Active non-communist opponents of the regime had to leave the country and had no impact on events in Italy. Any who stayed were hounded by the police, exiled to remote villages or, in some 5000 cases, were imprisoned in camps on one or other of Italy's Mediterranean islands (*Confino*). Mussolini felt sufficiently secure that he released some of them in 1932 as a humanitarian gesture to mark the tenth anniversary of the fascist regime.
- With the media censored or state-controlled there was no route by which opponents of the regime could make themselves heard and so those who were disaffected wisely chose to remain silent and unorganised.
- In any event, stability at home and apparent foreign policy triumphs – both backed by the full resources of state propaganda (see page 65) – ensured that, until the mid-1930s at least, Mussolini remained a popular figure.
- The first Italians actively to resist fascism in the 1930s did so from exile, fighting against Franco's fascists and their Italian fascist allies in the **Spanish Civil War**.

Many Italians may have been non-fascists and, from 1936, more and more of them, especially students and industrial workers, were disenchanted with the regime but, until after Italy entered the Second World War in 1940, there was no anti-fascist movement of note.

A FASCIST REVOLUTION?

In order to achieve power in the 1920s, Mussolini had disappointed his more radical followers by a series of accommodations with the Italian political establishment. In the early 1930s, there was much propaganda about fascist social and economic achievements, but these

Confino The most famous Italian sentenced to *Confino* was the communist Antonio Gramsci.

Spanish Civil War In the Spanish Civil War 1936–9 the nationalist General Franco received the support of Mussolini who sent him arms, soldiers and money. However, many Italians joined the International Brigade to fight against Franco. At the Battle of Guadalahara in 1937 Italians in the International Brigade defeated fascist troops.

remained largely set within the structures that the fascists had inherited.

New direction

The Ethiopian triumph of 1936 with its accompanying propaganda encouraged the regime to step up its efforts to create a more fascist society (see pages 93–5). However, the political implications of this new direction had still not been worked through before Italy found itself at war. The political centrepiece of the new radicalism was the law passed in January 1939, which abolished the Chamber of Deputies and replaced it with the Chamber of Fasces and Corporations whose members – all government appointees – would come from:

- the national council of the Fascist Party;
- the national council of corporations;
- the Fascist Grand Council.

The role of the monarchy

The Senate survived and was to play a part with the new Chamber in law-making but no reference was made to the role of the king in this regard. One of the last acts of the Chamber of Deputies had been to give both Mussolini and Victor Emmanuel the title of first marshal of the empire, placing them at the same level of prestige. At the outset of war in 1940 the king maintained his constitutional prerogative as head of state by placing Mussolini in charge of conducting military operations, rather than merely letting him seize that role. Victory in war would have left Mussolini in a strong position to enhance further his own powers at the expense of those of the monarch. Defeat in war saved the monarchy from Mussolini but Victor Emmanuel's association first with the fascist dictatorship and then, after the fascist regime's collapse in 1943, with the calamitous misconduct of the war, meant that the monarchy's days were numbered.

CONCLUSIONS

It is useful to see Mussolini's peacetime dictatorship as falling roughly into three phases:

- 1926–9 when the political emphasis was on constructing the authoritarian state, including the dictatorship (see pages 62–4);
- 1930–4 when the social and economic policies examined in AS Chapters 5 and 6 were the regime's main concern;
- 1935–40 when foreign policy issues and events became the regime's first priority (see AS Chapter 7). Italy also became distinctly more militaristic at this time, with men in uniforms everywhere, and with the regime making strenuous efforts after 1936 to create a more fascist society.

Mussolini established his political pre-eminence in the first phase. In the second, he did not really commit the regime to fundamental changes but was content to maintain his dictatorship and to make the best propaganda use of relatively modest social and economic innovations. He came into his own in the final phase, perpetually in military uniform and obsessed with imperial and foreign policy ambitions intended to making Italy great through military achievement.

SUMMARY QUESTIONS

1 What steps, taken from 1926 to 1929, helped to consolidate Mussolini's authoritarian state?

2 Why did the powerful fascist regime prove unable to provide Italy with efficient government?

3 In what ways did the fascist regime become politically more extreme in the late 1930s?

CHAPTER 5

Fascist Italy: the economy

INTRODUCTION

Italian economic policy soon became subordinate to Mussolini's political goals. In fascist theory, government direction of economic policy was central to building a strong state, capable of defending and developing Italy's national interests, which was in turn likely to involve military action. This assumption underpinned all of the main economic initiatives undertaken by the regime:

- establishment of the **corporate state** where, in theory, all economic activity and, by 1939, political life were to be organised through corporations, in which both workers and employers would be involved;
- the 1926 revaluation of the lira at Mussolini's personal insistence;
- state activity during the early 1930s depression to protect the banking system and key industrial undertakings;
- pursuit of economic self-sufficiency;
- the Battle for Grain;
- the Battle for Land.

THE CORPORATE STATE

The corporate state proved to be something of a mirage. It was intended to reorganise the basis of economic activity, eliminating labour problems, in order to create an efficiently functioning economy. The idea was copied from the system briefly introduced on a small scale in Fiume during D'Annunzio's 1919 occupation of the city and in origin owed something to the **syndicalist** movement. It owed much to the ideas developed before 1914 by Alfredo Rocco, previously a leading nationalist, for state-sponsored trades unions to control economic activity.

The legislation setting up the structure of corporatism was produced by Rocco between 1926 and 1928. Rocco set up, in each major area of the economy, *separate* corporations of workers and employers each of which would also have state-appointed officials on its committee. This dashed the hopes of syndicalist fascists, notably Edmondo Rossoni – once leader of the fascist unions but dismissed in 1928 – that the new corporations would control the factories and define economic policy. It did, however, reassure the employers who had feared that they were about to lose control of their factories. The corporations would now simply negotiate with each other about labour relations, including wage-rates. A Ministry of Corporations was set up in 1926 to regulate the working of the system.

However, in practice, the corporations – especially the employer corporations – emerged only slowly during the late 1920s and early 1930s and were dominated by the state-appointed officials.

- They played no part in defining economic policy or, indeed, in developing the economy.
- Most industrialists were suspicious of them and Mussolini failed to give them any backing.
- It took until 1934 before the system was fully established, with corporations formally set up in 22 areas of the economy.

The corporations lingered on, important perhaps in terms of everyday industrial relations but largely irrelevant to any assessment of national economic performance. They were frequently referred to in the regime's propaganda and impressed foreign visitors who took both their functions and their success at face value.

FEATURES OF FASCIST ECONOMIC POLICY

- By 1922, the fascist movement had abandoned the fierce anti-capitalist ideas of 1919 and the expansion of party membership after 1922 encouraged economic policy to move further to the right.
- From 1922 to 1925, Mussolini's coalition government

continued to pursue the liberal free-market trade and economic policies of its predecessors and, aided in part by the post-war international economic boom, the economy flourished. Exports of goods, particularly cars, rose sharply, unemployment fell and the economy prospered. Until 1925, the able finance minister Alberto De Stefani was able both to cut taxes and achieve a budget surplus but in that year the economic outlook darkened.

- A poor harvest in 1924 coincided with a decline in the international value of the lira and both contributed to worrying price inflation. Italy seemed to be at the mercy of international economic trends dictated by powers like the United States of America, to whom the Italian state owed vast sums of money in war debts. It was resentment at this subordinate situation in 1926 that prompted Mussolini to seek economic independence by introducing his two best-known economic policies – the Battle for Grain and the revaluation of the lira.

Currency revaluation – the *Quota Novanta*

In 1926, Mussolini made his most decisive contribution in economic matters when he pushed through a sharp **revaluation** of the lira, from 150 lira to 90 lira against the British pound sterling. His motives were political: a strong lira demonstrated a strong Italy and from this point Italian currency was over-valued against other currencies. This marked a turning point in economic policy as the free market was abandoned and the state increasingly intervened to regulate the economy, most directly by the introduction of tariffs on imports that were intended to protect both the new value of the lira and also favoured sectors of the economy from foreign competition. Stress was now laid on the need for an active government economic role in terms of regulating industrial relations, managing state finances and in developing the economy.

Effects of revaluation

- The revaluation hit Italy's export trade but, by making imports cheaper, benefited heavy industries, such as steel and chemicals, which relied on imported raw materials. These industries later provided the basis for an expanded rearmament industry and so supported the 'active' foreign policy, which became the chief characteristic of the fascist state.

- Tariffs on undesirable imports such as consumer goods and foodstuffs kept their price high and restricted demand.
- Long before Italy went to war the industrial basis for military adventure was, in this way, being established and the revaluation was presented to the Italian people in dramatic terms as part of a 'battle' for economic survival.
- The over-valuation of the lira also required that all the resources of fascist propaganda were deployed to convince Italian workers of the need to accept wage-cuts to bring wages in line with the value of the new lira. In practice this pressure was so successful that wages fell more than prices and the living standards of most working-class Italians fell markedly in order to secure Mussolini's revaluation.

Active state intervention in the economy
The depression

The most telling example of the fascist government's willingness to intervene in economic matters occurred when the world trade depression of the early 1930s hit the banking system. The banks, with too much money tied up in long-term loans to depressed industrial undertakings, were hit particularly hard and the government acted promptly to protect them.

The IMI and IRI These institutions concentrated on rescuing industry and banks by playing a key role in investigating industry.

- Through the Instituto Mobiliare Italiano (**IMI**) founded in 1931 and the Institute for Industrial Reconstruction (**IRI**) founded in 1933 the government bought the industrial securities deposited with the banks as security for loans and went on to buy the bank shares as well.
- Banks that survived the crisis were prevented from long-term lending, which increasingly became the responsibility of state agencies like the IRI.

This 'revolution in Italian finance' saved many small firms and individuals from ruin and was quoted approvingly, in Italy and abroad, as being in sharp contrast to the inactivity of other European governments. The historian Martin Clark, in *Modern Italy* (1996), considers that Italy survived the depression 'relatively painlessly' and that 'the banking system, although now state owned, was less vulnerable than before'.

After the depression
For the rest of the fascist period the government continued an active economic role through the ownership of businesses as well as through trade policy and import duties. This was not a programme of mass nationalisation of the industrial sector. The economy remained in private ownership and the government worked alongside and in support of large private firms. Many of the shares obtained by the IRI were later sold in order to offset the organisation's costs. Despite this, by 1939, the IRI had built up a dominant interest in some of the country's largest enterprises, including the Terni steelworks, the Ansaldo shipbuilding works and the L'Italia and Adriatica shipping lines.

Bureaucracy
State aid did not, in practice, always promote the national economic interest – for example, it encouraged firms to combine together in **cartels** and allowed the emergence of monopolies. State intervention in economic matters created a vast bureaucracy, operating controls, granting licences, manufacturing paperwork and all too often simply providing jobs for party members. Many members of Italy's middle classes may have benefited from having jobs in the bureaucracy but its existence did nothing for economic efficiency. The corporations, on the other hand, played little part in these economic initiatives promoted by the central government.

The aim of self-sufficiency (autarky)
Self-sufficiency became the most important **economic policy** aim from as early as 1930 and took on even greater urgency as **foreign policy** became more adventurous from 1935 onwards.

- It involved encouraging heavy industry, particularly industry with any military importance.
- It sought self-sufficiency in food supplies, especially grain.
- Both financial and trade policy were increasingly subordinated to the aim of autarky, with both working

---

KEY TERM

Cartel A union of business firms organised to control prices.

KEY THEME

Economic and foreign policy The fascist government encouraged self-sufficiency by redirecting its export trade towards its African Empire and, by trade agreements and import licensing policy, towards its new ally, Nazi Germany (see pages 114–22). In the late 1930s, these markets came to account for almost 50 per cent of Italian exports and, from 1936, economic policy became subordinate to the new direction in foreign policy.

to depress demand for consumer goods in order to reduce imports and provide surplus finance for heavy industrial and military spending.

- As a result, the living standards of industrial workers and the bulk of the peasantry were generally lower than in the 1920s, but to Mussolini this was a price well worth paying in order to build a nation ready for war.

After Italy invaded Ethiopia in 1935, the League of Nations imposed economic sanctions on the country and this led the fascist government to re-emphasise the thrust for self-sufficiency on patriotic grounds. The great increase in military spending after 1935 – financed by large-scale borrowing – led to government demand dominating the economy. In the late 1930s, between one-third and one-half of government spending went on the military – i.e. between 15 billion and 21 billion lira each year.

Economic inefficiency

State interference in the economy had an adverse effect on efficiency.

- Subsidies and the promotion of monopolies and cartels distorted the normal working of the market and had to be paid for through higher prices and declining standards of living for many Italians.
- In practice, self-sufficiency could never be realised in certain key areas, notably coal, **oil** and raw materials for the metal industries.
- The idea that Italy's African Empire could help make up deficiencies soon proved to be wide of the mark.
- Only with Germany's aid was there any hope of Italy's quest for autarky being fulfilled so that the direction taken by fascist economic policy in turn reinforced the logic of its post-1935 foreign policy but also left Italy dependent on its economically more advanced ally.

KEY THEME

Libya and oil Italy lacks natural fuel resources. From 1912 it controlled Libya, but Libya's vast oil reserves were only identified in the 1950s, long after it had ceased to be an Italian possession. The Italians had to export oil to Libya.

THE ECONOMY UNDER FASCISM

Industry

The 1926 revaluation of the lira meant that exporting industries, particularly cars and textiles, were badly hit as their products were priced out of world markets. The car industry used the home market to such effect that its workforce doubled in size during the 1930s, giving the best indication of a rising standard of living for at least some Italians.

- On the other hand, the steel industry, with cheaper coal and iron ore imports, and the chemical industry did well.
- Backed by heavy state subsidies the shipbuilding industry also developed rapidly.
- The massive programme of electrification and an impressive road-building programme also relied heavily on state initiative and state subsidies. The emphasis placed on heavy industry and on rearmament inevitably led to a switch in manufacturing resources to these areas.

Agriculture and the land

Mussolini, spurred on by the demands of self-sufficiency, had impressive schemes for land development. Large projects and dramatic gestures had great appeal to him. Mundane problems of rural poverty and the great economic divide between the progressive north of the country and the abject and immovable poverty of the south were usually ignored. He dreamed of an idealised rural Italy based on a society of independent, prosperous peasant farmers but he did nothing to bring it about. He was, in any case, unable to take radical steps either to reorganise farming or to make it more efficient for, at the heart of his agrarian policy, was a contradiction.

- Small, but inefficient, peasant farmers were important supporters of his rule.
- But the capitalist farmers of northern and central Italy had been some of fascism's earliest allies.

The Battle for Grain, 1925

The purpose of the **Battle for Grain** was to reduce the volume of foreign wheat imports, which were now subjected to high import duties.

- The policy benefited the large grain farmers of the **Po Valley** in the north.
- The state provided storage facilities and marketing

Mussolini makes the most of the Battle for Grain on land reclaimed from the Pontine Marshes near Rome. Here he is seen imitating the gesture of Romulus by cutting the first sod of the new city of Aprilla, the fourth town to be built on the reclaimed land.

agencies as well as training courses and publicity campaigns in new production methods.
- New areas of land were brought into wheat production, sometimes on unsuitable hill land in northern Italy.
- In the late 1930s, total wheat production was double what it had been in the pre-fascist era and 40 per cent higher than in the early 1920s.
- Wheat imports had dwindled to a trickle.

However, the Battle for Grain was far from an unqualified success.

- Italian wheat yields remained low and costs were high compared with those in France, for example.
- Much of the new wheat land was in the hot south and would have been better still-employed in the traditional production of olives and in providing pastureland. Cattle and sheep farming and fruit, especially olive and wine **production, declined.** The opportunity to turn these crops into a valuable export trade was lost, one more example of how the quest for self-sufficiency was pursued at the expense of economic efficiency and, ultimately, the living standards of many Italians.

Fascist propaganda announced the achievements of the Battle for Grain policy. In fact, the battle was, like so much of fascist economic policy, a success only in advancing the strictly political objective of self-sufficiency

KEY THEME

Decline in farming in the south Between 1918 and 1930, the number of cattle in the south fell by 20 per cent. The number of sheep fell by 18 per cent.

so that the country would have enough food in the event of war. It also helped the arable farmers in the north who were strong supporters of the regime. It made poor economic sense, perhaps best symbolised by Italy becoming an importer of olive oil.

The Battle for Land

In 1928 the 'Mussolini Law' outlined the regime's policy on **land reclamation**.

- Some drainage projects proved successful; the well-known Pontine Marsh scheme near Rome was, by 1935 providing land for settlement. The marshes were near Rome and provided a good propaganda opportunity for Mussolini. Even there much of the reclaimed land was lost again in the war period.
- In other areas, land reclamation projects were not even this successful and certainly came nowhere close to propaganda claims.
- For some years the actual reclamation of the land provided work for the unemployed and large subsidies for the great landowners who often administered the schemes but, by 1940, the programme had been abandoned.

Effects on peasant farmers

- Fascist propaganda stressed the need to revive the rural areas and to build up a strong peasantry, which was in turn linked with the Battle for Births (see pages 89–90).
- The other purpose of the Battle for Land was to revive rural Italy by altering the pattern of landowning for the benefit of small farmers at the expense of the large estates.
- In practice, however, the fascist regime achieved nothing in the way of land redistribution, which was, in any event, inconsistent with the central thrust of the more high-profile Battle for Grain.
- Subsidies benefited large landowners and fewer than 10,000 peasant families were re-settled on reclaimed land, for the drive for increased wheat production called for large-scale, machine-based farming methods, not hand labour on peasant plots.
- The small peasant farmers, despite being the backbone

of the regime in many rural areas, grew neither in numbers nor in prosperity during the fascist period. Except in the depth of the early 1930s depression, migration to the towns continued, despite local prefects and police being given powers to prevent and reverse it.

With regard to land-holding and the revival of rural Italy, as elsewhere, fascism proved to be a conservative force rather than one promoting radical change. In 1940, the peasants – 90 per cent of the farming population – owned only 13 per cent of the land while the richest 0.5 per cent of the population still owned over 40 per cent of the land.

ASSESSING THE FASCIST ECONOMIC PERFORMANCE

The depression

Fascist economic activity probably spared Italy the worst social and economic effects of the 1930s depression. Its policies safeguarded the banking system, built up heavy industries, bolstered the large landowning class and made Italy self-sufficient in wheat. The development of the electricity network, largely based on hydroelectricity stations exploiting Italy's water resources, and the extensive road-building programme owed much to **government encouragement** and subsidy.

Growth despite government policy

Developments elsewhere owed little or nothing to government policy. The expansion in light engineering, paralleling developments in the electrical and motor industries elsewhere in western Europe and the USA, provided the best example of economic growth despite government indifference. Some government policies failed: the battles for grain and land were far from unqualified successes and others were positively harmful to the economy – for example, the unquestioned investment in armaments and the high import tariffs protecting inefficient industries at the expense of Italian consumers.

Military needs

In the final analysis, fascism extolled military strength and the economy was directed to military needs. Other areas of the economy, notably the manufacture of consumer goods, suffered in consequence and the Italian national debt ballooned out of control. And yet, in 1939, after all the emphasis on armaments and military expenditure, Mussolini had to confess that Italy was not ready to join Hitler's war. By fascism's own criteria this was a fundamental failure.

SUMMARY QUESTIONS

1 In what ways did the 1926 revaluation of the lira mark a new direction in fascist economic policy?

2 How did the government try to support the economy during the world economic depression of the early 1930s?

3 Why did Italy pursue a policy of economic self-sufficiency during the 1930s? How successful was the policy?

4 Overall did the fascist regime help or hinder the Italian economy?

CHAPTER 6

Fascist society

INTRODUCTION

Fascism offered little in the way of a developed political philosophy and, once in power, the fascists could provide no detailed blueprint for reforming Italian society. They were, however, committed to the idea of a strong state and the belief that the citizen's central role was to serve the state. There were two principal reasons why the second aim could not be achieved easily.

- Fascist Italy was in theory a totalitarian state, but in practice totalitarianism failed because, in coming to power, Mussolini had fatally compromised fascist radicalism by a series of deals with well-entrenched conservative interests.
- Italy's persistent administrative inefficiencies blunted the fascist government's ability to impose its will and pursue its goals.

As a result, for many Italians the **pattern of everyday life under the fascists** had significant continuities with what had gone before. Above all, for almost all Italians in the countryside and many in the towns, the Catholic Church, since 1929 happily at peace with the political regime, flourished and, on a day-to-day basis, brought spiritual consolation to millions of the faithful. Politically, in the 1920s the fascists had struck a deal with conservative interests in the state and thereafter the working classes were kept in their place, but this was not the full story. The fascist state took an active interest in the everyday lives of its citizens, and, while such interest could be threatening, it did also lead to innovative social welfare and leisure programmes like the *Dopolavoro* (see pages 91–2).

KEY THEME

Pattern of everyday life under the fascists

- There were no dramatic economic upheavals such as those that occurred in the Soviet Union.
- The state institutions – police, courts, tax-collectors – seemed to function much as they always had and with the same people still in charge.
- Local government underwent more dramatic change but may well have been more efficient under the state-appointed *podestà* than it had been under the now-defunct elected local councils.
- Fortunately, Mussolini had honoured his pledge to curb the violence of the fascist *squadristi* and had crushed the violent potential of their left-wing opponents.
- In perhaps its most beneficial act, the fascist regime even destroyed the power of the mafia.

POULATION TRENDS

Employment

Patterns of employment provided continuity.

- There were as many small shops as ever, over half a million in the 1930s.
- Growing state bureaucracy and the expanding teaching profession provided more posts for the middle classes.
- Industrial jobs were found in the northern towns and provided a notably higher standard of living than the agrarian economy of southern Italy, for fascism did nothing to resolve the north–south divide that had dogged Italy since its creation.
- The establishment of a national **electricity** grid might have helped, but electricity cost three times as much in the south as it did in northern towns.

Migration patterns

The lower standards of living in the south drove many to emigrate. The United States of America had been the traditional magnet, but, as it closed its doors in the early 1920s, the emigrants trekked instead to the towns of northern Italy, some of which, doubling in size in the fascist era, acquired vast new but mean working-class suburbs. The difficulty the fascist state had in controlling its individual citizens was well illustrated by the total failure of its schemes to restrict this tide of **migration** by allowing only those with licences to move. The anti-migration measures may have illustrated the theoretical loss of freedom brought about by fascism, but in practice the efforts of the local authorities to enforce them were totally overwhelmed by the scale of the movement.

WELFARE ORGANISATIONS

A feature of the fascist state was the number and size of the organisations that were founded for social purposes.

- By 1940, nearly a half of the entire population was involved in one or other of them.
- These youth movements, student movements and the

KEY THEMES

Electricity was generated in Italy by water. Therefore the industry was based in the north where the hydro-electric turbines were driven by water from the Alps. By 1937 it produced 14.8 billion kilowatt hours.

Migration Industrial work meant that many Italians moved into growing cities. Rome's population doubled between 1921 and 1946, from 700,000 to 1.4 million inhabitants in the fascist period. During the 1930s, over 30,000 immigrants moved to the industrial city of Turin each year, almost all from rural areas.

leisure organisations (the *Dopolavoro*) promoted total loyalty to the *Duce* but also met social needs.

- As well as the inevitable uniforms and parades they provided opportunities to be involved in both voluntary work and paid employment.
- They were also an effective distraction from getting involved in political issues for even the local branches of the Fascist Party, which often carried out social work, deliberately avoided political discussions.
- All these bodies were imposed and organised from above. None acted as a route for the upward movement of ideas from the people to local and national leaders and in the end this seriously weakened the fascist state.

YOUNG PEOPLE

Early education policy

Although the fascist regime tinkered with **the school system** no revolutionary changes in the pattern of education were introduced. The influential first education minister, the philosopher Giovanni Gentile was, at heart, a conservative. Under him:

- there was an increased emphasis on the study of Italian history and culture, some of which was given a fascist slant and, perhaps surprisingly, practical subjects tended to be neglected at the secondary level;
- the emphasis was on raising standards by rigorous examination and so weeding out unsuitable secondary and university students: student numbers at these levels declined;
- primary education was generally neglected in the Gentile reforms.

Such conservatism disappointed those who had hoped for a fascist transformation of the education system. It suited the middle classes by providing education suitable for safe jobs in the state bureaucracy; in this it was a logical development of the compromises fascism had already made with the political establishment in order to gain power.

Growing fascist control of education

In the early 1930s, **fascist control of education** increased. The system served the interests of the middle classes by providing a route to suitable jobs: it was essentially a conservative structure. Church schools had survived and had become increasingly attractive to middle-class parents who could afford the fees. Their continued existence, part of the price Mussolini paid for his politically valuable accord with the Church, remained a major obstacle to the creation of a thoroughgoing fascist education system.

From 1937, under the new education minister Giuseppe Bottai, more radical reforms were planned, intended to make the education system more amenable to strictly fascist ends and to employ the schools and universities to create a truly fascist society.

Youth organisations

The regime had a greater direct **impact on the young** through the numerous youth clubs that were set up.

- By the late 1930s, the Italian youth movement and the fascist student unions had over 8 million members. The main youth organisation was the *Opera Nazionale Balilla* (ONB) with branches for different ages of both boys and girls from 8 to 21.
- These bodies together provided for children as young as 6 and students through to 26.
- From 1929, the youth movement was directed by the Ministry of National Education, which emphasised the importance of sport, gymnastics and military drilling.

The motto of the youth movement was 'Believe, Obey, Fight' and its central purpose was to produce a new generation of Italians worthy of the *Duce* and able to fight to create a great nation. Warlike and patriotic images were constantly emphasised. There were many rallies with youths dressed in suitable uniforms.

Rival organisations and criticism

Young people came under a lot of pressure to join these official clubs and rival organisations had many obstacles put in their way; for example, after 1931 Church clubs were not permitted to organise sporting activities.

Although Catholic youth clubs continued, the fascist youth movement was perhaps the regime's most successful propaganda agent. By 1939, it had done much to persuade a generation of young people that fascism was normal and part of the Italian way of life.

One curious feature of the regime's approach to young people was that it showed a relaxed attitude to university student **criticism of the regime**.

WOMEN IN FASCIST ITALY

Government policy
In its early radicalism fascism had appeared to offer women a wider, more responsible role in society. But that was in 1919 and as the movement grew in numbers both the *squadristi* and the newcomers to the Fascist Party promoted an increasingly conservative, indeed repressive, view of the role of **women under fascism**.

- The woman's role was to be in the home, the guardian there of moral virtue but naturally subject to the authority of her husband.
- The state discouraged the employment of women, sacking many in state-controlled enterprises like the railways and creating a climate where only a few jobs in private companies and domestic work were seen as suitable female employment.
- Women were also discouraged from secondary and university education but in fact numbers there increased greatly over those in pre-fascist times.

Women's organisations
The contradiction in all this was that the fascists created organisations for women.

- Their role in the state may often have been mundane but the half million members of Fascist Women did have a public role.
- The Fascist Party created women's *fasci* (groups) parallel to the male *fasci* but then directed the women members into neighbourhood welfare work, an extension of their expected role in the home.

Criticism of the regime
The regime tolerated hostile student union newspaper articles and films, apparently in the conviction that such outbursts were relatively harmless and also a useful safety valve.

Women under fascism – the vote In 1925, women were given the vote in local elections. It was an empty gesture, for changes in local government promoting the government-appointed *podestà* system meant that such elections were no longer held. Women received the vote in parliamentary elections only after the end of the fascist era.

An Italian girl proud of the portrait of Mussolini on her costume.

- Women were specifically forbidden to engage in political affairs but were seen as useful in distributing fascist propaganda.
- Women's organisations helped to arrange provision for family holidays and advice on bringing up children.
- Young women enjoyed greater social freedom than their mothers and grandmothers had. They were encouraged to take part in sport, with the best of them given substantial help to reach the highest levels, particularly in athletics where they could bring honours to the state.

The fascist ideal of the woman in the home was never achieved. In practice, the number of women in employment scarcely fell during the fascist period – another indicator of the limited power of the regime to create a fascist society against the quietly held convictions and interests of its citizens.

The Battle for Births

With fascist Italy geared to masculine ends and with military greatness seen as the most important of these, women's roles were always going to be seen as subordinate, except in one vital area – the production of enough young men able to fight for their country. **The Battle for Births** arose from the typically fascist idea of building up the nation's strength for unspecified foreign trials.

- Laws against contraception and abortion were strictly enforced.
- Bachelors paid heavy extra taxes, which raised 230 million lire in 1939.
- Family allowances were introduced in 1930.
- Loans to newly married couples were gradually written off as they produced children. By 1939 marriage loans had cost the state 89 million lire.
- Job promotion in the civil service was reserved for those men who had fathered children.

The campaign largely failed. Men remained bachelors or married later in life and the birth rate continued to fall. As the historian Martin Clark noted (*Modern Italy*, 1996): 'By 1936 there were 102.7 births per 1000 women of child-bearing age; in 1911 there had been 147.5.' This **population trend** was similar to that experienced in other west European countries in the inter-war period.

KEY THEME

The Battle for Births Part of the fascist drive for national greatness, this was a much-publicised campaign to increase Italy's population. However it did not work.

The campaign for births was a mix of propaganda and financial incentives; its comparative failure gives an interesting indication of the limits on the fascist state's ability to direct its citizens down paths they did not want to follow. In turn this raises important questions about the limits of totalitarianism and, indeed, the issue of whether Italy in the 1930s can really be described as a totalitarian state. (This topic is examined in A2 Section 4.)

THE CATHOLIC CHURCH

The Lateran Pact

Relations between the Church and the State were governed by the Lateran Pact of 1929 by which Mussolini had negotiated an end to the conflict that had existed since Italy was unified in the mid-nineteenth century. The Pact consisted of:

- a treaty setting up the Vatican City as a tiny independent state within Rome and with the Pope as the head of state;
- a financial settlement, which gave the Church some compensation for the lands it had lost when Italy was unified in 1870 – it received 750 million lire and 1 billion lire in state bonds;
- a religious **Concordat** that in practice established Catholicism as the state religion in Italy and accepted the survival of the Church administrative and religious structure independent of state institutions.

Cordial relations between Church and state

The agreement was a great triumph for Mussolini and marked the end of 60 years of animosity between the Catholic Church and the Italian state.

- Most Italians were delighted with this ending of the conflict between Church and state and in general it secured their unquestioning acceptance of the regime until at least 1936.
- The cordial relations survived a fascist assault on the **Church's youth groups** in 1931 that ended in a compromise limiting their role to religious activities.

The loss of their sports teams, especially football, made them much less of a threat to the fascists' own clubs.

- By 1938, more serious doubts were emerging within the Catholic Church over the increased belligerence of Mussolini's foreign policy and his newly introduced anti-Jewish policies, but, until that point, relations between Church and state were cordial and reconciled many Italians to the regime. This was important, for the Church and its servants were an important presence in Italian society at all levels from the humble parish priest through to the politically influential bishops and cardinals.

Mussolini had made very few material concessions in return for these huge advantages – a few acres of land and a modest financial payment to the papacy. The Concordat did, however, mean that Mussolini could no longer hope to create a totally fascist society with the state as the only focus of Italian loyalty. This compromise with the Catholic Church paralleled his earlier compromises on the road to power – with the monarchy and other state institutions. A thoroughgoing fascist revolution was now perhaps impossible.

LEISURE

The *Dopolavoro*

In an ambitious effort to link the people more closely to fascist aims and the fascist regime a systematic attempt was made to provide adult leisure programmes and facilities and to introduce welfare facilities. These programmes were known as the *Dopolavoro* and were administered by a government agency, the *Opera Nazionale Dopolavoro* (OND), set up in 1925.

- They were closely linked with the Fascist Party, which organised the programmes in the local areas.
- By 1939, 4 million people were members of the *Dopolavoro*.
- At first, education and skills training were an important aspect of the programmes but, as the numbers grew, the emphasis was placed on sport provision, heavily subsidised day trips, and holidays to the seaside, summer camps and cheap railway fares.

- Welfare for families in trouble remained an important feature of *Dopolavoro* work throughout the period.
- Wage rates for industrial workers were lower in the 1930s than in the early boom years of the fascist regime but any overall assessment of the workers' lot needs to take account of the facilities and enjoyment on offer through the *Dopolavoro*.
- The OND schemes provided marvellous propaganda opportunities for the regime, both with those who participated in the many activities and with admiring foreign observers.

Cinema

The cinema became the most important form of entertainment in the 1930s. The newsreels that were screened everywhere provided a useful outlet for propaganda about the regime's achievements.

The state put money into subsidising Italian film-making and into training technicians. However, the regime considered the average film an escapist piece of nonsense, too often inspired by US culture.

Sport

Sport also captured the popular imagination in this period and was used for propaganda purposes. For example, accolades for sporting achievement included:

Primo Carnera (right) and Max Baer fighting in June 1934.

KEY THEMES

World Cup victories 1934 and 1938 In 1934 Mussolini used the World Cup tournament, which was staged in Italy, to show his regime to the world. Italy, to his delight, won the tournament – beating Czechoslovakia 2–1 in the final. In 1938 the tournament was held in France. The Italian team held onto their title as champions, defeating France 4–2 in the final.

Cycling was the first popular mass sport in Italy. The first organisation to regulate cycling, the Touring Club Italiano, was set up in 1894.

- twelve Olympic gold medals in 1932;
- two soccer **World Cup victories**, in 1934 and 1938;
- a world heavyweight boxing champion (Primo Carnera) from 1933 to 1935.

Cycling and skiing also expanded greatly.

Such sporting activity and success affected the nation's self-esteem. It partly explains why so many Italians were, until a late date, content with the fascist regime.

CREATING A FASCIST SOCIETY, THE LATE 1930S

Militarism

From 1935, Italian foreign policy became more expansionist, and at home there was an associated increased emphasis on militarism and armaments along with outpourings of patriotic and warlike propaganda in newspapers, cinema newsreels and on the state radio. Following the Ethiopian triumph of 1936, and ironically as the early fascists were becoming middle-aged and had often lost their radical edge, the state attempted to impose a series of stricter fascist measures on society. In 1934 the regime launched a campaign to reform customs.

- There was a growing fashion for donning uniforms and wearing medals by the military.
- Regulations were introduced requiring civil servants and teachers to wear uniforms at work. All the new social organisations had their own uniform; fascists of course had the black shirt.
- Attempts to re-create ancient Roman styles led to official attempts to ban handshakes in favour of the fascist, and allegedly Roman, clenched-fist salute.
- The military and fascist militia marching style was changed to the dramatic goose-step, again allegedly Roman in origin.

Social changes

The new emphasis had a more significant side.

- In 1937, a new Ministry of Popular Culture, *miniculop*,

was set up to manipulate opinion and take control of the direction of all cultural activity.

- Also in 1937, the various fascist youth organisations were placed in a new body, the Italian Youth of the Lictors (GIL), with an increased emphasis on physical and military training.
- The new educational reforms of Giuseppe Bottai, introduced in 1939, were intended to establish 'a fascist system of education', though this was never clearly defined. There was a drive to centralise the education system and to control the schools and youth clubs, which were now to be incorporated within them. In 1940, there were proposals to impose a national school timetable that would run across the year, regulating and combining the activities of the schools and the clubs.
- There were official attacks on 'bourgeois values' and an emphasis on the need to embrace fascist discipline and determination in their place.
- Perhaps the most serious development was the publication of the Race Manifesto in July 1938, which marked the beginning of **Mussolini's purge against Jews.** Anti-Semitism had never previously featured in Italian fascist theory or practice and its introduction now was probably a direct result of the much closer relations being forged with Nazi Germany. The manifesto was followed by race laws banning marriages between Italians and Jews, banning Jews from the Fascist Party and expelling foreign Jews. The persecution also fitted in with Italy's new imperial role and with the efforts to create a tougher, 'cleaner' fascist society.

Among the young, especially students, there was **growing cynicism** of the regime.

Political changes

These social changes, both trivial and serious, were accompanied by important political changes. In 1939, the Chamber of Fasces and Corporations replaced the Chamber of Deputies and new titles and honours were created for Mussolini (see pages 62–6). These moves may well have been the first stages of an attack on the still surviving political role of the king.

Arguably, from around 1936 fascism began to revert to its

KEY THEMES

Mussolini's purge against Jews In the 1920s, Mussolini had a Jewish mistress and this is sometimes cited as illustrating his lack of anti-Semitic feeling prior to falling under Hitler's influence. His daughter Edda, however, revealed on her deathbed in 1995 that, when she had told her father in 1929 she wished to marry a Jew, he had exploded and told her: 'The Jews are my worst enemies.'

Growing cynicism The government's new extremism encouraged cynicism. Some of the extremism was a little absurd (for example, the goose-step and the endless saluting), but some was more sinister (the racial laws). The latter made the Church authorities more openly critical of the regime.

more radical revolutionary roots after years of lethargic despotism. It is difficult to be absolutely certain about this because war, and then defeat in war, intervened in the experiment. Cynics might argue that the social changes often seemed merely cosmetic and that the new direction was simply another of Mussolini's fads – one in which he would soon lose interest and which he certainly lacked the administrative ability and sustained sense of purpose to bring to fruition.

CONCLUSIONS

Acceptance by the Italian people

Until the regime drifted into unpopular foreign-policy adventures and commitments, in the late 1930s, most Italians accepted it.

- They did not commit their lives to fascism and the service of the state.
- Despite an overmanned and over-active police presence the state did not totally dominate their lives; it was never so active in this respect as the shorter-lived Nazi regime in Germany.
- Silenced opponents apart, Mussolini seems to have been generally popular, although the propagandists did a good job in this respect.
- Italians were proud of many of their country's achievements.
- The majority were able to get on with their own lives and it was easy to acquiesce in what, over the years, became the normal way of life. This was possible because, for most of the period, the fascists had no political programme to transform society and because Mussolini himself did not have the energy or the application to drive through radical changes.

Mussolini's many compromises on the road to power denied him the opportunity of creating a truly fascist state, whatever that might have been, but they made it easier for most Italians to live in harmony with the inefficient conservative state that Italy continued to be. Fascist social policy was a laughable failure in terms of controlling and ordering society for some great fascist purpose, but for many years it did have the great merit of winning the Italian people's acceptance of the regime. For much of the fascist period the regime must have seemed to many Italians no worse than the confusions and corruptions of earlier liberal regimes.

Changing attitudes, late 1930s

A change in public attitudes began in the late 1930s. Even before war came, the links with Nazi Germany were not popular with the general public. The much publicised Rome–Berlin Axis in 1937, the German occupation of Austria in 1938 and the Pact of Steel in 1939 all raised anxieties among thinking Italians about the direction taken by Mussolini's foreign policy. Italian anti-fascist volunteers – communists and socialists – fought valiantly against Franco's forces in the Spanish Civil War and even in defeat established links among themselves. News of their existence and their exploits reached the tiny dissident groups still inside Italy via foreign radio stations. The first signs of disillusion with the regime and an opposition movement were evident even before Italy allowed itself to be drawn into Hitler's war.

SUMMARY QUESTIONS

1 In what ways did the fascist regime try to control the everyday lives of the Italian people?

2 What part did fascist educational and youth policies play in promoting loyalty to fascism?

3 What was the purpose of the Battle for Births? How close did it come to succeeding?

4 What were the 1929 Lateran Pacts and why were they so important to the fascist regime?

5 What evidence is there that, in the late 1930s, Mussolini was set on creating a more truly fascist society?

6 What signs were there, even before war came in 1940, of a more critical attitude to the fascist regime?

CHAPTER 7

Italian foreign policy, 1922–40

INTRODUCTION

In 1922, there were many possibilities regarding international relations for Italy, though it did seem likely that at some point the intensely nationalist nature of fascism would require an ambitious foreign policy. The country's interests were dictated by its position as a Mediterranean power fronting the fragmented Balkans region. Across the Mediterranean beckoned the prospect of Italy at last becoming a European imperial power. The outcome of the First World War had not been as disappointing as Mussolini claimed: territorial gains to the north had provided a secure Alpine frontier and, above all, it had destroyed the Austro-Hungarian Empire. Italy had been on the winning side in the war and was able to play a full part in the conduct of European international relations, albeit as a junior partner to France and Britain.

In practice, until 1935 Mussolini simply responded to events and generally his efforts enjoyed only modest success. Italy was able to exert only limited power and influence at a time when European international relations

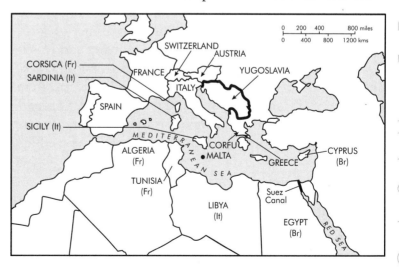

An Italian lake.

were dominated by Britain and France, the two leading powers in the **League of Nations**. For much of that period, European politics were conducted within the framework of the Paris Peace Conference settlement, which seemed to bring real stability in the late 1920s. This stability began to break down after 1933 when Hitler came to power in Germany and began forcefully to challenge the European order created in 1919. France and Britain were alarmed and unsure how to react to Hitler. In these more troubled circumstances, Italy became more important to the plans of the other powers and Mussolini could be gratified at the attention he received. The international problems of the 1930s also provided him with opportunities to pursue long-cherished dreams and, from 1935, the course of Italian foreign policy changed dramatically.

Throughout the period Italian foreign policy was controlled by Mussolini personally and he was increasingly treated by the other powers as a major European statesman. Britain and France saw Italy as a key element in balancing the power of a newly resurgent Germany. In their anxiety to placate Mussolini, they often seemed to exaggerate his abilities as a statesman and certainly over-emphasised Italy's industrial and military power, both actual and potential.

LEGACY OF THE FIRST WORLD WAR

Paris Peace Conference

The First World War of 1914–18 destroyed three great European empires – those of Austria, Germany and Russia. The leaders of the victorious powers, with Britain, France and the United States pre-eminent among them, had to re-draw national frontiers across central and eastern Europe. Italy's influence on the outcome was limited to arguing for as much new territory on its northern frontier as possible.

The territorial arrangements made at the Paris Peace Conference in1919–20, and most importantly in the Treaty of Versailles that was drawn up there, set the geographic and political context for international relations in Europe through to the outbreak of the Second World

War in 1939. Italy's foreign policy had to be conducted within that context.

- With the defeat of Germany, US forces quickly returned home, and the USA, though never totally isolationist, rapidly reduced its involvement in Europe and declined to become a member of the newly founded peace-keeping organisation, the League of Nations.
- Germany was disarmed and almost bankrupt so that, for more than a decade, France and Britain dominated European international relations. In the 1920s and early 1930s Italian foreign policy had to take account of this and temper ambition accordingly.
- The establishment of a new **communist state, the Soviet Union**, in eastern Europe was a matter of great concern to all the capitalist countries, including Italy.
- The war also left a legacy of unrest and instability and in the early 1920s there were several revolutionary attempts to seize power in central and east European states.

In Italy fascism was itself a response to that danger and its success in 1922 owed much to fears of the communist threat.

Stability, mid- to late-1920s

In the mid- and late-1920s, a new political stability and economic prosperity seemed to emerge in Europe.

- The Soviet Union remained isolated but Germany was drawn back into participating in international affairs.
- Many of the newly founded nations managed to establish more stable governments.
- The international economy recovered and with it international trade; war damage was being repaired; national finances restored; and new industries established.
- A series of international **political initiatives** marked this new stability.

World economic crisis, 1929–33

Hopes that Europe had at last recovered from the war and that a new era had dawned were dashed in 1929. The financial crisis in the USA swiftly spread to Europe and

KEY THEMES

A communist state, the Soviet Union Officially founded in 1922. It followed the successful communist takeover of Russia in October 1917. It was a one-party state, which controlled the economy according to socialist principles. During the 1920s and 1930s it was viewed with great suspicion by the other, capitalist, nations, of Europe. After its dreams of a world communist revolution proved to be illusory, the Soviet Union drew back into isolation, distrusted by the other European powers both for its potential power and its revolutionary ideology.

Political initiatives Italy's new stability in the mid- to late-1920s was marked by a series of these including, most notably, the 1925 Locarno Pact, which gave international guarantees of western European frontiers, and the 1928 Kellogg–Briand Pact, which renounced war and was eventually ratified by 61 nations.

expanded into a general trade recession with the most dramatic consequences for industrial production and employment. As world trade shrank, nations retreated inwards to defend their own markets: economic protectionism replaced free trade.

ITALIAN FOREIGN POLICY, 1922–35

Until 1935, Mussolini's conduct of foreign policy was quite cautious and usually aimed to be respectable.

Fiume

Failure to obtain the north Adriatic port of **Fiume** at the 1919 Paris Peace Conference had been a major blow to Italian pride for which the port's continuing status as an international free city provided no consolation. (For a map showing Italy's northern frontier and Fiume, see page 12.) Mussolini also inherited Italy's wider ambitions to dominate the Adriatic through possession of lands on its eastern coastline but he, and the liberal foreign office staff he had inherited, showed diplomatic skill in ditching the less realistic of these.

By striking bargains with the new Kingdom of Yugoslavia in 1924, Mussolini finally secured that country's acceptance that Fiume was part of Italy, and it was duly annexed. It was important to Mussolini that this could be presented at home as a great triumph, securing D'Annunzio's legacy and so quelling any fascist criticism of his failure to stand up for wider Italian interests in the region.

Corfu

Following the assassination of an Italian general, General Tellini, on Corfu in 1923 the Italian navy bombarded the Greek-controlled island, which controls the mouth of the Adriatic. The murder was an excuse to implement a plan already prepared and was pushed through on Mussolini's personal instructions without consulting the Italian foreign office. The attack itself was bungled and led to unnecessary civilian casualties. Eventually, pressure from Britain and France forced withdrawal of the Italian forces. This episode was also presented to Italians as a great national triumph,

Fiume Became part of Italy in 1924. It had no economic or strategic importance but was simply an important symbol of Italian national aspirations.

protecting Italian interests in the region, but in practice it was most important in showing Mussolini's willingness to act impulsively and violently in international matters in a region where important Italian interests required consistent and well-considered policies. Its outcome also demonstrated the limits of Italian power to defy the major European powers.

Albania

Italian forces had controlled Albania during the First World War but withdrew in 1920, after which the country was plagued by civil war. Mussolini interfered in Albanian politics, allying with the parties supporting Ahmed (later King) Zog. In 1926, he established an Italian **protectorate** over the country. Albania can be seen as a first step in fascist imperial expansion and was, by the late 1920s, increasingly treated as part of Italy with plans to settle Italian peasants there. These proceeded at a leisurely pace and had not advanced far when, in 1939, the country was formally annexed and declared to be part of the Kingdom of Italy.

Libya

Italy took Libya from the Ottoman (Turkish) Empire in 1912, but local Berber rebels had never been defeated. From 1922 to 1925, the Italian army worked to bring these desert tribespeople under control and the fascist authorities then planned, despite continuing guerrilla warfare, to introduce large-scale Italian settlement of the country. In the early 1930s, Italian measures became more repressive, including the establishment of mass concentration camps and the erection of a barbed-wire barrier from the Mediterranean coast deep into the desert in order to cut the Berber supply route from Egypt. By 1932, the country was at last pacified, though only the coastal strip was firmly under Italian control (see map on page 97).

The attempted **colonisation of Libya**, a thinly populated desert-state, brought no economic benefits to Italy and was conducted purely for reasons of national prestige. Despite a huge government propaganda effort it aroused little enthusiasm among the Italian people.

see map on page 97

KEY TERM

Protectorate When one country controls another.

KEY THEME

Colonisation of Libya
Libya was not a popular destination for Italian emigrants. In 1928 only 2500 Italians lived in the country. The plans for up to half a million Italian settlers were never close to being realised. In a conscious attempt to link the fascist regime with past imperial glories, Italy devoted a great deal of effort to restoring, and sometimes 'improving', many of Libya's splendid ancient Roman sites.

North-east Africa

In the 1920s, Italy also mounted successful military campaigns to assert full control of the north of Somalia, which Britain and France had accepted as an Italian area of influence in the late nineteenth century. But here, and in Eritrea – an Italian colony since 1889 – dreams of large-scale Italian settlement in the region remained unfulfilled.

The Locarno Pact (1925) and the Kellogg–Briand Pact (1928)

Mussolini was able to present Italy as a major European power when – along with Britain, France and Germany – he signed the Locarno Pact guaranteeing the integrity of north European frontiers. He was again able to pose as a major European statesman when he joined 60 other nations in signing the Kellogg–Briand Pact renouncing war. Both of these actions, which seemed to symbolise the more settled climate of international relations emerging in the late 1920s, were more in the nature of gestures than serious commitments, but their propaganda value was fully exploited within Italy.

The frontier with Austria

The fragmentation of the pre-war Austro-Hungarian Empire and territorial gains at the 1919 Paris Peace Conference left Italy with a secure northern frontier, which reached to the Brenner Pass, the main route to the newly established German-speaking Republic of Austria (see page 19). This happy state of affairs lasted until 1934 when the Nazi regime in Germany first started to interfere in Austrian domestic politics with a view to uniting the two German states. Mussolini, who had earlier helped to bring about a right-wing takeover in Austria, now moved to protect the integrity of that state. In 1934, he moved Italian troops to the Austrian border in order to discourage Hitler from developing his ambitions against Austria. Naturally, there was a **reaction to his Austrian policy.**

The Stresa Front, 1935

Mussolini's aim in early 1935 was to make Italy a foremost diplomatic power. The Stresa Front was set up by Britain, France and Italy at a conference held at Stresa in the Italian lake district. The three powers issued a joint protest

KEY THEME

Reaction to Mussolini's Austrian policy The 1934 episode produced a great outburst of anti-German feeling within Italy. Mussolini's action had protected important Italian interests and, at this point, he seemed to be an important stabilising influence in European international relations.

at German rearmament contrary to the Versailles Peace Treaty and pledged themselves to resist any such unilateral repudiation of peace treaties when this might endanger the peace of Europe. It was the high-water mark of Mussolini's working with the western democratic powers.

Being linked with Britain and France in this 1935 agreement appealed to Mussolini's self-importance. Despite his **true motives** in hosting the Stresa Conference, he was once more acting the role of major European statesman and his arrival at the venue by speedboat enabled him to cut a dashing figure.

Stresa did not mark a change in Italian priorities: it was a diplomatic manoeuvre in advance of the colonial war that came later in the year. In fact, all three Stresa powers hoped that the very existence of the Stresa Front would make any further action by them unnecessary, and it was Britain that first undermined that hope by signing a separate naval agreement with Germany.

The importance of Mussolini's personal role, 1922–35

In the 1920's Mussolini's foreign policy had much in common with the foreign policies of the liberal states, so the foreign ministry officials had little problem at first in operating fascist policy, which probably helped in the agreement with Yugoslavia over Fiume.

It was only as fascist control within Italy was firmly established that Mussolini became determined to make an impression on the international scene.

ITALIAN FOREIGN POLICY, 1935–40

The international context: new European tensions

The world economic depression of the early 1930s showed how fragile the earlier optimism had been and had the most profound impact on European politics through to the outbreak of war in 1939.

All governments faced new and difficult problems about

Mussolini's true motives at Stresa These were almost certainly less to do with providing Italian forces to stand up to Hitler than ensuring an arrangement with Britain and France that would leave him free to pursue his imperial dreams in Africa, while at the same time giving him some guarantee that others would check any revisionist plans in Europe that Hitler might embark on.

how to deal with the social distress created by economic dislocation and associated mass unemployment. One direct consequence in all the democratic nations was the increased support for more extreme parties of both the left and the right. Democracy did not seem to be working. In particular, the depression gave a boost to the fortunes of the German Nazi Party and helped Hitler to power in January 1933. He was committed to redressing the injustices which, he argued, had been done to Germany at the Paris Peace Conference. These included ending the ban on German rearmament and the recovery of the lands that, he argued, were rightly German but which had been handed to other nations. Germany was still potentially the most powerful European state and the establishment there of an undemocratic and expansionist government undermined the fragile peace that had seemed to be emerging before the economic catastrophe of 1929. On **the road to war, 1933–9**, European politics revolved largely around German ambitions and German diplomacy.

A revolution in Italian foreign policy, 1935–40

The new international climate inevitably affected Italian foreign policy and eventually led to a total change in its direction.

- At first, Mussolini was understandably alarmed at the threat the new German regime's ambitions posed for Austrian independence and, potentially, for the security of Italy's northern frontier.
- The re-emergence of an increasingly aggressive Germany revived French fears for its own security. France therefore would be less capable of or interested in checking Mussolini's ambitions in the Mediterranean and in Africa.
- **The failure of France and Britain to stand up to Hitler** and also their failure to use the League of Nations to contain aggression made Mussolini contemptuous of the western democracies.
- Conversely, Mussolini became increasingly impressed with, and excited by, the power of Germany and the vigour of its new authoritarian government. The Nazis and the fascists seemed to have much in common, not least their hatred of communism and their desire to

The road to war, 1933–9
1933, Adolf Hitler became Chancellor of Germany and took the country out of disarmament talks and the League of Nations

1934, Mussolini blocked German pressure on Austria

1935, Formation and collapse of the Stresa Front. Italy invaded Ethiopia

1936, Hitler and Mussolini created the Rome–Berlin Axis. Italy and Germany supported Franco in Spanish Civil War.

1937, Italy joined Germany and Japan in the Anti-Comintern Pact.

1938, Germany annexed Austria and at Munich gained the Sudetenland from Czechoslovakia.

1939, Germany annexed the rest of Czechoslovakia. In August Germany signed a non-aggression pact with the Soviet Union and in September invaded Poland. Britain and France then declared war on Germany. Italy remained neutral.

1940, Italy entered the war.

KEY THEME

The failure of France and Britain to stand up to Hitler In 1934–5 Germany was allowed to start rearming and in 1936 remilitarised the Rhineland, both breaches of the 1919 Versailles Treaty. In 1935 Britain negotiated a separate naval agreement with Germany contrary to the agreement it had reached with France and Italy at Stresa.

KEY PLACE

Eritrea In 1890 the Italian Prime Minister Francesco Crispi united Italy's two colonies on the Red Sea (Massawa and Assab) to become the country of Eritrea.

re-draw the political settlement imposed by the western democracies at the end of the First World War.
* German and Italian national ambitions seemed to be compatible, with Hitler, looking to territorial gains in northern and eastern Europe, leaving Italy free to create a Mediterranean–African empire.
* By 1938, these positive attractions of a closer German connection had outweighed Mussolini's initial concerns over the integrity of Austria and, from that point, Italy moved swiftly into Germany's embrace and, in 1940, became its ally in a major European war.

ETHIOPIA

The origins of the war against Ethiopia (Abyssinia)
* In the late nineteenth century Italy had acquired two disappointingly unproductive colonies – **Eritrea** and Somaliland in north-east Africa (see map below) – but, itself only finally united in 1870, had fared less well than Britain, France and Germany in the scramble for empire in Africa.
* When the German colonies were seized and redistributed to the victorious powers after the First World War, Italy had again been denied any share.

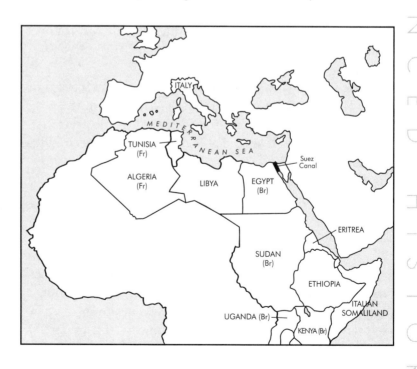

Mussolini and Africa. The region including Ethiopia and neighbouring countries is often referred to as 'the Horn of Africa'.

- Italians had come to resent their imperial inferiority and the Libyan adventure had been a response to this feeling. Fascism, a nationalistic and militarist movement at heart, was a natural vehicle for imperial ambitions.
- After 1922, Mussolini with his dreams of making Italy 'great' and himself important, was inevitably an imperialist. The entire theme of linking fascist Italy to the glory of the ancient Roman Empire went in the same direction.
- The dreams simply lay dormant until fascism was established at home and conditions in Europe were right for an attempt to create an Italian fascist empire in Africa. The first condition was met by 1929 and by 1932 Libyan resistance had at last been broken, freeing experienced troops and resources for a new adventure.

From 1932, when Mussolini had again taken personal control of foreign policy, there had been an emphasis in Italian domestic policy on the build-up to economic self-sufficiency and military strength in readiness for an assault on Ethiopia, the last truly independent state in Africa. It had common borders with the two Italian colonies and was generally regarded as falling into Italy's zone of economic influence in Africa. It was also one of the very few regions in Africa where British or French interests were not already firmly established. The country was vast but backward and **Emperor Haile Selassie** had only intermittent control over its warring tribes and mountainous terrain.

The war started with Italian military attacks in October 1935, following a border incident at Wal Wal on the Ethiopian border with Italian Somaliland in the previous December, in which several Italian soldiers had been killed. Interestingly, Mussolini himself hesitated to order an attack, fearing the complications of a difficult military campaign. It was fascist officials in the foreign ministry who pressed the case and even conjured up the vision of it as a base for a far bigger Italian empire in Africa, perhaps even stretching to the Atlantic coast. There was in any case a danger that economic penetration of the region by other powers, including Japan, would undermine Italy's prime position. By 1934, Hitler's recent arrival in power in Germany was troubling the western powers, but Hitler

Emperor Haile Selassie 1891–1975 Ruler of Ethiopia from 1916 to 1974. He succeeded in arousing international indignation and much personal sympathy at the Italian attack on his country, but failed to secure effective help in its defence. He lived in exile in Britain during the years of the Italian occupation (1936–41). Army officers deposed him in 1974.

himself was not yet strong enough to cause trouble on Italy's northern frontier. Mussolini now committed himself to planning to attack Ethiopia and mounted an internal propaganda campaign to soften up the Italian people for what was about to happen.

At the Stresa Conference in 1935, Mussolini formed a definite impression that neither Britain nor France would try to block an Italian annexation of Ethiopia, an impression reinforced by his access to secret British government papers, which stated that Britain had no important interests in Ethiopia. Since before 1914 both Britain and France had accepted that Ethiopia was in the Italian area of influence in East Africa.

But he was almost certainly deluding himself and ignoring some direct unofficial hints to the contrary. He had managed to convince himself that the British were too worried that Italy might, if opposed, go on to seize both the Sudan and Egypt, to take any action. More realistically he also felt that Britain was too concerned about the rise of extremism in Germany to act decisively against Italy. In short, the international climate seemed favourable for an adventure that was required for domestic and personal reasons.

Following the Wal Wal incident there was a steady build-up of substantial Italian forces and munitions in both the Italian colonies. The dead Italian soldiers at Wal Wal, and the claim that Italy was bringing to an end appalling conditions of slavery, served as Mussolini's excuses for this build-up of forces in Somaliland and Eritrea, and this despite the fact that the League of Nations, at Ethiopia's own request, was conducting an enquiry into the border incident. There was nothing secretive about the build-up: all the supplies had to go through the British administered Suez Canal and, in any case, the warlike preparations were given maximum publicity within Italy. This was to be **the great test of the fascist state**.

The campaign

The conquest of Ethiopia took from October 1935 to May 1936.

- The Ethiopian forces, split into rival groups and poorly armed, were not ready to fight a modern war but, thanks to the mountainous terrain and the primitive state of the roads, a substantial military effort was needed over several months to defeat them.
- In all, 400,000 Italian troops were sent to the campaign and this, together with an unnecessary mountain of equipment, led to a great deal of muddle and incompetence.
- In the early fighting the regular army was given second place to the Fascist Militia, which proved an ill-organised and ill-equipped force.
- The lethargic, elderly Emilio de Bono, a leading fascist, was made the commander of the invading forces. He was soon replaced as the advance came to a halt largely because of transport problems.
- His successor, Marshal Badoglio, used regular troops to fight a more energetic and much crueller campaign, including the use of poison gas dropped from planes, until his forces reached the capital **Addis Ababa** in May 1936.

The war had in fact been fought inefficiently.

- Fortunately for the fascists, the enemy was so much weaker that this did not matter except in terms of delaying unduly the enjoyable victory celebrations.
- The Italians had committed over 400,000 men to this small colonial war and lost 1500.
- The colossal over-provision of men and materials on the other hand had cost the equivalent of two years' normal state spending and was to start off a vicious upward spiral of state debt.
- Nor was Ethiopia really conquered. The Italian attack had united its warring tribes, which now proceeded to wage a series of guerrilla campaigns that the Italian occupation army was scarcely able to contain even by employing the utmost barbarism in its treatment of the population.
- Fierce guerrilla fighting continued throughout Italy's five-year occupation of the country and at times reduced the area under Italian control to little more than the

HEINEMANN ADVANCED HISTORY

few main towns and the tank-patrolled main routes between them.

KEY THEMES

Mussolini, Britain and France Mussolini appeared genuinely bewildered that the two imperial powers opposed Italy's own imperial claims, especially in the light of the deal at Stresa and in an area of the world where their own interests were not involved. Their own public opinion had forced them, perhaps half-heartedly, to support the League sanctions.

The Hoare–Laval Pact Negotiated between the British foreign secretary, Samuel Hoare, and the French prime minister, Pierre Laval, it would have handed over a large part of Ethiopia to Italy. A public outcry against the pact led to it being abandoned.

International reaction

The international reaction (including that of **Britain and France**) did not prove as accommodating of Italian ambitions as Mussolini had assumed it would.

- Ethiopia was a member of the League of Nations, ironically there because of Italian sponsorship in the 1920s, and now Haile Selassie demanded the League's action against the aggressor.
- The Italian action provoked widespread international condemnation and the members of the League of Nations voted in November 1935 to apply economic sanctions against Italy as an aggressor and in order to force its withdrawal from Ethiopia. The sanctions meant there would be no arms sales to Italy and League members would ban the import of Italian goods.

In December 1935, Britain and France attempted a compromise position, the so-called **Hoare–Laval Pact**. They had to abandon it in the face of pro-Ethiopian outrage, particularly in Britain. The pact and then its abandonment succeeded in both discrediting the League and destroying the Stresa Front.

Fortunately for Mussolini the sanctions that were introduced proved ineffective: crucially, oil was not embargoed and certain countries – Germany, Japan, the USA – did not support any of the sanctions. Once Italian control of Ethiopia had been secured the sanctions were quietly dropped.

The fact that the British government did not feel its garrison in the Suez Canal Zone could close the international waterway against the steady flow of Italian reinforcements moving south from the Mediterranean to the Red Sea denied it the obvious means of ending the attack almost immediately. It seems likely that neither the British nor the French government was prepared to oppose Italy too vigorously lest it led to war, as Mussolini threatened in public speeches. Their sanctions annoyed Mussolini greatly but did not hinder the war effort.

Crowds celebrate the arrival of Gigli in Addis Ababa, Ethiopia, October 1936. The slogan on the banner reads, 'To whom does the empire belong? Duce! Duce! To us!'

Reaction in Italy

The attack on Ethiopia at first divided Italian opinion, despite the full-scale propaganda campaign launched by the regime and co-ordinated by Mussolini's son-in-law, **Galeazzo Ciano**, at this time minister for press and propaganda.

The nation only swung behind the military effort when the League of Nations introduced its sanctions. Mussolini was then able to present the war as one for national survival against 52 other nations. Once the initial difficulties experienced by the Italian army had been overcome and when Addis Ababa was taken the propaganda machine, with a good story of easy victories to tell, ensured enthusiastic support for the war from all sections of society.

- About 20 million people listened to Mussolini's radio broadcast in May 1936, proclaiming victory in Ethiopia.
- The war greatly increased the size and importance of the propaganda industry, and the patriotic feelings that it promoted meant that the fascist regime reached its high point in terms of public support and popularity.
- It was a considerable personal triumph for Mussolini. The generals, diplomats and the king had all opposed the war or counselled caution but the *Duce* had persisted, and victory and a new empire had been

Galeazzo Ciano 1903–44
Mussolini's son-in-law, Ciano was Italian foreign minister from 1936 to 1943. In this role he was always strictly subordinate to the *Duce*. In 1939, he advised Mussolini not to enter the Second World War; in 1943, he voted to end the fascist regime. Despite his wife's desperate attempts to save his life he was shot by a fascist firing squad on Mussolini's personal instructions. His diaries later became a major source for historians studying Italian foreign policy.

secured in a few months and with fewer than 2000 casualties.

The outcome
In Ethiopia
- After his capital had been taken, Haile Selassie fled to Britain and organised opposition ended.
- Victor Emmanuel was crowned Emperor of Ethiopia, in a ceremony of fascist splendour.
- But the territory proved to be a source of great expense and, in the brief period to 1941 in which it remained under Italian control, failed to provide settlement or trading opportunities for its conquerors.
- A policy of systematic brutality had to be adopted to keep the country pacified. In this sense the conquest was an empty victory with an Italian army of occupation camped precariously amid a hostile native population.
- If Italy became engaged in a European conflict newly conquered Ethiopia would be very difficult if not impossible to defend.

State expenditure (in million lire)

Year	Expenditure	Deficit
1934–5	20,926	–2,195
1936–7	40,932	–16,230
1939–40	60,389	–28,039

In Italy
- The heady victory encouraged the regime to press on with plans to create a truly fascist state that were to dominate government domestic policy through to 1940.
- In particular, the war against native Africans produced a new racist emphasis in government thinking and played a part in encouraging the anti-Jewish campaign that began at this time.
- The war had been very expensive. It had forced up government borrowing and had diverted industrial production into armament production. It contributed greatly to the poor **state of the Italian economy** in the years to 1940.
- The war, and international sanctions, encouraged the government to even greater efforts to achieve economic

KEY THEME

State of the Italian economy By 1939 the Italian budget deficit stood at an astonishing 12,750 million lire. This was partly due to the regime's social policy but also to the Abyssian war.

self-sufficiency, autarky; this was understandable but in practice unattainable.

- Victory and belief in his own propaganda made Mussolini over-confident in terms of both his own political and military judgement and of Italy's military might. This was made more dangerous by the widespread cult of the infallible *Duce* and by Mussolini's total isolation from any source of criticism. In particular, he developed an exaggerated contempt for Britain and France.

Internationally

- With the capture of Addis Ababa organised Ethiopian resistance was at an end and, in July 1936, the League of Nations ended its ineffective economic boycott of Italy.
- The League's failure to protect one of its members further undermined its credibility, which had already been damaged by its failure to defend China against Japanese aggression or to act against Hitler's rearming Germany in defiance of the Treaty of Versailles (1919).
- Sanctions had failed to save Ethiopia, but they did destroy the common front built up at Stresa between Britain, France and Italy. There had always been a selfish element in the thinking of all three Stresa powers, but the common stand they had taken on German expansionism could have been developed to block Hitler's later moves. This possibility was now at an end, and relations between Italy and the other two powers deteriorated steadily from the time of the Ethiopian war, opening up a new and potentially dangerous stage in Italian foreign policy.

THE SPANISH CIVIL WAR, 1936–9

Civil war between right- and left-wing forces broke out in Spain in July 1936, conveniently two months after Mussolini had proclaimed Italy's victory in Ethiopia. It led to three years of extremely bloody conflict, prolonged by the intervention of foreign powers. Given the warlike nature of Italian fascism and Mussolini's dreams of dominating the Mediterranean it was perhaps inevitable that there would be **Italian intervention in the Spanish Civil War**.

KEY THEME

Italian intervention in the Spanish Civil War

- Italian 'volunteers' were the first foreign troops to arrive in Spain in support of General Franco's right-wing nationalist forces.
- Italy eventually sent 70,000 men to Spain (compared with Nazi Germany's 10,000) as well as approximately 700 aircraft and almost 1000 tanks.
- Foreign help has been described as fundamental to the nationalist victory and, if so, Italy's was by far the largest single contribution.

Mussolini's motives

Mussolini's motives for intervention were straightforward.

- He sought further military glory to add to the Ethiopian victory.
- He rejoiced at the thought of the expansion of fascism.
- He saw in nationalist Spain an ally for Italy's pretensions in the Mediterranean, possibly including Italian naval bases established in mainland Spain.

The consequences of Italian intervention

The consequences were more far-reaching than Mussolini had contemplated.

- It crippled Italian public finances and, added to the burden of the Ethiopian war, imposed a strain on the Italian economy that seriously reduced its ability to maintain an independent foreign policy in other areas. This at a time when the power of Nazi Germany was growing rapidly.
- It made relations with France, and to a less important extent Britain, even more complicated and provided yet another obstacle to these countries co-operating in other areas of interest.
- Intervening alongside Germany materially helped draw Italy into closer relations with that power.
- Mussolini's dream of a **Mediterranean ally** to offset the power of France and Britain proved to be short-lived.

THE BALKANS

East from the Adriatic Sea was the natural region for a newly powerful and ambitious Italy to establish its presence, but Mussolini made little progress in building up his country's power and influence there.

- The new Kingdom of Yugoslavia was too large to be easily intimidated and French interest in the region remained strong.
- By the early 1930s, Albania was completely under Italian influence. Italy's unopposed invasion of the country in April 1939 was an empty gesture and, aping the expansion of its German ally, contributed more to fascist

Franco: a Mediterranian ally? Once in power, Franco proved to be singularly ungrateful to the foreign powers that had helped to place him there. Italy made no strategic or other gains for the 11,000 casualties its forces suffered and during the Second World War Franco kept Spain resolutely neutral.

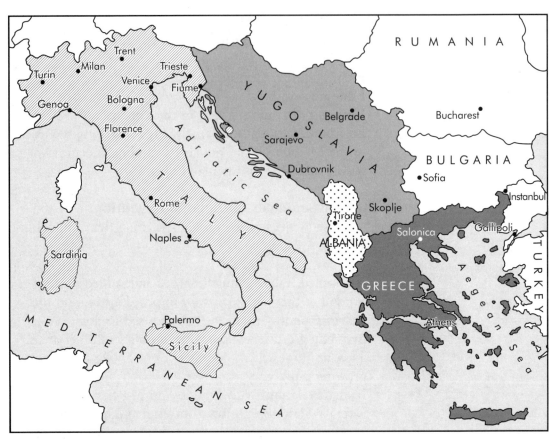

Italy and the Balkans in 1926.

propaganda than it did to any real assessment of Italy's true economic and political interests.

- Overall Mussolini, with his dreams set across the Mediterranean and in Africa, failed to develop an Italian presence in the lands that had so recently been part of the Austro-Hungarian Empire.

THE GERMAN ALLIANCE

From the end of the Ethiopian war Mussolini's foreign policy was based on a highly exaggerated opinion of Italian military strength reinforced by the belief that any war between fascist and non-fascist powers would be over in weeks rather than months. His public and parliamentary speeches offered the Italian people a totally unrealistic view of what Italy would be capable of in any future war.

Italy's move from one camp to the other in an increasingly divided Europe was perhaps the most significant

Mussolini addressing the Senate, 30 March 1938. (Left of Mussolini is the secretary to the Fascist Party, Starace; to his right is Ciano, the foreign minister.)

The British press agency note accompanying this picture read:
'In a dramatic speech in Rome yesterday Mussolini emphasised Italy's preparedness for war. He spoke to the Senate on the estimates for the army, navy and air force and said that 9 million men could be mobilised ready for a quick war. He spoke in the capacity of minister for war, the navy and air, and all ministers attended the Senate.'
A separate press report of the same Senate meeting quoted Mussolini as saying that he was making his plans on the assumption of 'a very quick war'.

diplomatic development of the period and severely restricted British and French options in countering Hitler's ambitions. By it Mussolini made his most significant mark on European affairs but not in the way he had planned.

Italy's move to an alliance with Germany developed by stages.

The collapse of the Stresa Front
A new coolness set in among the Stresa partners as Britain did a separate naval deal with Germany in 1935. The rift became more serious when Britain and France applied the League of Nations' economic sanctions against Italy over the Ethiopian invasion in 1935–6.

The impact of the Spanish Civil War
The military aid provided to the nationalists by both Germany and Italy was viewed by Britain and France with

great suspicion and was seen by them as extending the Spanish conflict in dangerous ways. Equally, it brought Italy and Germany together in a common cause, though this should not be exaggerated for their interests in Spain were not identical. Mussolini dreamed of setting up a second fascist power in the Mediterranean area with attendant military advantages for Italy. He committed many more men and much more aid to the nationalist cause than Germany. Hitler was happy to see the war drag on, leaving a weakened Italy at odds again with France and Britain and so increasingly dependent on Germany.

The Axis

The appointment of Mussolini's son-in-law Ciano as Italy's foreign minister gave a new impetus to the move towards closer relations with Germany.

- He visited Berlin in October 1936 at a time when Mussolini was furious at uncomplimentary references to himself in the British press, and also soon after the election of a left-wing government in France.
- In Berlin, Ciano received a flattering welcome and also assurances that, while Hitler was preparing if necessary to go to war against France and Britain, Germany was seeking new territory only in central and eastern Europe. Hitler had no wish to get in the way of Italian ambitions in the Mediterranean area.
- In return for these assurances Italy accepted the right of Germany to rearm and, more surprisingly, formally acknowledged German predominance in Austria.
- Both countries agreed to work more closely together in Spain and to hold military and intelligence discussions.
- Within days Mussolini had announced in a public speech that a new Rome–Berlin Axis had been formed, around which European affairs would now revolve. This public identification of the new partnership then led to use of the term 'Axis Powers' to identify the partners and later also their ally Japan.

Although Mussolini continued to see Italy as an independent power able to mediate between other European powers he had, in fact, made a decisive move that placed his country firmly in the German camp in any

Non-intervention in Spain
In September 1936, Britain, France, Germany and Italy signed an agreeement not to intervene in the Civil War in Spain. Britain and France stuck to the agreement; Germany and Italy ignored it. The flouting of the agreement raised tension between Italy and Britain and France.

future crisis. The new relationship soon affected Italian policy in a number of areas – for example, the fascist persecution of Italy's small Jewish population. Mussolini's respect for Germany was further enhanced when, in September 1937, he visited Hitler, who went out of his way to lay on displays of German military might and Nazi prowess.

The Anti-Comintern Pact, November 1937

Mussolini decided to join Germany and Japan in the Anti-**Comintern** Pact to oppose the spread of international communism, which the other two powers had signed in November 1936. In December 1937, Mussolini emphasised their common front when he followed Hitler in withdrawing from the League of Nations.

The Anschluss, March 1938

In March 1938, with a bare minimum of notice to Mussolini, Germany invaded Austria and swiftly incorporated the state into a greater Germany. Despite his earlier assurances to the Italian people, Mussolini took no action to prevent or reverse this. Hitler was grateful but Austria's fate aroused intense frustration and anger in Italy, and public discontent with the fascist regime was as great as in the first days of the Ethiopian war.

Cordial relations with Hitler were restored less than two months later, after the Führer visited Italy, so that during the crisis over Czechoslovakia in the summer of 1938 Mussolini convinced himself that the real challenge facing Italy came not from Germany but from British naval domination of the Mediterranean.

Italy, exhausted by its commitments in Ethiopia and Spain, could do little but accept its new ally's expansion southwards. A powerful Germany with a frontier bordering northern Italy's German-speaking provinces was a high price to pay for adventures elsewhere. It made Mussolini increasingly dependent upon German goodwill.

The Munich Conference, September 1938

Mussolini was an important figure at the **Munich Conference**, which saw the first stage in Germany's

KEY TERM

Comintern This was the international organisation devoted to spreading communism. Founded in 1919, it lasted until 1943.

KEY THEME

The Munich Conference
Held in September 1938, this followed intense German pressure on Czechoslovakia to hand over the Sudetenland, which had a majority of German-speaking inhabitants. At the Conference, Britain and France, in order to avoid a possible European war, forced the Czechs to cede the region to Germany. This appeasement of Hitler failed to end his territorial ambitions and in March 1939 Germany occupied the rest of Czechoslovakia. From this point appeasement, previously a neutral term for calming things down, became a term used to indicate the disreputable, cowardly conduct of foreign policy.

dismemberment of Czechoslovakia. It was he who, at the height of the crisis, responded to a request from the British prime minister, Neville Chamberlain, and arranged this conference of the European powers in an effort to resolve peacefully German claims for Czech territory. During the crisis, Mussolini was wooed by all sides and appeared to represent an uncommitted major power. He gained some personal prestige and enormous self-satisfaction from his 'statesmanlike' mediation between the other powers, but in practice he had simply carried out deals agreed earlier with Hitler and was rapidly becoming the junior partner in the alliance with Germany. The Munich meeting and the agreement there, by which France and Britain accepted the German territorial claims, confirmed Mussolini's contempt for the feeble western democracies and for their leaders personally. Unfortunately, Mussolini threw away his reputation as a mediator, won at Munich, when he antagonised a newly resolute French government and united its divided people by making a series of crass demands on French territory, in particular Corsica, Nice and Tunisia. The resulting abrupt loss of influence in Paris threw Mussolini back into Hitler's arms. Mussolini's options had begun to run out.

A step backwards? November 1938–March 1939

In 1938 and indeed into 1939, Mussolini may still have seen himself as manoeuvring between the two camps into which Europe was rapidly dividing. Over several months, he avoided any closer military alliance with Germany and, in November 1938, entertained Chamberlain in Rome. In March 1939, he was badly shaken when Hitler invaded what was left of Czechoslovakia without giving him advance notice. In practice by this stage he was committed to the German alliance. Germany seemed to be re-drawing the map of northern Europe and, by checking France, would give Italy the opportunity to become the dominant power in the Mediterranean region. Carefully orchestrated hysterical anti-French demands in the Italian parliament gave a better indication of Mussolini's intentions than did the window-dressing of the Chamberlain visit. In these last months of peace, Mussolini persisted in his ambitions to obtain the French islands of Corsica and Tunisia and his entertainment of the British prime minister was perhaps a first step in undermining the Franco–British alliance.

KEY THEMES

Pact of Steel An open-ended commitment, not a defensive alliance. Each country was required to come to the assistance of the other in the event of war, regardless of who had started the conflict. Mussolini had convinced himself that the guarantee to Greece was part of a British and French manoeuvre to encircle Italy with hostile powers and the pact with Germany was his response.

Reactions in Italy to the German alliance A propaganda offensive meant that the Italian people appeared to receive this new alliance with wild enthusiasm. Later, leading figures claimed that they had been opposed to the pact, or at least dismayed by it, but by the time they made these claims the war had started to go wrong for Italy. How much King Victor Emmanuel III, by whose executive authority the deed was done, knew in advance remains an open question. He later claimed that he was kept in total ignorance until after the event but, by the time he spoke, he too was facing the harsh realities of military defeat.

Albania, April 1939

In April 1939 Italy occupied Albania and made Victor Emmanuel its king. The invaders met little resistance, for the country had been an Italian **satellite** for many years. However, within Italy the annexation provided great propaganda for the *Duce* and was presented as creating an Italian lake of the Adriatic Sea. The seizure provoked the despised French and British into giving military guarantees to Greece and Romania, which in turn infuriated Mussolini.

The Pact of Steel, May 1939

Mussolini and Ciano took Italy into a full military alliance with Germany in the **Pact of Steel**. Despite his belligerent talk he had, until this point, been cautious about being tied to Hitler by a formal military alliance. He prized his role as an independent figure in European diplomacy and greatly over-estimated Italy's ability to act alone in the event of military action. The initiative for a formal tie came, surprisingly, from Germany. The Germans did not value Italy's military capacity, but in the event of war they at least wanted the assurance that Italy could neutralise the Balkan region and tie up British and French forces in the Mediterranean. More importantly, and noting what had happened at Munich, the British and French would be aware of this and so would hesitate to take strong action wherever provoked.

The initiative came with the visit of Hitler's deputy, Hermann Goering, to Rome in April 1939, which was swiftly followed by meetings between the foreign ministers of the two countries, Ciano and Joachim von Ribbentrop. It was, however, a spur-of-the-moment decision by Mussolini to proceed immediately with a formal pact with Germany and, without consulting the Fascist Grand Council or foreign ministry officials, he instructed Ciano to seek both an offensive and defensive alliance. There was little discussion between the representatives of the two countries and the paperwork was rushed through with indecent haste. All this on the *Duce*'s whim.

The Italy–German alliance raised the tension in Europe another notch and made a general European war all the more likely. The Pact of Steel certainly marked the most serious international obligations Italy had ever undertaken, and ones that were to lead the country to total disaster. The frivolous way in which these daunting commitments were arrived at is perhaps the most damning indictment possible of Mussolini's way of conducting his country's foreign affairs.

The Pact of Steel completed, on very disadvantageous terms, Italy's move into alliance with Germany.

- It may have been intended to promote Mussolini's ambitions in Africa and the Mediterranean but it also threatened to trap a militarily unprepared Italy into supporting German expansionist plans in northern Europe.
- If German actions provoked a general European war then Italy's forces would almost certainly find themselves fighting both France and Britain, on land and sea. This would present a more serious test of fascist militarism than that provided either by the ill-equipped and disunited troops of the Ethiopian army or by the ill-organised forces of the Spanish republicans.
- It is therefore surprising that the Italian government did not insist that the pact be followed by military discussions between the new allies but in fact no steps were taken to make the alliance a strategic reality.

ITALY'S DILEMMA, 1939–40

Mussolini had enjoyed the prestige of being centre stage at Munich, but he despised those who hailed him as a peacemaker. He wanted the fascist state that he had created to win glory in war. It is possible that he had not appreciated the nature of the commitments that Italy had undertaken in the Pact of Steel. Ciano, however, did realise the implications and, in May 1939, persuaded Mussolini to tell Hitler that, although Italy stood by the terms, it was essential that any war should be postponed for three years.

Germany in Poland
Hitler did not trouble to reply but, in September when Germany's invasion of Poland precipitated what became the Second World War, he demanded that Italy stand by

KEY THEMES

Nazi–Soviet Pact Signed on 23 August 1939, this marked a revolution in international relations. Germany and the Soviet Union, previously bitter enemies, agreed not to go to war with each other and to remain neutral if either were to be attacked by a third country. This opened the way for Hitler to attack Poland, which he did on 1 September 1939, thus starting the Second World War.

Neutrality The fact that Italy remained neutral in 1939 is one of the greatest contradictions of Mussolini's Italy. Throughout the dictatorship Mussolini claimed that he had transformed the Italian nation to be ready for war. But when war broke out, Italy declared neutrality.

its pact obligations. In the interim he had largely kept the Italians in the dark as to his plans to attack Poland and, more devastating still, had on 23 August 1939 signed a non-aggression **pact with the Soviet Union**, again without any warning, much less consultation, with Mussolini. The news had a shattering effect on Italian fascists, who had believed that the central core of fascism was its total opposition to communism. Hitler's secrecy enabled Ciano to persuade Mussolini that Italy, despite its obligations under the Pact of Steel, must keep out of the war. On 26 August, Ciano sent to Berlin a long list of war supplies, including 17,000 military vehicles, which the Germans would have to supply to the Italians before they could honour their treaty obligations.

Italy stays out of war

The Italians were so out of touch with what Hitler intended that they even attempted, hours before the Germans attacked Poland, to call a European conference for 5 September. Mussolini then used German secrecy, which he denounced as treachery, to declare that Italy would be a 'non-belligerent' in the war that had broken out on 3 September 1939 between Germany and Britain, France and, of course, Poland. Having to do this offended him greatly – for example, he carefully avoided using the term '**neutrality**' to describe Italy's war status.

- Mussolini resented his own and Italy's unheroic roles but made some efforts to mediate between the two sides in the war.
- The first months of the war were indecisive and Italian industrialists made good profits selling arms to both sides, including orders for a thousand planes from Britain and France, to the fury of the ill-equipped Italian forces.
- Despite the obvious economic advantages of neutrality, Mussolini fretted increasingly about not being involved in the war. This was entirely understandable, for fascism's message had always been about the need for national greatness proven on the battlefield. He saw Italy becoming a second-class nation denied its rightful territorial gains in the Balkans and the Mediterranean region.

In March 1940, Mussolini and Hitler met at the Brenner Pass on the German (previously Austrian)–Italy border and this may have stiffened Mussolini's resolve.

Mussolini joins war

This phase came to an end in April 1940 when the German forces gained a series of stunning victories in western Europe, overrunning Denmark and Norway before sweeping through Holland and Belgium and bringing France to the point of surrender. Hitler's plans for these campaigns had been well in hand when he and Mussolini had met only three weeks earlier but, in a revealing indication of the relative importance of the Axis partners, he had not chosen to mention them at the meeting.

Mussolini could no longer stall. He wanted his share of the spoils of victory and was equally concerned that, if he still did not act, then the victorious Germans might well use their new power against Italy, claiming the German-speaking valleys of north Italy. The scale of the German successes silenced Italian doubters, including Ciano and Victor Emmanuel, who only claimed to have been against the decision when the tide of war had already moved decisively against Italy. On 10 June 1940, Italy declared war on Britain and a France already on the verge of surrender.

Mussolini and Hitler meet at the Brenner Pass, March 1940. On the right is the Italian Foreign Minister Count Galeazzo Ciano.

SUMMARY QUESTIONS

1 What were the constraints on Italian foreign policy in the period from 1922 to 1935?

2 Explain how Italian foreign policy took a new direction in late 1935.

3 Why did Mussolini attack Ethiopia in 1936?

4 How did the Italian attack on Ethiopia affect international relations in Europe?

5 How did the Spanish Civil War affect international relations in Europe?

6 Identify the main stages in Italy's moves towards alliance with Germany in the 1930s.

7 Explain your understanding of the claim that 'by 1939 Mussolini's foreign policy options were running out'.

CHAPTER 8

Italy at war

INTRODUCTION

- Italy fought alongside Germany from June 1940 to September 1943.
- In July 1943, Mussolini was removed from office by the king and was then arrested, only to be freed in a daring raid by German troops.
- Italy then entered the war on the Allied side but made little contribution, except extensive anti-German guerrilla activity, in a grimly defensive campaign in which the Allies slowly pushed the German army northwards.
- The war in Europe came to a general end before all of Italy was freed from what had become an oppressive German army of occupation.
- Approximately 400,000 Italians – military personnel and civilian – were killed in the Second World War.
- Both pre-war failures and strategic wartime mistakes contributed to Italy's dismal military record.

Italian forces fought in several theatres of war. Despite many individual acts of bravery and good general discipline, their record was uniformly undistinguished. It was also in distinct contrast to the army's achievements in defending the country's northern frontier during the First World War. There are many reasons for this.

INADEQUATE PREPARATION FOR WAR

By the late 1930s, Italy was essentially a military state. Its internal propaganda stressed the likelihood of the country being involved in a major European war and from 1935 the *Duce* was advising his civil servants and military leaders that war was coming. From 1936, with involvement in Spain and the closer relations with Germany, the structure of a future conflict seemed more predictable. Mussolini's international ambitions and the rhetoric that accompanied them had, however, made little impact on Italy's economic and defence policies.

Military strength
Almost nothing had been done to prepare Italy for the heroic military role that the *Duce* envisaged.

- Various pre-war claims boasted that Italy would be able to put an army of 8–9 million, or even 12 million, into the field when the demands of war required it. Even the lower figure would have been close to three times the number of men in the Italian armed forces in the First World War and, in practice, in the Second World War Italy's armed forces never reached the size or the efficiency of those deployed by the much despised liberal governments which had fought the First World War.
- All branches of the armed forces were ill-supplied:
  - the army with almost no tanks;
  - the navy with too many battleships but, because the admirals refused to believe that planes could bomb ships at sea, almost no aircraft carriers;
  - the air force with too many bombers, too few fighters (647 and 191 respectively: Martin Clark, *Modern Italy*, 1996) and, crucially, no knowledge of the secrets of radar.
- Defences against aerial bombing scarcely existed.
- There was no one other than Mussolini to combine the efforts of the separate armed services and no general staff to plan war strategy.
- There was a lack of co-ordination in ordering military supplies so that the three armed forces competed with each other and no attempt was made to standardise equipment.
- Each service had its own intelligence network but in practice Italy's international espionage network was woefully inadequate so that its knowledge of the likely reactions and military capacity of other powers was limited.
- Additionally, in the three years immediately prior to the outbreak of the Second World War, the troubled occupation of Ethiopia and intervention in the war in Spain continued to devour the country's military strength.

The economy
Little had been done to prepare the economy for war.

- In theory the Battle for Grain would make Italy self-sufficient in food, except that the much acclaimed wheat production was heavily dependent on imports of fertilisers. Such supplies and, more seriously, imported supplies of oil on which all the armed forces depended, were all too likely to be disrupted in any war.
- Although there was a pattern of state interference in industry in peacetime, this was never built on to ensure the efficiency of essential war industries.
- The notion of a co-ordinating ministry to organise a future war effort was never achieved. Instead, money and raw materials were squandered on a series of splendid fascist building projects that bore no relation to military needs.

Propaganda
- In these last years of peace, Mussolini continued to insist on the remarkable strength of the Italian military machine.
- Fascist **propaganda**, as efficient as ever, rammed the message home. Even before Italy went to war propaganda had lost touch with military reality.
- Most serious of all, Italian military and civil leaders began to believe in their own propaganda. No one questioned either the figures or the plans. Even the most absurd claims for Italian military might were accepted.

Propaganda In 1938, for example, the number of army regiments in each division was reduced from three to two and, instantaneously, the propagandists referred to the army's 60 divisions instead of the much less impressive 40 divisions.

Mussolini's leadership
Mussolini was the sole source of major policy decisions and long before war came he had allowed himself to be deluded by his own propaganda. The gap between militaristic rhetoric and military reality almost suggests that Mussolini did not in practice seriously intend to go to war and certainly he never faced up to the likely impact of a long modern war. Italy's tragedy was that, under fascism, no one was able to question the basis of the *Duce's* logic. Fascism's great triumph had been to sweep both critics and common sense under the carpet.

FAILURES OF STRATEGY

Italy's unpreparedness for war was reluctantly
acknowledged in September 1939 but had not been
remedied when war came in June 1940. The major
weaknesses and mistakes of the war period resulted from
that fact. Only an overwhelming German victory could
ensure a triumphant Italy. Its fate was in the hands of
others.

The Mediterranean theatre of war

Woeful strategic mistakes were made here.

- Italian planners made no move to capture the
  strategically vital island of Malta, which continued to
  function as a British naval base throughout the war. By
  1942 British submarines and planes based at Malta were
  inflicting crippling losses on Italian convoys taking
  supplies to north Africa. With no aircraft carriers the
  Italians were not able to command the western
  Mediterranean but a determined assault on Malta could
  have secured their supply route to north Africa.
- The Italian army in its Libyan colony did not have the
  military capability to drive the British forces out of

**The crucial position of
Malta in the
Mediterranean.**

Egypt and so gain control of the Suez Canal, which would have opened the Red Sea route to its otherwise isolated colonies in Ethiopia, Eritrea and Somaliland. This was all the more strange since the most consistent aim of Mussolini's pre-war foreign policy had been to turn the Mediterranean into an Italian sea.

- There was no assault on the British base at Gibraltar, commanding the western entrance to the Mediterranean.
- Most surprising of all, Mussolini failed to take up a German offer to occupy defeated France's colony of Tunisia, complete with its modern naval base at Bizerta.

Wider miscalculations

The **lack of long-term war objectives** left Italian strategy at the mercy of Mussolini's intuition.

- In the summer of 1940, Mussolini was determined to take full part in the invasion and subsequent humiliation of Britain and for this purpose sent 300 Italian aircraft to Belgium. They lacked the range and the speed to be of any use there but could have been invaluable in pressing attacks on British targets in the Mediterranean theatre of war.
- The decision to imitate German victories, by invading Greece in 1940, had far more serious consequences when the Greek army counter-attacked and invaded Italian-held Albania. Until a few weeks before the invasion of Greece, Italian military planning in the Balkans had been entirely geared to an attack on and the subsequent dismemberment of Yugoslavia. The efforts of its invading forces were not co-ordinated; the army was under-equipped and its supply lines through Albania were totally inadequate; and no account had been taken of the effects of the onset of winter on the mountain passes that the Italian army had to capture and cross.
- In June 1941, it was perhaps inevitable, given his close ties with Nazi Germany, that Mussolini should follow Hitler in declaring war on the Soviet Union. He then insisted, against German wishes, on sending a large Italian force to the Eastern Front where its lack of tanks and inadequate motor transport made it completely ineffective and where it suffered great losses of men.

KEY THEME

Lack of war objectives
Mussolini's approach was completely inconsistent and he was prepared to fight anywhere. Italy found itself at war first with Britain and France; it then invaded Greece; sent troops to fight the Soviet Union; and then declared war on the USA.

Even German military leaders would have preferred these resources to have been used in the Balkans and in north Africa, but Mussolini was too anxious to share both the glory of victory and the plunder in the Soviet Union to see what Italy's real strategic interests were.

WARTIME WEAKNESSES WITHIN THE MILITARY

Greece
- The invasion of Greece in October 1940 had coincided with a mass demobilisation of the army that had just fought against France. No attempt was made to resolve this contradiction.
- The size of the Greek army, and its fighting capacity, were underestimated.
- Mussolini assumed that simply bombing Athens would lead the Greeks to surrender. In this war the navy suffered a decisive defeat in March 1941 at Cape Matapan because the air force failed to come to its aid.
- The army invaded Greece, but was soon in full retreat back into Albania, simply because it could not ship its supplies across the Adriatic, through Albania's single suitable port, in the time envisaged.

North Africa
Greece represented fascist Italy's most important military campaign. Defeat there, followed by rescue by the German army, coincided with the rout of Italian forces in Libya by a numerically vastly inferior British force whose 30,000 men made prisoners the vast majority of Italy's army of 200,000.

- In this campaign, which opened with an **Italian attempt to seize Egypt** and the strategically crucial Suez Canal, Mussolini refused German offers of transport and tanks. But his army was defeated because, in a war of swift movement across vast areas of desert, its transport support was so inferior to that of the British forces.
- Here, too, German forces came to Italy's aid and took over the campaign.

KEY THEME

The Italian attempt to sieze Egypt The Italians invaded Egypt in September 1940 but in December 1940 and January 1941 were driven back almost 1000 miles into Libya, past Benghazi. This rout was only reversed following the arrival in Libya of large numbers of German troops, who drove the British army back to the Egyptian frontier.

Italian, German and Hungarian POWs on their way to a Soviet POW camp after the great offensive of the Red Army, January 1944.

- With the Suez Canal still in British hands the fate of the 250,000 Italian troops in Ethiopia and the east African colonies was also settled and they surrendered with the minimum of resistance.

Defeat

Italy's early defeats in the war had a serious impact on military morale and its contribution to what became Germany's war in north Africa became less and less significant. The final defeat of Italy, in Africa and then in Sicily, involved Allied victories over German armies. The Italian navy, however, played one last significant though scarcely heroic role when its ships surrendered to the British. This totally altered the balance of naval power and not merely in the Mediterranean. It released Allied warships for the 1944 invasion of German-occupied France.

FAILURE TO DEPLOY THE COUNTRY'S RESOURCES EFFECTIVELY

The Second World War is commonly described as a **total war**. This was never the case with Italy where Mussolini, for reasons of morale and propaganda, preferred to keep up an appearance of peacetime normality.

- There was no general call-up of men into the military forces.

KEY TERM

Total war Involving the total commitment of all the nation's resources to the task of fighting.

- Rationing of food and consumer goods came slowly and at most patchily.
- A vast black market emerged which directed resources to the rich at the expense of the war effort.
- Private cars continued unrestricted far longer than in other belligerent countries. Luxury goods continued to appear in the shops.
- Factories were not involved only in the manufacture of war goods because it was considered important that they be ready to compete in the prosperous international economy that would surely follow the swift fascist victory. Even some merchant shipping was kept out of the war for this reason and civilian industry was encouraged to build up stocks of raw materials for the expected post-war boom.
- The armaments industry took until 1942, by when Italy's military plight was all too evident, before its output began to move seriously above peacetime levels.
- Once the tide of war turned against Italy, the peasant farmers started hoarding food and selling it on the black market. Food shortages then developed in the cities and led to the first strikes of the war period.

In short, fascist Italy, which had so long preached the virtues of military readiness, proved remarkably inefficient in fighting a long-term war. Everything had been based on Mussolini's assumption that victory would come quickly. (For more on this aspect of the war period see pages 132–4.)

INADEQUATE LEADERSHIP

It was Mussolini who had mesmerised Italians with his vision of fascist greatness and created the strongly centralised state based on himself. His most serious mistakes were strategic but increasingly he became a bottleneck in the task of fighting the war. Important decisions were endlessly delayed as he dealt with trivialities; they were then based on the *Duce*'s intuition, which no one dared to challenge. The despatch of ill-equipped planes and infantry to the Russian Front was merely the most dramatic example of this substitute for strategic planning.

Mussolini avoided the reality of the war. He rarely went anywhere near military action, even to inspect the bombing damage inflicted on Italy's northern cities. He consulted less and less with his military commanders and increasingly lost touch with reality; in a final irony, he came to rely on his own propaganda.

THE HOME FRONT

The wartime economy

The Italian army's difficulties (see page 125) are partly explained by shortage of arms and equipment.

* The economy was not able quickly to respond to wartime demand because of shortages of fuel and raw materials. Before entering the war Italy had been using over 3 million tonnes of oil each year but, once engaged in the war, the only supply of oil was from Romania and amounted to about 1.5 million tonnes, less than half of Italy's normal peacetime demand.
* Hydro-electricity could not be quickly expanded and the only source for coal was Germany, which needed all that it could produce for its own use.
* As a result steel production, essential to the war effort, fell in the first two years of the war from 2.3 million tonnes in 1938 to 1.9 million tonnes in 1942 and, as Allied bombing increasingly disrupted industrial production, to 1.7 million tonnes in 1943. Peacetime production had, in any case, been only one-tenth that of Germany and the Soviet Union, illustrating the lightweight nature of Italy's contribution to the war effort (Martin Clark, *Modern Italy*, 1996).
* Because of the shortage of raw materials and inadequate power supplies, neither of which even the most energetic manufacturers could do much to combat, armament and military transport production declined sharply at the onset of war. (Clark indicates that production of military vehicles by the two major manufacturers halved in the first year of the war from some 5000 to 2500 vehicles.) The manufacture of armaments increased slowly from 1941 to 1942, but then soon declined once more, thanks largely to heavy Allied bombing of the main industrial areas.

Mussolini avoided the reality of the war He had a network of secret underground passages built in the grounds of his home in Rome. Ten metres below ground, there was a main shelter of reinforced concrete with gas-proof doors and air filters together with a private shelter with a separate spiral staircase providing escape to the street above. Rome's city council only admitted to the bunker's existence in 1994. Mussolini's son, perhaps anxious to protect his father's image, said that Benito, a sufferer from claustrophobia, would not have dreamed of entering the shelter but that 'the authorities' had insisted on building it. The gas-proof doors were presumably there because most inhabitants of Rome expected the city to be subjected to Allied gas attacks that would kill them but preserve the historic buildings of the city. Rome was in fact never subjected to air attack, perhaps because the papacy devoted much diplomatic effort to preventing it happening.

- The fact that before 1940 the state had systematically controlled the country's major firms and that this continued during the war did not to any great extent change wartime business patterns or increase production in line with wartime demand. In many respects the fascist economy in the Second World War failed to function as efficiently as had the liberal economy in the First World War.
- As in the First World War factories were subject to military discipline and, until the heavy bombing raids in the second half of 1942, there were few labour disputes. But this could not compensate for failures in the supply of raw materials.

The war also brought **shortages of food, domestic fuel and essential consumer goods** such as soap, clothing and shoes.

- Food shortages were made worse by the second year of the war, owing to the conscription of young farm labourers and peasants into the army and to a sharp decline in the production of artificial fertilisers because of a lack of imported raw material for the chemical industry.
- German demands that Italy should continue to export food made shortages worse. Food was strictly rationed and this in turn encouraged the development of a black market as farmers evaded the official prices set for their produce. Because of this, many peasants became reasonably prosperous and certainly lived better than anyone in the towns.
- Industrial wages may have kept pace with the official prices, but these bore no relation to what was actually charged on the black market.
- The economy was further disrupted by the regime compelling civilians to go to work in Germany (200,000 were sent in 1941 and perhaps twice that number in 1942).

Italian society at war

- It was the industrial workers – particularly in the cities of Genoa, Milan and Turin – who suffered the worst of the bombing attacks that were so disruptive of production and which increased in intensity in 1942.

KEY THEME

Shortages of food, domestic fuel and essential consumer goods
In October 1941 bread was rationed at 200 grammes a week for most people (reduced to 150 grammes in March 1942). Potatoes, beans, lentils, milk, cheese and eggs were also subsequently rationed. In the same month shoes and clothing were rationed, private cars banned and the heating of buildings restricted. To prevent illegal trading, food markets were placed under Fascist Party control and savage punishments, including the death penalty, were made available to deal with those hoarding food.

Thousands of houses were destroyed (25,000 in Turin alone) and tens of thousands of people left these cities to live in the surrounding countryside.

- In April 1942, normal hours of work in heavy industry were set at 12 per day, 72 per week, but with 14 per day allowed in exceptional circumstances.
- By 1942 there were virulent press campaigns against 'defeatists and grumblers' who were accused of links with the British and with international communism. The penalties for listening to enemy or neutral broadcasts were trebled to a maximum of eighteen months imprisonment.
- Early in 1943 there was a series of short strikes protesting in theory about wages but in practice at conditions of life generally and indeed at the very continuation of the war.
- Left-wing agitators reappeared in these towns, which had in the 1920s been strong centres of socialism. The fascists had to rely on a heavy police and military presence, including the widespread use of police informers, in their efforts to keep control.

Loss of public support for the war

- As the bombing intensified civilian morale plummeted and the powerful **propaganda machine** became less and less convincing. Italy's reasons for going to war had never been clearly spelled out and became ever more obscure in late 1942 as military defeats became all too common on both the Soviet and the North African fronts.
- People lost all faith in the state-controlled radio and turned instead to broadcasts from the neutral Vatican City or, at considerable personal risk, those from the BBC.

Collapse of the Fascist Party

From the fascist regime's point of view the most sinister internal development was the collapse of the Fascist Party organisation. Nationally, it was badly led by a succession of weak secretaries and, under the ceaseless pressure of bad military news, had collapsed locally months before the fascist regime nationally was officially brought to an end.

The destruction of the Galleria Vittorio Emanuele in Milan, August 1943, after Allied bombing.

MUSSOLINI'S DOWNFALL

Mussolini replaced as prime minister

In 1942, the war in north Africa was clearly being lost and Italian public support for the war was ebbing away. Leading Italian fascists began to contemplate making a separate peace but soon realised that Mussolini would never agree to this. The Allied conquest of Sicily and the likely prospect of an invasion of mainland Italy provoked them to take action.

- In late July 1943, Mussolini was persuaded to call a

meeting of the Fascist Grand Council, the first since 1939, and was wrong-footed when the council voted, 19 to 7, to ask King Victor Emmanuel III to give back to parliament and the other **constitutional bodies** all the powers Mussolini had taken from them.

- When, the next day, Mussolini tried to override this, and to continue governing with new ministers, the king, at last and far too late, found the courage to stand up to him. Mussolini was arrested and replaced as prime minister by the aged soldier Marshal Badoglio.
- The *coup*, opening a road to peace, was widely welcomed among the public and not resisted by the fascists, many of whom sought to work under the new regime.

Leader of the Republic of Salo

The Germans had to prevent the total collapse of their Italian Front and did so with remarkable success so that Italy had to face two more years of fighting, this time on its own soil. The *Duce* was rescued by German paratroops and, as Italy entered the war on the Allied side, he was made the puppet-leader of a fascist republic, the Republic of Salo, in northern Italy where a vicious civil war ensued. Mussolini permitted, perhaps organised, the executions of leading fascists who had betrayed the movement. The best-known victim was his own son-in-law, the ex-foreign minister Ciano.

The Fascist Party in the puppet republic denounced the treachery of the king and renamed itself the Fascist Republican Party, which in theory at least had almost half a million members. For many months, with the Allied advance blocked by the German army, the republic maintained the myth of business as usual. A party convention was held and produced a radical political agenda, including worker takeovers or state control of many large businesses. Government and local government remained in the hands of the traditional office holders and functioned as usual.

The real power, however, lay with the German occupying forces and they used it with as much savagery as they had done in other parts of German-occupied Europe. The remnants of the Italian army and the police force gradually

The role of constitutional bodies The best evidence of Mussolini's failure to transform Italy was the continuity in the influence of many sections of the political establishment. The king kept enough power to be able to dismiss Mussolini in 1943. The civil service, police and legal systems stayed in the hands of the same individuals and class of people who had run these institutions before 1922. The localities were run by Prefects who, again, were not necessarily fascist. Mussolini relied on the Prefects and the institutions mentioned above to keep order.

disintegrated or evolved into private armies like the initial *squadristi*, backing one or other leading fascist. Roberto Farinacci was still prominent at this level. By the end of 1944, violence and lawlessness had become the norm, with attacks on suspected anti-fascists and on Jews alongside plunder and destruction for its own sake. Mussolini, who had not wanted to be head of the German-dominated republic lest he be branded a traitor, was helpless in the face of the growing anarchy. In December 1944, the faithful rallied to hear him for one last time in Milan and responded with enthusiasm to his oratory.

Execution

By early 1945, after prolonged resistance, the German forces in Italy were in full retreat and no longer had use for their puppet. Abandoned by his family and by all but a dozen followers, Mussolini and his long-time mistress, Clara Petacci, tried to escape across the frontier to Switzerland but were captured about 50 kilometres short of their objective by Italian communists. On 28 April 1945, just one week before Germany itself surrendered, **they were shot.** Their bodies were taken to Milan where Mussolini made his final public appearance, his body mutilated and strung upside down for public vilification by a vengeful mob.

SUMMARY QUESTIONS

1 How did lack of preparation before the Second World War contribute to Italy's poor military performance during the war?

2 In what ways did mistakes by Mussolini bring about Italy's defeat in the Second World War?

3 Examine the view that Italy's wartime experiences on the Home Front provide the best indication of the failure of fascist social and economic policies in the 1930s.

4 Why did the fascist regime collapse in 1943?

AS ASSESSMENT

INTRODUCTION

All three English examination groups – Edexcel, AQA and OCR – offer the opportunity of taking an AS level in Italian history in this period.

- The Edexcel module 'Italy: the Rise of Fascism 1918–25' requires candidates to answer one two-part essay-style examination question from a choice of two in a 1-hour paper.
- OCR's option 'Europe 1890–1945' contains within it four study options on different topics, one of which is 'Italy 1919–45'. In this 1-hour paper there is only one two-part question on each study option so that, if the Italian question does not appeal to you, you have to look elsewhere. The two parts of the question are likely to come from different parts of the period – for example, the OCR specimen paper question asks in (a) for an explanation of why Mussolini came to power and in (b) for an assessment of how successful he had been by 1939 in making Italy a stable and prosperous country.
- The AQA Option J module on 'The origins and consolidation of Totalitarian States, 1918–39' requires the study of the Soviet Union and *either* Nazi Germany *or* Fascist Italy. In a 1½-hour paper it is assessed by two three-part source-based questions on historical explanations and interpretations. Both questions have to be answered. There is no choice in the first of these, but there is the opportunity to use knowledge of Italian history to answer *some* of the sub-questions on, for example, the development of state control or the role of the leader in totalitarian regimes. The second question can be answered almost entirely from knowledge of Italian history, though some idea of the European context of inter-war totalitarianism would be a useful asset. AQA also has some AS Italian history in its Option H module 'The effects of World War One, 1915–1924', which is assessed by a coursework essay.

These descriptions of AS examinations are based on the first two sets of papers issued by the examination groups. They will almost certainly be modified in some ways in the future. Examination candidates must be aware of this and make sure that they get copies of up-to-date syllabuses and current examination papers.

Edexcel

The period covered in the Edexcel syllabus at AS level is very brief and will require candidates to have detailed knowledge of Italy from the end of the First World War through to Mussolini establishing his authoritarian rule by the end of 1925.

AQA

The same Edexcel material will provide a sound basis for two of AQA's three modules – the origins of totalitarianism in Italy and the internal crisis in Italian democracy 1918–22 – but, in order to cover the AQA syllabus fully, candidates will also have to study 'the consolidation of the totalitarian regime through to 1939'. In this broader syllabus they will also have to be aware of some aspects of Soviet history from 1919 to 1939.

OCR

The syllabus for the Italian study option covers the period from 1919 to 1945 and provides no choice of questions. It seems probable that most candidates will study Italy as their favoured area for a question but also prepare some material from a second study option. Studying Italy alone is a higher risk strategy but has obvious advantages in terms of the range of work to be undertaken.

Once the syllabuses have operated for several years it will be important to check this informal advice against the papers actually set by the exam groups and modify it in the light of experience. In any event, make sure that you see and understand the examination syllabus of your exam group at an early stage of your studies. Study and practice of the questions set in previous AS papers will be invaluable.

A STUDY AND REVISION STRATEGY

- Study in terms of examination questions. History is about problems, 'How?', 'Why?', 'With what consequences?'. Organise your reading and your notes in terms of such problems.
- Read, or at least survey several times, each of the chapters in this book that are relevant to your own syllabus. Do not try to memorise too many facts. It is the overall understanding that is important.
- Try to read actively and ask questions of what you are reading. Questioning an account of a, perhaps trivial, act by Mussolini could, for example, lead you on to the big decisions and moments in his life.
- Get a full picture of Mussolini. For good and ill he dominated Italy in these years and he is likely to loom large in most of the essays you write about Italian political life in the fascist period.
- Leave plenty of time before the examination to re-read some of the module content. Continue during revision to think in terms of asking questions about the

historical material and also in constructing outline answers to likely questions. Draw up a list of revision themes in order of priority and get through as many as revision time permits.

EXAMINATION TACTICS

- Do the obvious as a matter of course – note the exam date and time, which option paper, how much choice, any compulsory questions.
- In any exam you will have limited time to think about and plan your answers on different topics. You must divide your time effectively between the questions and sub-questions. There are severe limitations on any candidate's ability to raise the overall mark by doing brilliantly in just one part of the answer. It is much better to give each question and sub-question a fair share of the time available, relating this to the maximum number of marks available in each case.
- Do not write out the question. Do not list purely factual knowledge as your essay plan.
- Remember that you face a direct question; try to give a direct answer.

ESSAY QUESTIONS

Question in the style of Edexcel

1a Describe the main reasons for government instability in the period 1919 to 1921. (15)
 b Why was there a crisis of government in 1922? (15)

Reading
Before answering this question you should read Chapter 1 (pages 6–27).

How to answer this question
In 1a you are asked for the *main* reasons, so do not leave a major area out. On the other hand, you will not have time to go into detail about how these reasons emerged in an earlier period and how they interacted on each other. In 1b you can refer in passing to the earlier events you have covered in 1a, but the bulk of your answer must be specifically on 1922.

Plan for 1a
You need to refer to at least the following reasons.

- No one party had enough seats to form a government alone; explain how the electoral system caused this.

- The two largest parties (socialists and the *Popolari*) would not work together. You could refer also to the fear of the left felt by many Italians.
- Coalition governments centred on the liberals were therefore required but, after Italy's entry into the war in 1915, the leading liberals would not work together. So coalitions were unstable (give examples) and relied on smaller parties (cite Giolitti's deal with the fascists).
- Mounting violence from left and right also created instability. Use the D'Annunzio occupation of Fiume, and refer particularly to fascist tactics and growing power in the cities. The collapse of law and order.
- Disillusion in society and economic problems after the war. Keep this brief. Aim to show how it created government instability

When writing, remember the following.

- The question is on 'government instability' and not on the general ills affecting Italian society, so keep your answer focused on the question.
- Avoid merely describing what happened. Write in short paragraphs with each moving on to a new reason for instability. D'Annunzio at Fiume offers a very good example of the dangers of describing events at too great a length. A book could be written about this episode, but all you want and have time for is a direct statement on how it added to government instability.
- Try to provide a one-paragraph conclusion. One way to do this might be to indicate what you think was the most important reason for instability underpinning the other reasons you have provided.

Style
Here is an example of a paragraph on the mounting violence creating government instability.

> *One reason for increased government instability was the developing violence in society at large which gave the impression that the government was losing control. In 1919, D'Annunzio and armed followers in uniform seized control of the disputed port of Fiume and held it for many months, defying the Italian government. Their success encouraged other groups to use direct action to settle grievances. In 1920–1, there were many examples of workers occupying factories, and peasants forcibly occupying land, disrupting the economy and arousing fears of a communist takeover. The fascist* squadristi *deliberately copied D'Annunzio's paramilitary tactics down to the blackshirt uniforms. They destroyed socialist trades unions in the countryside and fought pitched street battle with their socialist enemies in the cities. Many respectable people, who would normally have supported the government, were so frightened of the socialist threat that they came to support the fascists as the best hope against a left-wing coup.*

This is not intended as a perfect answer, but it does try to use important detail to illustrate one reason for instability without getting entangled in long passages describing what happened. Remember that you will have several other paragraphs to write on other reasons before the answer to 1a is complete.

Plan for 1b
You have already covered the background in 1a and must now concentrate on 1922. In the body of this part of your essay you need to explain:

- fascist control of major provincial towns and the increased violence; growing numbers and increased support – the fascists could not be ignored;
- the inability of the government to handle this situation; its greater fear of the communist threat; inability of leading democratic politicians to work together; paralysis of Facta's government; the king's dilemma; the issue of army loyalty;
- the skilful way in which Mussolini put pressure on the other parties in the crisis.

Style
A possible final paragraph to this essay could read:

> By 1922, fascist squadristi *controlled many of the towns and were accepted by the local leaders there, government orders were ignored and in the final crisis it was this loss of control that destroyed prime minister Facta's liberal government and led to Mussolini being asked to form a government. Fascist violence had grown so strong that the king even feared that there could be a civil war if he used the army to end it and so refused to back his prime minister.*

Question in the style of OCR

1a Explain how Mussolini rose from obscurity in 1919 to become prime minister of Italy in 1922. (30)

b Assess Mussolini's success by 1939 in turning Italy into a totalitarian state. (60)

Reading
AS Chapters 1 and 2 both have relevant material for 1a though, with only 30 marks involved, you will need to select only the most directly relevant points. AS Chapter 4 will provide the basis for 1b, but consider consulting A2 Section 4. Above all, be aware that, in this 1-hour paper, the two-part question format means you must write concisely, stick to the main points and use the limited time to maximum advantage. In the light of the mark allocation try to spend twice as long on question 1b as on question 1a.

Plan for 1a

Explain:

- the political confusion and government instability after the war, making a new political direction seem attractive;
- how Mussolini skilfully exploited post-war disillusion by his oratory and his journalism;
- the importance of the fascist *squadristi*, in country and in town, in building up the movement;
- the 1921 deal with Giolitti, which gave the fascists seats in the Chamber of Deputies;
- Mussolini's balancing act using both legal manoeuvres in parliament and exploiting fascist street violence to gain support;
- 1922 government paralysis and how Mussolini exploited it via the threat of the March on Rome;
- how in 1922 the politicians and the king caved in to the threat.

An effective conclusion could be that he became prime minister by a mixture of legal and illegal methods, each dependent on the other and all skilfully masterminded by Mussolini. You will have to explain the post-war political confusion very briefly; it is important in understanding what happened, but the question is on the rise of Mussolini and not on the Italian situation in general. It is important that you answer the question directly.

Plan for 1b

- Start with a simple definition of totalitarian (one sentence, not a long debate).
- Explain Mussolini's personal dominance in almost all aspects of *government* but add that the king survived and would eventually dismiss him.
- Explain how the state interfered in the *economy* especially labour relations, but also indicate the limits of this – capitalism survived outside the corporate state, both small and large firms and of course the peasant farmers.
- Examine how the state interfered in *society*; give specific examples – police activity, fate of opponents, the *Dopolavoro* and youth movements controlling leisure. Again indicate that there were limits, especially the survival of the Catholic Church.
- Conclude by writing that Mussolini had altered Italy. He personally controlled politics, citizens were less free of the state than pre-1922 and the state had a big say in economic matters. But not totalitarian because too much of the earlier Italy survived (class structure, king and Church) and because fascism was too inefficient (too half-hearted in Italy compared with Nazi Germany) to impose its controls on everything. Much of Italian life still went on outside the control of the state.

Now assume that you prefer to argue that Italy was clearly a totalitarian state. Draw up an essay plan and write a concluding paragraph on these lines.

Question in the style of Edexcel

1a How was Mussolini able to survive the Matteotti crisis? (10)
  b What steps did he take, in the course of 1925, to establish 'strong government' in Italy? (15)

Reading
You should read AS Chapter 3 before attempting to answer this question.

Plan for 1a
A useful start would be to indicate, at paragraph length, what the Matteotti crisis was, then how it threatened Mussolini. It is important not to embark on a longer descriptive account of the details of the crisis or you will not have time to construct an answer to the question. A plan, paragraph by paragraph, might look like this:

- Matteotti's attack on the conduct of the 1924 election, his subsequent disappearance and murder, the high-ranking fascist suspects, the issue of Mussolini's involvement;
- the threat of a parliamentary vote of censure, of uncontrollable public protest or of dismissal by the king;
- the failure of any parliamentary threat (the poor tactics of the opposition walkout but also stress the size of the fascist majority in the Chamber plus the use of intimidation of members). Later the poor timing of the release of evidence incriminating Mussolini at Christmas so that the impact was lost. Opponents never worked together;
- the failure of opponents to arouse public opinion, especially the failure of the unions to call a general strike or of the socialists to organise public demonstrations. Also refer to the effectiveness of government propaganda and to the support Mussolini still enjoyed as the best hope of avoiding a communist revolution;
- the king's failure to dismiss Mussolini, but remember the lack of public protest, the fascist majority and the continuing support of Mussolini by non-fascist members of the coalition government. Why should he act?
- Mussolini's resolution in the face of the threat, particularly the impact of his speech in January 1925, declaring the setting-up of strong government.

Plan for 1b
This requires a descriptive account of the measures indicated in AS Chapter 3, but included in the description should be enough comments to show that you are aware of the significance of each stage:

- the speech of 3 January 1925 as a turning point in Mussolini's reaction to the mounting criticism;
- Mussolini preventing the Aventine Secessionist opponents returning to the

Chamber and the collapse of the other political parties;
- the press law;
- the *Legge Fascistissime*: the importance of each of which needs to be spelled out;
- the efforts to bring the *squadristi* leaders into line and to control the Fascist Party;
- Mussolini becoming political head of each of the armed forces and tightening his control of the civil service.

A possible, but brief, conclusion could be that strong government still needed further steps at the end of 1925 – for example, in January 1926 Mussolini was made 'head of government'. From 1926 to 1928, the Rocco Laws provided a framework for state control of labour relations and saw socialist and Catholic trades unions wither away. In 1929, the Lateran Pact secured general agreement for his regime.

Question in the style of AQA

Read the source extract provided and then answer questions a, b and c which follow.

What gave them [the fascists] their chance after the First World War was the collapse … of the old ruling classes and their machinery of power, influence and hegemony [leadership]. Where these remained in good working order there was no need for fascism.

(Adapted from E. Hobsbawm, *The Age of Extremes*)

1a In the context of Italy from 1919 to 1922, what is meant by the 'old ruling classes'? (3)

 b Explain why Mussolini was able to establish a one-party state in Italy. (7)

 c 'Repression became the keynote of the state.' With reference to fascist Italy in the 1930s explain why you agree or disagree with this statement. (15)

Plan for 1a
With only 3 marks available be brief: make reference to the narrow pre-1914 franchise; to middle-class domination of parliament; use the term 'Liberal State' and have one sentence on *trasformismo* coalition politics; name two leading liberal politicians.

Plan for 1b
Again you will have to be brief. Indicate the weakness of the Liberal State and the appeal of fascism in the 1920s, but then concentrate on 1925 and give specific information on what happened to allow Mussolini to establish his position. You will need to say why no one blocked this – the mistake of the Aventine Secession and the king's failure to act must both be mentioned.

Plan for 1c

With 45 minutes available to answer all three parts of this question, even here you will not have time for a full essay answer. The simplest way to plan this answer is to decide quickly whether you will argue agreement or disagreement. It would be useful, however, to show that you understand there may well be another side to the issue.

Another route might be to open by arguing that at first sight there is a lot of truth in this claim (or assert the opposite) and have an opening paragraph giving a few reasons why this looks to be so. Then state clearly that nevertheless you do not find this convincing and, for the rest of the essay explain, in separate paragraphs, why this is so. Whatever you do make sure that your verdict on the statement is clearly stated – even if you have gone for a mixed verdict.

SOME FINAL EXAM TIPS

- Make any essay plan brief and in abbreviated note form. Plan a structure; do not just list factual information.
- Structure your essay plan around paragraphs. At the end of actually writing each paragraph ask yourself whether you are still giving a direct answer to the question as set. Or have you been side-tracked into just describing what happened?
- Do not use slang or casual English. Historians use technical terms (executive, legislature, proportional representation, constitutional monarchy, constituency, pragmatic, patriotism, chauvinism, propaganda, even *trasformismo,* and lots more), so take a pride in knowing their meanings and using these and other terms correctly. Be proud of an extensive vocabulary. Your ideas deserve the most professional presentation.
- Practice planning and writing timed essays in exam conditions long before the actual examination.

A2 SECTION: ANALYSIS AND INTERPRETATION

INTRODUCTION

This part of the book is based on the explanations offered in the AS part so it will be useful to students taking AS modules as well as to those going on to study fascist Italy at A2 level. The opportunity is taken here to expand points of interpretation that could only be dealt with briefly earlier in the book. Each A2 section is organised around the issues and problems that have attracted historians and examiners, and each contains a brief comment on past historical writing on the subject matter. The sections cover the following major issues.

- **Section 1: Why did Mussolini become prime minister in 1922?** Examines the long-term weaknesses of the Liberal State, the impact of the First World War and the confused state of Italian politics from 1919 to 1922.
- **Section 2: Why was Mussolini able to acquire dictatorial powers?** Discusses Mussolini's intentions after 1922, and examines the significance of the Acerbo Law and the Matteotti crisis before assessing the steps he took to achieve dictatorial powers.
- **Section 3: What were the main features of fascism?** Looks at the development of fascist ideas in the 1920s and 1930s, relates them to the construction of the fascist state and tries to set fascist Italy in a wider European context.
- **Section 4: Was fascist Italy a totalitarian state?** Defines totalitarianism, examines the efforts made to create a totalitarian political structure and considers whether Mussolini was ever in a position to establish totalitarian control over the Italian people.
- **Section 5: What was Mussolini's role in the fascist state?** Examines Mussolini's political role and also the huge propaganda that surrounded him, leading on to the cult of the *Duce* and his dreams of a new Italian people.
- **Section 6: Analysing fascist Italy: central issues.** Considers the myths and reality of the corporate state, the efficiency of the fascist economy and the effectiveness of fascist economic policy, and the issues of how popular and how oppressive the fascist regime was.
- **Section 7: Analysing Italian foreign policy, 1935–40.** Examines the factors influencing foreign policy and, in particular, Mussolini's desire for an Italian Empire. It explores the importance of the Ethiopian war as a turning point in European relations and analyses the subsequent

moves made by Italy to form an alliance with Nazi Germany. There is a section on the links between foreign and domestic policy, and a final attempt to analyse the successes and failures of Mussolini's conduct of foreign policy.

SECTION 1

Why did Mussolini become prime minister in 1922?

KEY POINTS

An explanation of how Mussolini became prime minister in 1922 needs to take account of the following.

- **The long-term political weaknesses of the Italian state.** The narrowly based franchise and the weakness of political parties meant that political life, revolving around a few leading liberal politicians, was very unstable. Short-lived coalition governments dominated politics until the emergence of new parties – socialist and Catholic – made these more difficult to form.
- **The dramatic impact of the First World War on Italian politics.** Coalitions had revolved around middle-class, middle-of-the-road liberals, but these groups were bitterly divided over Italy entering the war. The war also challenged Italian governments with vast new economic and social problems that proved politically disruptive.
- **The political confusion of the 1919–22 period**. The system of liberal coalitions (the *trasformismo* system) broke down in the new political conditions after the end of the war. The liberals needed new partners to enable the system to go on working and yet they did not want to work with the socialists whom they saw as a potentially revolutionary danger to the state.
- **The positive appeal of fascism.** This rested on the possibility that fascism would end the political drift and provide solutions to Italy's economic and political instability. It owed much to Mussolini's skills as a publicist and in controlling and directing the movement.
- **The role of the king.** Why did Victor Emmanuel III fail to block Mussolini?

HISTORICAL INTERPRETATIONS

The British liberal historian G.M. Trevelyan, born in 1876 and studying Italian history before 1914, was impressed with the strength of the Italian state and by its political stability (*Garibaldi and the Making of Italy*, published in 1911). He later considered the effects of the First World War to be the agent that destroyed this achievement. Marxist historians on the other hand, most notably the Italian communist leader Antonio Gramsci, writing in Italian and largely after being imprisoned by the fascists in 1926, pointed out the many weaknesses of liberal Italy and blamed liberal politicians and a feeble king, bowing to the interests of big business, for allowing the fascists into office. Another contemporary, G. Salvemini, who went into exile after the fascist regime was established, blamed the events of 1922 on the Catholic Church for blocking attempts to form an anti-fascist coalition, and the authorities of the Liberal State, especially the army, for condoning fascist criminal activity (*The Origins of Fascism in Italy*).

Later Denis Mack-Smith, in his splendidly readable *Mussolini* (1982), stresses the crucial role of the fascist leader in manipulating a complex situation. Martin Clark, in *Modern Italy* (1996), emphasises the many structural weaknesses and differences at the top of Italian political life, which at the crucial moment prevented non-fascists working together to block Mussolini's progress. He is anxious to stress that there was nothing inevitable about the eventual fascist takeover; if, at crucial moments in 1922 and later, events had taken a slightly different course, as they well might have done, then Italian politics could have continued on a democratic course.

WERE THE LIBERALS RESPONSIBLE FOR MUSSOLINI BECOMING PRIME MINISTER?

Liberal weaknesses

Liberal politicians had led most of the pre- and post-war Italian governments, maintaining themselves in power (usually briefly) by doing deals with fellow liberals in order to construct coalitions based on personalities rather than political programmes. In consequence, important domestic problems had no systematic attention and serious public disaffection with the regime went unattended. From 1919, these leaders behaved as though their political world was unchanged either by the vast expansions of the electorate in 1912 and 1918 or by the events and the outcome of the First World War. In this sense it was the liberal system, *trasformismo* politics, rather than individual liberal leaders, that failed Italy. The war dealt a fatal blow to the liberals by producing a deep divide within their ranks between interventionists like Salandra and Orlando and those like Giolitti and the majority of liberals in the Chamber of Deputies for whom taking part in the war was folly. The two sides never again worked together effectively and many of the interventionists felt closer ties to Mussolini on this issue than they did with those who had opposed intervention. The lack of an electable central political party – able to command a parliamentary majority and committed to a specific political programme – led to the politics of drift and despair after 1919.

Individual Liberal State politicians certainly made mistakes that, with hindsight, were helpful to Mussolini.

- Orlando introduced votes for all men in 1918, creating an electorate that was much more difficult to control or persuade to stay within the normal bounds of traditional party loyalty.
- Nitti introduced proportional representation, based on vast constituencies and complex lists of candidates, in 1919; this greatly helped the electoral prospects of small parties, like the fascists.
- Giolitti, the grand old man of liberal politics, included fascist candidates on his government lists of candidates, in order to block the socialists in the 1921 election; this made fascism respectable and gave its followers their crucial parliamentary breakthrough, with 35 members of the Chamber.

Mistakes in 1922

The mistakes continued in the 1922 crisis when Facta, who saw himself simply as a caretaker until Giolitti chose to re-enter the fray, acted too late in trying to introduce martial law in order to combat the fascist threat. In 1922, all the liberal leaders were too willing to listen to Mussolini's half-promises of curtailing the violence once he was in government. Perhaps most culpable of the liberals at this point was Giolitti – the one man in the 1922 crisis who might have been able to form a government without Mussolini but who chose not to be in Rome at the crucial time. Arguably, the many twists and turns of *trasformismo* politics had exhausted all the possible combinations capable of providing the state with effective government. The **political divisions** at the heart of Italian liberalism, brought about by Italy's entry into the First World War, were largely responsible for this, creating distrust and dislike between individuals and groups.

KEY THEME

Political divisions
The divisions over the entry of Italy into the First World War in 1915 were not healed by peace in 1918. Indeed, they acted to cripple the Liberal State thereafter as they made coalition politics virtually impossible.

Liberal miscalculations

The dilemma for the parliamentary liberals was that, by 1922, their power to influence or control events in the towns of northern and central Italy was very limited. There the police, the courts and even detachments of the army had such sympathy with the anti-left-wing aims and the direct methods of the fascists that it was difficult to see how fascist violence and intimidation in these areas could be controlled. It is true, however, that by continuing to talk of political deals with Mussolini, leading liberals undermined the position and the will of those local authorities that might have acted against fascist anarchy. Equally, liberal unwillingness to negotiate with socialists and trades unionists also prevented an anti-fascist stand in the name of restoring law and order. The main charge against the bankrupt leaders of liberalism must be that they preferred a deal with Mussolini to a possible alliance with the left.

By the autumn of 1922, the most eminent liberals – the conservative Salandra and even the more democratic Orlando, Nitti and Giolitti – had convinced themselves that the best way out of the looming crisis was to appease the fascists. Most liberals had reached the same conclusion, with many right-wing liberals feeling that fascist violence was an acceptable answer to socialist subversion of the state. In 1922, liberals like Giolitti stood aside, believing that, once Mussolini was given responsibility within the parliamentary framework, he could be tamed and would in turn tame his violent followers. Others welcomed the formation of the new government, not only as offering the best prospect for ending the unruly behaviour of the fascists but also opening up the welcome new prospect of an alignment of liberals and fascists, able to defend Italy from socialists and communists.

In the light of traditional Italian political practice this might have seemed an entirely reasonable assumption. Such a view, however, ignores the fact that Mussolini, unlike earlier politicians, was made prime minister not because of his parliamentary political significance but precisely because of the escalating violence perpetrated by his followers. The liberal leaders chose to ignore this inconvenient fact and paid a high price for their miscalculation in the years after 1922.

WHY DID LEFT-WING OPPONENTS FAIL TO HALT THE RISE OF FASCISM?

Fear of socialism

In crucial ways the actions of 'the left' actually helped the fascist cause. When peace came both socialist groups and trades unions expanded and became more ambitious. Some simply sought a better deal for their members but the success of the 1917 communist revolution in Russia encouraged many urban activists to dream of an Italian workers' state. The series of strikes in 1919 and 1920, the *Biennio Rosso* (Two Red Years), terrified industrialists who, whenever possible, simply bought off trouble. Repeated widespread strikes in the transport industry were especially disruptive. At the same time, left-wing-inspired food riots forced local authorities to impose price controls on goods, thereby destroying the normal working of markets and the businesses of middle-class shopkeepers. This apparent anarchy produced fury and fear outside the ranks of the left activists. It culminated in September 1920 in a widespread four-week long worker Occupation of the Factories, which looked dangerously like the first step in an economic revolution.

In northern and central parts of Italy the unions were able to disrupt the rural economy and force their demands on the landlords, in many areas taking over the supply of labour in the crucial harvest period.

The fascists were able to exploit this upheaval because a sorely puzzled government did little about it. From this point, they were able to present themselves as the most effective defence against industrial anarchy, acting as strike-breakers and attacking trade union leaders and offices. Meeting the threat of force with the use of force, and challenging the left's control of the streets, they attracted enormous sympathy and support from the beleaguered middle classes.

Failure of the socialist general strike

Early in 1921, the Socialist Party (the PSI) split and a new **Communist Party** was formed. The new party was tiny but demonising. It provided much effective propaganda for the fascists and also an excuse for them to take direct action on the streets. Even after this split, the Socialist Party still refused to make formal pacts with the liberal groups, to block Mussolini. The final mistake of the Italian left, having at last formed a loose coalition, the **Alliance of Labour**, was its decision to call a 24-hour general strike in August 1922 in order to block any fascist entry into government. This again frightened respectable opinion and yet attracted very little support from the workers.

The fascists organised 'volunteer' strike-breaking groups and claimed to have saved the country from a communist revolution when the strike rapidly collapsed. As the government drifted and hoped for the best, it was this action that gained the fascists so much moderate support that future political stability seemed to demand their inclusion in any future government. The left had again played into Mussolini's hands by making him seem to be the country's best defence against a godless communist revolution.

WHAT ROLE DID CONSERVATIVE INTERESTS PLAY?

Fascist sympathisers in the Catholic Church

It seems unlikely that Mussolini could have entered government, much less become prime minister, without the active goodwill of right-wing groups and individuals. Many in Italy preferred the prospect of a fascist presence in government to the apparent imminent danger of a left-wing revolution. These sympathisers included the hierarchy of the Catholic Church, where the election in February 1921 of a new Pope, Pius XI, created a more strongly anti-communist feeling. From that point, the papacy worked to eradicate left-wing influences within the Catholic Party (the *Popolari*) and did much to undermine the Alliance of Labour's call for an anti-fascist general strike. The new Pope perhaps saw in the fascist advance an opportunity to improve the official status of the Catholic Church in Italy, an issue that liberal governments had continued to ignore. At this crucial time, papal influence was used to oppose any

KEY THEMES

Communist Party
The party was committed to the revolutionary overthrow of the democratic state and the creation of a communist state on the Russian model.

Alliance of Labour
With the abject failure of the general strike the Alliance of Labour rapidly disintegrated and, even in industrial urban Italy, the demoralised left retreated as the fascist gangs seized control of the streets in more towns.

notion of closer co-operation between the *Popolari* and the liberals, thus seriously weakening any hope of a viable anti-fascist coalition.

Other support for the fascists

Large industrialists, impressed by fascist strike-breakers opposing trades unionists, had already provided funds for the movement. Two of Italy's best-known industrialists, Pirelli the tyremaker and Olivetti the typewriter manufacturer, were among those who, in 1922, urged liberal leaders to bring the fascists into a coalition government. Many conservative groups – notably police officers, members of the army, rural landlords, middle-class businesspeople – also had sympathy with the fascists' stand against the left and, in the crisis of 1922, these sympathisers often played a significant role in paralysing local opposition to the fascist takeover of the great towns. Others joined the Fascist Party and helped in its organisation or in producing party propaganda.

When the traditional leaders of urban society stood aside, the path of the **fascist advance** was made much easier. It was crucial to Mussolini's success in 1922 that his followers succeeded in gaining control of the streets and then the local administration of the great northern towns. The key local government officers, the prefects, did little to resist fascist violence, usually seeing left-wing agitators as the enemy to be dealt with.

WHAT PART DID THE FASCISTS PLAY?

Fascist seizure of the towns

Mussolini became prime minister as the result of a bluff, but it was a bluff based on a reality: the dominant position established by the fascist *squadrismo* in the northern towns. The threat to march on Rome never materialised but it was this solid **control in key urban areas**, illustrating the scale of the fascist advance, that frightened even reluctant liberal leaders into seeking a compromise with Mussolini.

Mussolini's control of his followers was not total

The great danger for Mussolini came from these same groups and their growing impatience with his cautious search for a deal with the government rather than risking a violent overthrow of the political system. For months, Mussolini worked to keep his more violent followers in check but, in 1921–2, he could not take their loyalty for granted. In July 1921, he had almost lost control of the movement when in the Pact of Pacification he attempted to promote a deal between the fascist and the socialist trades unions, which led to resignations from some and a visit by others to ask D'Annunzio to become their leader. Mussolini was saved on this occasion only by the mutual distrust between the leaders of the various local *squadristi*.

Fascist advance
In 1922, the fascist advance in northern Italy was so relentless that the prefects lost effective power in their own localities. The one exception, Cesare Mori in Bologna, who had resisted fascist violence, was swept out of office when fascist gangs from other towns moved into Bologna and forced his removal.

Control in urban areas Roberto Farinacci took violent control of Cremona and Italo Balbo led rural landless labourers to seize Ferrara.

During 1922, Mussolini had to work to retain their loyalty as the pace of their illegal action increased and his threat in October to march on Rome and seize control of the capital was forced on him by this need to keep ahead of his followers. It is wrong to see Mussolini, masterly bluffer though he was, as in total control of fascism's destiny in 1922. The fascists did not march on Rome; they arrived there by train and lorry, and only *after* Mussolini had been made prime minister. As they strutted in their uniforms around the streets of the capital it is tempting, with hindsight, to see them as rather absurd figures of fun but in reality their crude violence in Italy's other cities had not been at all amusing. It had been brutally effective in making Mussolini indispensable to the liberal leaders and to the king.

WHAT WAS MUSSOLINI'S ROLE?

1919–21

Mussolini's considerable journalistic skills, on daily display in his newspaper *Il Popolo d'Italia*, and his well-practised role as a mob orator were at the heart of fascism's appeal. In 1919, the fascists were only one of several militant groups who sought solutions to Italy's problems by bringing down or bypassing its parliamentary constitution. By 1922, however, the fascists were the group that mattered.

Mussolini kept clear of the early fascist violence but soon appreciated its importance and was happy to exploit the violence of others. It was Mussolini who promoted the semi-military appearance of the movement and developed its tactic of taking control of the streets – at best by semi-legal means – from the socialists and communists. He also quickly backed the stratagem of winning support from right-wing elements in the countryside by sending gangs of fascist thugs, the *squadristi,* to attack rural trade union activists and offices. Mussolini copied D'Annunzio to give the movement the potent paramilitary symbol of the blackshirt uniform and also promoted the fascist salute.

Above all, Mussolini had the flexibility to drop the left-wing political programme of 1919 in favour of an appeal to the disgruntled right-wing elements in society. At the same time, he made himself more acceptable to conservative groups in Catholic Italy by either toning down or abandoning his own strongly held atheist beliefs. This approach also involved pursuing a respectable parliamentary path, which led first to the creation of the Fascist Party (*Partito Nazionale Fascista,* PNF) and then, in the 1921 elections, to the fascists joining the coalition grouping of candidates led by the liberal politician Giolitti. By these means the fascists secured 35 seats in the Chamber of Deputies.

Many of Mussolini's more militant followers were suspicious of this new respectability. Not least of his achievements was that, with some difficulty as with the Pact of Pacification, he managed to hold the movement together and retain his own control over it. Most importantly, it was Mussolini who orchestrated the colossal bluff of 1922 that led directly to his becoming prime minister.

1922

Mussolini appeared to face a choice between using the fascist *squadristi* to sweep him to power or do a deal with some of the liberal leaders and so become a parliamentary leader. He, unlike the more extreme *squadristi* leaders, was shrewd enough to realise that the fascist street fighters could never bring him to power. The more successfully they used violence to take power the greater the danger that the army would move against them: it was certain that the army would never allow the violent overthrow of the monarchy, and once the army moved the fascist squads would be swept away. Mussolini's appreciation of this and his continuing to negotiate with the liberal leaders was his first great contribution to the fascist takeover.

His second contribution was his success in keeping his own followers in check for sufficient time to allow his negotiations to bear fruit. Mussolini proved to be a masterly negotiator, offering vague compromises to the traditional political leaders and, at the same time, keeping them divided from each other. As his opponents became more nervous about where the violence was going to lead next, he unleashed his threat of a fascist March on Rome to 'restore order' there. With this threat hanging over the government, Mussolini raised his price for restraining his followers from four government posts for the fascists to himself being made prime minister. The king then had either to stand up to the fascists or agree Mussolini's terms.

A political deal

In these last tense days Mussolini kept his nerve. He stayed in fascist-dominated Milan, safe from a counter-*coup*, and negotiated by telephone until the king offered him the post he had demanded. Only then did he leave for Rome, by train. By being prepared both to use the threat of violent takeover and yet holding out a political compromise to his opponents, he had achieved a prize that violence alone would never have given him and one that his parliamentary position at the head of 35 deputies certainly did not warrant. In the last days of the political crisis of 1922, Mussolini was the key figure in bringing the fascists into office.

WHY DID THE KING REFUSE TO INTRODUCE MARTIAL LAW?

Mussolini became prime minister because King Victor Emmanuel III invited him to form a government. Fascist illegality during 1922 had driven the king to this step although, at the last minute, it had looked as though he would resist the fascist advance by establishing martial law and using the army to confront the fascists. He first agreed to prime minister Facta's request to sign a martial law decree and then, in the early morning of 28 October, dramatically changed his mind and refused to do so. The reasons for this royal change of mind have been much debated.

KEY THEMES

Fascist resistance to the army The fascists had already seized strategic government buildings in towns across north and central Italy.

Mussolini's bullying tactics In a speech in September, Mussolini had sought to reassure the king and the army that, provided they did not oppose the fascists, their roles were safe.

Bringing the fascists into government Salandra, for example, thought that such a move was essential for public order. He had felt unable to form a government after Mussolini had refused to join it.

- Much later he claimed that he was unsure of the loyalty of the army if it were called on to challenge the fascists, with whose objectives many officers had great sympathy. General Diaz assured the king of the army's loyalty but famously added: 'The army will do its duty, however it would be well not to put it to the test.' Facta, on the other hand, had satisfied himself that the Rome garrison would indeed do its duty.
- **Fascist resistance to the army** might well have led to considerable bloodshed and possibly all-out civil war.
- The king's cousin, the Duke of Aosta, a known fascist sympathiser and living conveniently close to the fascist headquarters in Perugia, might have used any turmoil as an opportunity to try to oust Victor Emmanuel.
- The king may well have been convinced that, in view of lamentable liberal weaknesses, fascist participation in government would provide welcome strength against a left-wing *coup*. Victor Emmanuel was almost certainly more perturbed by the danger of such a *coup* than by the fascist threat.
- Mussolini's claims were arguably within the constitution; at the point when the king changed his mind he was asking only for four fascist ministers in Facta's government. **His bullying tactics** were regrettable but not impossible to understand and it was certainly not worth risking a calamitous civil war to prevent him from entering the government.
- The king was very much influenced by pressure from his prominent subjects, particularly northern industrialists, that Mussolini was preferable as prime minister to the liberal Giolitti with his record of giving in to trade union demands at the time of the 1921 factory occupations.
- All the liberal leaders whom the king had consulted had either positively advised him to **bring the fascists into government** or were at least resigned to that happening.

Factors such as these provided satisfactory reasons for avoiding or at least delaying a crisis and this fitted in well with the king's character. Once the king had abandoned Facta and any intention of declaring martial law, Mussolini was in a strong position to increase his demands and promptly did so. In the final analysis, it was only the head of state that could legally make Mussolini prime minister: Victor Emmanuel saw this action as the easiest way out of his problems. In a parliamentary monarchy, power normally resides in parliament; but, when abnormal times have been allowed to develop, then the actions of the monarch can be of crucial importance.

A REVOLUTION OR A MISCALCULATION?

The kindest comment on the democratic politicians and others, including the king, who stood aside and let Mussolini become prime minister, is that they miscalculated. They had seen the possibility of a coalition government led by Mussolini as just another turn in the game of *trasformismo* politics. A period in office, they calculated, would keep Mussolini busy: the responsibility of running the country would tame him and his followers. In any event, given his lack of political experience, it would not be difficult for his colleagues from the other coalition parties to keep him under control. But they were wrong and, by the end of 1925, the democratically elected politicians had been either swept away or forced to do private deals with Mussolini. They had underestimated their opponent.

The fascist regime was later inclined to refer to the events of 1922 as 'the Fascist Revolution' even complete with a calendar of the fascist era dating from that year. But 1922 was not a revolution: rather it was a deal between fascism and the conservative forces in the country, especially the key handful of liberal leaders. Mussolini too had to pay a high price for the way he came into office. He secured the tacit support of the king, and so the army, but found that, as a result, he had to accept and work within the existing power structures of the Liberal State.

CONCLUSIONS

Mussolini became prime minister largely because a consensus emerged, at least among non-socialist political and social leaders, that he must be given a chance to resolve the country's crisis. Their own suspicions of the 'threat' from the left blinded them to the fascist violence that had, in fact, done much to create the crisis. The fascists took over because the middle classes had become convinced that, since the end of the war, successive governments had totally failed to combat the spread of socialism. The Alliance of Labour's failed general strike of August 1922 produced a belief that it had only been fascist intervention that had saved Italy from a left-wing coup. Once this was widely agreed the fascist involvement in government became a necessity. The precise terms on which it was achieved were, however, dictated by Mussolini.

SECTION 2

Why was Mussolini able to acquire dictatorial powers?

KEY POINTS

An explanation of the origins of Mussolini's dictatorship needs to take account of the following.

- **The constitutional position after 1922.** In 1922, Mussolini became prime minister by constitutional means, although these were backed by the threat of violence and a potential breakdown of law and order brought about by the fascist *squadristi*. In 1922–3, most Italians assumed that Mussolini would continue to act within the normal constitutional limits and, indeed, that his period in office would be quite short-lived. From 1922 to 1924, he led a coalition government in which fascist ministers were in a minority.
- **The Acerbo Law.** In 1923, the fascists pushed through the Acerbo Law on electoral procedures which, after the 1924 election, transformed the basis of their political power, giving them almost two-thirds of the seats in the Chamber of Deputies.
- **The Matteotti crisis.** The key turning point of the period came in 1924 with the murder of the socialist leader Matteotti, reaction to which threatened Mussolini's position. He eventually reacted boldly, denounced his critics and instituted a series of measures to suppress them that amounted to the creation of an authoritarian state.
- **The authoritarian measures of 1925–6.** These destroyed any legal basis for opposition to the one-party regime that they established and gave control of the media to the fascists. There was surprisingly little opposition to these far-reaching measures.
- **The consolidation of the regime 1926–9.** In these years, the Rocco Laws laid down the basis for the corporate state and the control of labour relations. In 1929, in the Lateran Pact, the state made its peace with the Catholic Church. The opposition to the new fascist order melted away and, more surprisingly, the Fascist Party and its individual members lost most of their influence.
- **The emergence of Mussolini's personal dictatorship.** By 1929, the over-centralised pattern of government with authoritarian rule from above, the vast state propaganda machine and the personal cult of the *Duce* were all in existence. The parliamentary constitution, intact in 1922, had been destroyed and Mussolini was exercising a personal

dictatorship with almost no opportunity for his edicts to be questioned or challenged.

HISTORICAL INTERPRETATIONS

Historical discussion has tended to centre on the precise nature of Mussolini's intentions in the years 1922 to 1925. It is clear that he intended to create a strong government and an authoritarian regime; this the fascists had proclaimed loud and clear in their constant criticisms of the failed liberal regime, but this could have been done within the *normal* political framework as many non-fascists wanted. Did Mussolini seek normalisation of Italian politics on these purified lines, only to see this intention destroyed by the depth of the Matteotti crisis and the need to respond radically to it? Or was he, from the outset, plotting to create a one-party state with himself having supreme power? Martin Clark, in *Modern Italy* (1996), spells out the argument for normalisation, wrecked by the Matteotti murder, without totally committing himself to it. In *Fascist Italy* (1995), John Whittam sees Mussolini as being under intense Fascist Party and *squadristi* pressure to act radically but failing, prior to 1925, to advance towards a fascist regime because of the compromises of 1922 and the fragmented nature of fascism itself. In his analysis, the Matteotti crisis provided the opportunity, but even then Mussolini had to be pushed to seize it. Other recent writers rehearse the issues but tend to take the view that Mussolini was always intent on a dictatorial system of government and simply had to bide his time during the coalition years 1922–4. In *Italian Fascism* (1995), Philip Morgan argues that from 1922 Mussolini and the fascists wanted and worked for an authoritarian state in which the Fascist Party would in practice have a monopoly of political power – this was not normalisation. In an earlier book *Mussolini* (1982), Denis Mack-Smith is more definite: 'Despite the fact that he temporarily observed existing constitutional forms, Mussolini was intent on becoming a dictator', and 'Mussolini continued to express distaste for parliamentary government but did not yet [1923] judge himself strong enough to think of recasting the constitution.'

DID MUSSOLINI INTEND TO CREATE A DICTATORSHIP FROM 1922?

The case against: parliamentary government

When Mussolini became prime minister those who welcomed his appointment expected strong government to end the anarchic violence and the government drift that had marked the post-war period. That is why parliament was content to give him emergency powers to govern by decree and later agreed to the radical alteration in the electoral system in the Acerbo Law because this would provide stable government in place of shifting weak coalitions. Note that Mussolini, appointed constitutionally, continued to defer to the king and to work through parliament, attending the Chamber of Deputies for important debates and creating the Fascist Militia as a means of controlling the more violent *squadristi*. No attempt was made to undermine state institutions: the police, the army, the civil service and the courts continued with their normal functions. The powers of the monarchy and the Senate remained untouched and unthreatened.

At the time of the Aventine Secession, Mussolini argued that it was his opponents who, by walking out of the Chamber, acted unconstitutionally. It was only in the Matteotti crisis – when the continued attacks of his opponents threatened to destroy his government and himself – that Mussolini counter-attacked. He acted (after considerable hesitation) when confronted by the leading *squadristi ras*, who saw all their work and achievements being undermined by their leader's procrastination. He was goaded by his followers, who threatened to withdraw their support of him, into the powerful speech of January 1925 and into the decisive changes towards strong government that followed it. The prolonged and deepening Matteotti crisis was a watershed in the move from a parliamentary government to one-party dictatorial rule. Without it an authoritarian state would probably still have emerged, but conceivably within the normal constitution of the Italian state.

The case for: creation of fascist institutions

There is no doubt that some of the fascist leadership, notably Farinacci, wished to destroy the Italian constitution and replace it with a fascist state. Mussolini was more cautious but, in the years 1922–4, the trend towards an all-embracing one-party state is clear, with the creation of new fascist institutions placed alongside the state apparatus.

- The Fascist Militia was partly an instrument for keeping control of the *squadristi*. It also served as a paramilitary defender of fascism, using violence systematically to neutralise its enemies, as in its destruction of any opposition in the crucial 1924 election. While it existed as a private police force for fascism, normal democratic politics would be impossible.
- The Fascist Grand Council, which met regularly in its early years and was always under Mussolini's close control, dealt not only with Fascist Party matters but also co-ordinated the coalition government's business and so ensured that fascist ideas prevailed. Key decisions were often made in the Grand Council rather than in the cabinet, undermining the notion that this was a coalition government.

Both the Militia and the Grand Council indicated that, whatever happened to the coalition government, the fascist structure was there to stay. This was not normal *trasformismo* politics but was intended as a permanent change in the conduct of political life.

Before 1924, the fascists were using the state authorities to harass and impede their opponents on local councils and in socialist labour organisations. In important industrial concerns and in the agricultural regions of north and central Italy fascist labour syndicates established exclusive negotiating rights, which brought important sections of the economy under their control.

The Acerbo Law made the government list of candidates all-important in **elections to the Chamber of Deputies**. Collaboration with the fascists was a dangerous business: when the *Popolari* proved unsatisfactory partners they were first turned out of government and then the Catholic Church was both bullied and bribed to undermine their status as an independent political party.

By 1924, fascism had spread its influence widely and was already undermining institutions that presumed to have independent power in the state. It was not yet a dictatorship or a one-party state, but the direction in which the fascists were driving was clearly signposted. This is not surprising: in his speeches in the Chamber of Deputies, Mussolini had made no effort to hide his contempt for the deputies or for democratic parliamentary government. The Matteotti crisis did not send Mussolini and the fascists off in a new, totalitarian direction. It simply speeded up their progress along a route clearly marked out from the moment Mussolini became prime minister.

The Matteotti crisis

On balance it seems probable that the fascist desire for strong government would eventually threaten democratic politics and lead to one-party rule and dictatorship. One does not have to go as far as Mack-Smith (see page 160) and envisage Mussolini coolly plotting to become dictator from as early as 1922. Mussolini had to make too many compromises to achieve office legally and fascist ideas were too varied for this to be the case. But the trend towards the fascists dominating, swallowing up or destroying individuals and independent institutions, is clearly marked from an early stage. The Matteotti crisis speeded up this process, carrying it to the logical conclusion of a one-party state dominated by the *Duce*.

WHY DID MUSSOLINI'S OPPONENTS FAIL TO PREVENT HIM BECOMING A DICTATOR?

Non-fascist groups had been unable to work together to prevent Mussolini becoming prime minister in 1922 and the central weakness in their position – the mutual hostility between the liberals and the left, the

Elections to the Chamber of Deputies In 1924, those wishing to become deputies had to be on the fascist list and after the election the fascists controlled the all-important state funds. They had become the only source of patronage for the constituencies and this, for example, brought the traditional leaders of the south into the fascist orbit.

socialists and communists – continued to undermine their effectiveness in subsequent years.

The liberals

Most liberals preferred a fascist government to the danger of a full-blown socialist regime. They welcomed Mussolini's coalition government as offering much needed stability. In the early years of Mussolini's ministry, 1922 to early 1924, liberal politicians continued to base their actions on the same fatal miscalculation that had dominated their actions at the time of the March on Rome, namely that Mussolini was a politician in the coalition tradition of *trasformismo* politics. At worst, he would try to impose a much-needed control over the warring factions in the state and, in any event, his government was unlikely to survive for long. Liberal leaders not only contributed to a massive vote of confidence in the new government but also granted Mussolini emergency powers to rule by decree for twelve months, including the power to pass laws without consulting parliament.

KEY LAW

The Acerbo Law
This law fundamentally modified the proportional representation system employed in parliamentary elections and proved a turning point in the parliamentary position of the Fascist Party.

In their anxiety to end the anarchy of the 1919–22 period, the liberals underestimated Mussolini's real intentions, most seriously when, in 1923, they gave their support to the **Acerbo Law**. At this point the liberals expected to be the main electoral beneficiaries of this legislation. In the 1924 election, many liberals followed through the logic of this support and happily joined the electoral lists of fascist candidates because they provided the best prospect of protecting their personal political positions.

The *Popolari*

Any hope of presenting a united front against the Acerbo Law was in any case lost when the members of the Catholic Party split over the issue. This split was largely brought about by pressure from the Vatican, which increasingly saw the fascists as the best bulwark against godless communism and worked to undermine the leadership of the Catholic Party, which was seen to contain men, like Sturzo, with undesirable left-wing sympathies.

The Aventine Secession

The most important opposition failure after 1922 came with the murder by fascist thugs of the socialist leader Giacomo Matteotti. As the press increasingly held Mussolini and his immediate circle responsible for this outrage his position became distinctly vulnerable. Opposition deputies – mainly socialists, *Popolari* and left-wing liberals – walked out of the Chamber and took to meeting as a separate body. This tactic failed disastrously and has since been treated with some amazement by historians. The action conveyed a sense of moral outrage at what the fascists had done but was politically inept because the only place where the fascist government could be overthrown was in parliament. The aim behind the so-called Aventine Secession was to put pressure on the king to dismiss Mussolini. It failed because Victor Emmanuel, like the Vatican, was unwilling to promote the fortunes of socialists and communists or indeed to run the risk of provoking fascist violence by dismissing Mussolini. In this the king remained true to his 1922 strategy, which appeared to be vindicated when right-wing groups – including prominent liberal leaders like Giolitti – remained in parliament. It was then possible for Mussolini to claim that those who had withdrawn had acted unconstitutionally while he had continued to uphold the status of parliament. It remained only for the Vatican to block any thought of the *Popolari* co-operating in a replacement anti-fascist government with the liberals for the entire Aventine strategy to collapse.

The Rossi memorandum

There was no doubt that the Matteotti crisis posed a serious threat to Mussolini's position. But the absence of effective parliamentary opposition allowed him to recover his nerve. In another tactical error evidence pointing to his personal involvement in the Matteotti plot only emerged at a late stage, and was then badly mismanaged by his opponents. Cesare Rossi, a disgruntled fascist, issued a memorandum to opposition newspapers directly implicating Mussolini in the murder. But he did so over the Christmas holiday period when it was difficult to pursue the charges, so the impetus created by the memorandum was quickly lost. Liberal leaders like Giolitti and Salandra, the natural leaders of any move against the government, looked on complacently. The socialists and communists failed to challenge the Fascist Militia in the streets and Mussolini was safe.

WHY WAS THERE GENERAL ACCEPTANCE OF THE EMERGING DICTATORSHIP?

The memory of pre-1922 chaos was still strong. As long as Mussolini was seen as just another coalition prime minister trying to restore some sense of order to Italian political life and society, then he could command widespread acceptance. Mussolini's reliance on and support of the **traditional state machinery** made such acceptance easier and this was enough to see him through the period 1922–4. The basis of fascist support had in any case widened since 1922, particularly with the merging of the right-wing Nationalist Party into the Fascist Party in March 1923, which greatly increased its strength in the south of the country.

Most Italians accepted the electoral changes made by the Acerbo Law as contributing to much-needed political stability and did not see its immediate consequence – the creation after the 1924 election of a fascist-aligned government committed to Mussolini's support – as being particularly sinister. It seemed preferable to the earlier near anarchy and, crucially, better than the evident danger of a communist revolution. The

Matteotti murder and subsequent political crisis was a matter of much greater concern to the political classes in Rome than it was to the average Italian. **Conservative groups** all feared the violent anarchy that would result from any attempt to unseat Mussolini. In contrast, the murder of a socialist seemed of little consequence. Even the socialists and communists failed to rise up in protest. The public were prepared to ignore Mussolini's rough tactics because the general direction, towards a stable society, seemed to be the right one. Additionally, they were lulled into this lethargy and acceptance by Italy's strong economic performance in the early 1920s, part of the worldwide post-war economic recovery for which Mussolini's government received undeserved credit.

WHAT WAS MUSSOLINI'S OWN ROLE?

In 1922, Mussolini's position was far from secure even within parliament; by 1929, he was unchallenged in the state. His own actions contributed to this happy outcome to a significant degree

- First, he posed as a **moderate politician**.
- He showed great skill in preventing a crisis by keeping his more radical party members in check. Crucial in this regard was his initiative in setting up the Fascist Militia, which provided his party followers with an honorary role but one with no real political power. In 1925, he reined in and then placed in impotent exile the most violent of the fascist leaders, Roberto Farinacci, and carried out a thorough purge of the more violent of the remaining *squadristi* leaders. He nevertheless used the potential threat of fascist violence to browbeat possible opponents into silence, notably doing so at the climax of the Matteotti crisis.
- He showed political skill in winning the support of the papacy and industrial leaders for his regime. This was also evident when, in 1923, he dismissed the *Popolari* members of his coalition government and later went on to win liberal support for the Acerbo Law.
- He showed political courage and decisiveness when, on 3 January 1925, he confronted his opponents in the Chamber at the height of the Matteotti crisis and set his government on a new, more authoritarian, course. But this was not a decision taken in a vacuum. In the face of the post-Matteotti reaction to fascist violence, the fascist *squadristi* were becoming increasingly restive and threatening to take direct action against their opponents, with or without Mussolini. Mussolini had to act decisively in order to keep control over the *ras*.
- In the far-reaching constitutional changes from late 1925 to 1929, Mussolini played a central role. Only his enormous prestige with the public and his dominant role in parliament enabled these changes to be carried through. It was appropriate that, in December 1925, a law was passed creating an entirely new post for him – as head of government.

In this role he was responsible not to parliament but to the king who alone could dismiss him. After 1925, Mussolini took on more and more ministerial responsibilities and became, for example, head of all three branches of the armed forces. This did not lend itself to efficient government but certainly set the pattern of centralised government for the remainder of the fascist period.

WHAT HAPPENED TO THE FASCISTS?

The Fascist Party in the 1920s

The aftermath of the March on Rome, with Mussolini installed as prime minister, proved a sad disappointment to rank-and-file fascists. There was no fascist revolution and no sharing out of lucrative jobs at the expense of the established civil service hierarchy. Mussolini's followers had to be content with modest and largely ceremonial roles in the newly formed Fascist Militia. In the next twelve months they saw their party's ranks swollen by the influx of half a million opportunists anxious to protect their career prospects and also the merger with the Nationalist Party whose members were a far more conservative force than the fascist radicals of the pre-1922 period.

The *squadristi*

After 1922, Mussolini was anxious to compromise with other parliamentary groups and a return to large-scale fascist violence by the *squadristi* could only disrupt his progress. A handful of *squadristi* leaders were demoted and some even expelled from the Fascist Party, but many of these leaders were, for the moment, immune from such action because of their power in their own localities. Men such as Farinacci were disappointed with Mussolini but they were not yet powerless.

The limits of their patience with Mussolini's parliamentary tactics were reached during the Matteotti crisis and 30 of the *ras* visited him at the end of 1924 to demand the creation of a full fascist regime. It was this that prompted Mussolini to abandon his attempts at compromise with his non-fascist opponents and made him decide to counter-attack. The existence and the potential for violence of the *squadristi* were at this point as vital as they had been in 1922. The fear of the anarchy the *squadristi* could create if unleashed by Mussolini made many of the political elite, and especially the king, who alone could remove his prime minister, hesitate to challenge the fascist leader, however much they disliked his actions and distrusted his explanations of the Matteotti murder. In 1924, Mussolini survived because the *squadristi* existed.

However, Mussolini's fascist supporters lost their power when he created 'the strong state', which he had promised at the critical moment of the Matteotti crisis. The new, post-1925 order was based firmly on the traditional state authorities and not the Fascist Party, much less the *squadristi*. Further, once the crisis was surmounted the more radical *squadristi* leaders were purged, including eventually the most powerful and extreme of all, Farinacci, who was driven into police-supervised exile in the small town of Cremona.

The Fascist Party in the 1930s

The Fascist Party in the 1930s was also purged of radical undesirables and was more closely supervised by its central officers. Under the new party secretary Augusto Turati, it became subservient to the leader's will, providing a variety of social activities and serving as a useful sounding board for the regime's increasingly bombastic propaganda. The fate of the Italian Fascist Party in these years and through to the end of the regime was, of course, in distinct contrast to the central role of the Nazi Party in Hitler's Germany. But Adolf Hitler, in his early days in power, had ruthlessly swept away or cowed any competing sources of authority in the Nazi state. Mussolini reached personal ascendancy by making himself indispensable to the existing Italian authorities. There was no role in Mussolini's very personal control of fascist Italy for a powerful and trouble-making fascist party. Nor did Mussolini have any radical programme of reform on Nazi lines that might have provided a role for his more committed followers.

HOW WAS THE STRONG STATE CONSTRUCTED?

At the height of the Matteotti crisis, Mussolini took the precaution of introducing censorship of the largely hostile press and prohibited meetings by opposition parties. These emergency measures were followed in late 1925 by further measures against his opponents and in November the members of the Aventine Secession were physically prevented from re-entering the Chamber. Those left in parliament put up no effective opposition as anti-fascist parties were banned and all non-fascist parties were either closed down by the authorities or dissolved themselves before that fate overtook them. Legislation in 1928 turned Italy into a one-party state by requiring that all election candidates had to appear on one authorised list, drawn up by the fascist syndicates and approved by the Fascist Grand Council. The election of 1929, despite these restrictions, was still accompanied by fascist intimidation of anyone who appeared at all critical of the regime. A stream of anti-fascist politicians, recognising their impotence, went into exile abroad; others were imprisoned or banished to remote districts. At the same time, the Catholic and socialist trades unions, copying the non-fascist political parties, closed down, leaving all labour issues to the fascist unions. Laws were passed providing for permanent press censorship under which opposition party newspapers were closed down. Other papers were bought from their owners and all journalists were required to belong to the relevant fascist union. By these means, the press became a totally reliable servant of the fascist state.

The Fascist Party in the 1930s Its officers were now appointed, not elected; its councils, including the Fascist Grand Council ceased to meet; its newspapers disappeared; and it ceased to have any influence on policy.

The state became sharply more repressive as laws passed in 1926 made any opposition to fascism illegal and set up the **Special Tribunal** to provide military-style trials for anyone accused by a prefect of being a danger to public order. Police powers over individuals whom they considered undesirable were from this point unchecked. Police numbers and police activity increased greatly. It became impossible to question or to challenge the fascist regime. Accompanying the repressive measures was a growing reliance on state propaganda to convince any doubters of the real achievements of fascism.

However, important as this propaganda was in winning a largely unquestioning acceptance of the regime, it is arguable that the Lateran Pacts with the Catholic Church were Mussolini's single greatest achievement. They provided the regime, warts and all, with a large measure of general acceptance that was only dissipated in the late 1930s by the introduction of more radical domestic policies and by an increasingly reckless, and eventually catastrophically unsuccessful, foreign policy.

CONCLUSIONS

The central issue in this section relates to Mussolini's intentions. Was he committed to imposing a fascist dictatorship from his arrival in office in 1922 or was he driven to this by the reaction, among both opponents and supporters, to the crises brought on by the murder of Matteotti? The means and the ease with which the dictatorship was established remain major topics of debate among historians, as do the roles of both the fascists and their opponents in the new 'strong state'.

Special Tribunal for the Defence of the State Set up in 1926. It applied military law in the trials of people accused of terrorism and other political crimes and could impose the death penalty, but in practice rarely did so.

SECTION 3

What were the main features of fascism?

INTRODUCTION

There was more to fascism, even in its earliest days, than well-organised street violence and bullying of opponents. Fascist ideas continued to develop, notably in defence of the emerging Mussolini dictatorship in the late 1920s and in response to the evolving European situation in the late 1930s. As a system, fascist philosophy was never as structured, as revolutionary or as interesting as **Marxist-based communism,** nor as coherently focused as aspects of **Nazism,** but it did exist and it did adapt to changing circumstances.

KEY POINTS

An examination of the main features of fascism needs to recognise the following.

- **Fascist philosophy changed over time.** Fascism developed in Italy in the shadow of the First World War and in the context of a rapidly expanded and relatively uneducated electorate. In 1919, it offered a left-wing political agenda; by 1922, it had moved sharply to the right.
- **Fascist action first.** Fascist philosophy was not the powerhouse that created the fascist state; it came afterwards, rationalising what had been done.
- **National greatness.** Despite the diversity of early fascist ideas, the concept of national greatness and how it could best be achieved became and remained the central theme of fascist philosophy
- **Cult of the *Duce*.** From 1925, fascist writings increasingly involved explaining and justifying Mussolini's dictatorial rule.

HISTORICAL INTERPRETATIONS

One of the most concise accounts of 'the doctrine of fascism' appears in Denis Mack-Smith's *Mussolini* (1982), where he argues that fascist ideas were confused and inconsistent. The essence of fascism was action and the attempts to provide a fascist philosophy were not the source for political activity but merely an attempt to justify what had been done at an opportunistic level. Eric Hobsbawm makes the same point in *Age of*

KEY THEMES

Marxist-based communism
Based on the ideas of the nineteenth-century German philosopher Karl Marx, and advocating a society where property was owned by the community and economic activity controlled by the state.

Nazism The right-wing nationalist authoritarian creed of Hitler and the German Nazis. It had much in common with fascism but added to it a virulent racism which became its driving force.

Extremes (1994), arguing that theory was largely decorative and that 'Mussolini could have readily dispensed with his house philosopher Giovanni Gentile'. Mussolini's stress on 'permanent revolution' was a convenient cloak for the ever-changing fascist policies. There was, for example, no reference in the early writing of Mussolini or Gentile to racism being part of fascism but, by 1939, it played a prominent part in fascist policy. A useful chapter in John Whittam's *Fascist Italy* (1995) takes a similar line but looks more broadly at the fascist leadership's 'search for an ideology'. In *Modern Italy* (1996), Martin Clark sees the essential feature of fascist Italy as the concept of 'a warlike society'. Most writers agree that fascist attempts to define their ideology were made more difficult, if not impossible, by the contradiction between the vision of a revolutionary movement and the conservative nature of much of their support and many of their policies. R. Griffin, in his source book *Fascism* (1995), argues that Italy's fascist regime was durable because Mussolini refused to impose a rigid set of doctrines on his followers; but this also helps to explain his failure to create a truly fascist society.

HOW DID FASCIST IDEAS DEVELOP IN THE 1920S?

Early fascist ideas

The early incoherence of fascism's philosophy is not surprising, for its **early supporters** came from many different backgrounds and had varying motives for joining the movement. They became fascists because they sought practical solutions to their post-war problems. This delayed the emergence of a common ideology. The rapidly changing pattern of Mussolini's own political ideas illustrates the problem:

- from opposition to pre-war imperial adventures in Libya and against involvement in adventures in Europe to a fervent pro-war stance after 1914;
- from republicanism and fierce atheism, 1919–22, to acceptance of monarchy and realisation of the need for conciliation with the Church;
- from socialism to capitalism.

In these years, fascism evolved by seizing opportunities and reacting to events and, at Mussolini's insistence and to the annoyance of many of his more radical followers, by discarding radical political and left-wing-inspired social policies.

Nationalism and patriotism

Despite the diversity there was even then a common theme that held the movement together ideologically. A mixture of nationalism and patriotism came through from the privations and the 'victories' of the First World War. In the early post-war period it was combined with a

KEY THEME

Fascism's early supporters These supporters included a wide range of people – for example:

- disgruntled peasants;
- a few great industrialists;
- officers and men from the rapidly disbanded army
- students;
- lower middle-class professionals
- many small shopkeepers.

fierce anti-socialism, for the socialists had been opposed to the war, and a raft of radically democratic political ideas and socio-economic policies: rural fascists, for example, wanted reorganisation of the countryside and agriculture on syndicalist, co-operative lines.

It has been claimed, however, that the early fascists were more easily identified by what they were against than by what they stood for. Above all, early fascism was opposed to the Italian liberal establishment and so to the corrupt and convoluted games of parliamentary politics that had repeatedly betrayed what the fascists saw as the true interest of the nation. More positively, before the movement came to power, fascism's central 'great idea' was a call for the rebirth of Italy, a call to national greatness that would require a revolutionary change in political direction.

Economic philosophy

The limited development of these ideas arose in part from the nature of the early movement based on the *squadristi*, led by the local *ras* and committed to action, particularly violence against those who opposed them, rather than to debating and evolving a party philosophy. The one coherent thread of ideas running through early fascism came from the syndicalists who had a vision of syndicates of workers as the basis, not just of the economy but also of the political structure of the state. Flirtations with such theories in 1919, along with the aim of outbidding the socialists in terms of economic restructuring, had been quietly abandoned by 1922 in favour of less radical ideas that would not offend the great industrialists and landlords who became the valued paymasters of the party.

In 1921, the creation of the Fascist Party alongside the *squadristi* called for a need to develop a party programme; this encouraged the definition and radical reshaping of fascism's political aims. By the time Mussolini came to office in 1922, fascism was committed to the private ownership of property, a private enterprise economy and, at least temporarily, *laissez-faire* (market-driven) economics. Its most outrageously revolutionary political demands – republicanism, for example – had also been sensibly muted.

Coalition government, 1922–5
Normalisation

The ostensible aim in these years of coalition government was to work within the framework of normal politics; this reflected the loss of the radical edge as the Fascist Party grew and absorbed self-seeking individuals and political groups like the nationalists. Fascism remained poised between the contradictions of working within the political system and producing a radical revolution. In practice, Mussolini and the fascists would never escape the compromises they made to achieve office in 1922, but this did not mean that fascist ideology did not continue to evolve.

Fascist revolution

Squadristi leaders such as Farinacci continued to press for a more thoroughgoing fascist revolution, which would replace the role of traditional state institutions with government by the Fascist Party enforced by the Fascist Militia. The radical *squadristi* leaders wanted to set up a one-party state in which labour relations would be controlled by the fascist syndicates and the media controlled by the Fascist Grand Council. At the very least they wanted strong government that would deal firmly with the enemies of fascism and place political power in their own hands.

Emergence of totalitarianism, late 1920s

It is important to realise that, after 1922, fascism's direction became more and more closely associated with **Mussolinism**. His intentions and ideas for the future of fascist government in the years 1922–4 have been hotly debated (see pages 160–2) and, in the late 1920s, the emergence of his personal dictatorship in the context of the 'strong state' stimulated the further development of fascist ideology.

Mussolini himself drew attention to the concept of totalitarianism in a speech in 1925 (see pages 55–6), using it to identify the growing control of the fascist state over wide areas of everyday life as well as to indicate the changing direction taken by the state with the elimination of rival political parties and institutions. In the same year, he summed up his meaning in the phrase: 'Everything within the state, nothing outside the state, nothing against the state.' These ideas on the function of the state, and the role of the individual within it, mark a revolutionary change from the philosophy that had prevailed in liberal Italy since its inception. Fascism, unlike communism, may not have been driven by a coherent set of revolutionary ideas but it had, in response to circumstances, arrived at a revolutionary view of the nature of the state.

Italian totalitarianism owed its success to Mussolini but its origins lay in Italian involvement in the First World War when there was a total state commitment to the war effort. It was Alfredo Rocco, sponsor of key administrative economic and constitutional legislation and later minister of justice, who inspired Mussolini with ideas of totalitarianism in the late 1920s. Responsibility for the development and publicity of the underpinning rationale rested with Giovanni Gentile, creator of the *Enciclopedia Italiana*.

In 1932, Mussolini published in the *Enciclopedia* his much debated 'Doctrine of Fascism' which, alongside the more substantial writings of Gentile, sought to present a justification for 'totalitarianism' and by so doing legitimise his personal dictatorship. The central concept of Gentile's writings is that the purpose of an individual's life is necessarily totally committed, and subordinate, to the purposes of the state.

WHAT WERE THE MAIN DEVELOPMENTS IN FASCIST THOUGHT IN THE 1930S?

The corporate state

The most original fascist political innovation, in theory, was the creation and development of the corporate state from the late 1920s, reaching its climax only in 1939 as Italy faced the prospect of a European war. (Its foundation is explained in AS Chapter 5 and its performance analysed in A2 Section 6.)

The cult of ancient Rome

Under fascism there was a growing obsession with the achievements and monuments of the ancient Roman Empire, often referred to as *Romanita*. It was a deliberate fascist attempt to set Italian national greatness within a glorious historical context.

- Fascism's symbol and name came from the bundle of twigs carried by ancient Roman magistrates and representing the virtues of discipline and authority.
- Ancient history saw a remarkable revival in schools and universities and, surprisingly for an allegedly modern movement, fascist education promoted a revival of the study of Latin and classical literature.
- Modern buildings and squares, like the Foro Mussolini, consciously copied classical Roman styles.
- Mussolini's title of *Duce* was taken from the Latin *dux* (leader).
- The fascist salute and the goose-step marching style of the army were claimed to be inherited from Rome's imperial past.
- A great deal of money was spent on archaeology, excavating and restoring Roman sites in Italy and in the newly conquered province of Libya. Many of Rome's medieval remains were disposed of in order to reach and display the monuments of the ancient world that lay beneath them. When ancient sites were disappointingly bare imaginative steps were taken to improve them, as at **Sabratha** on the Libyan coast.

The cult of the *Duce*

The concept of the strong leader became central to fascism when Mussolini's dictatorship was established in the late 1920s. From then, through to the moment of his fall in 1943, state propaganda was geared to providing a relentless stream of images of Mussolini as the destined leader of the fascist nation. The full resources of youth groups, newspapers, radio – often amplified across city squares – and, most powerfully, of cinema news bulletins, were committed to this. The indoctrination of the Italian people in the wisdom and leadership qualities of the *Duce* became a central activity of the fascist state. It paid off in the much-repeated graffiti 'Mussolini is always right' scrawled on walls all over Italian towns.

The cult of the strong leader had featured in European literature from the late nineteenth century onwards but had not figured largely in the early days of fascism, when the fiercely independent status of the separate local leaders was notable. It developed in Italy as a rationalisation of Mussolini's personal dictatorship. There were images of Mussolini:

- the scholar, writing learned articles for the *Enciclopedia Italiana*;
- the man of culture, in a widely distributed photograph of him playing the violin;
- the man of action leading by example, bare-chested and helping to bring in the grain harvest;
- the athlete, running bare-chested along holiday beaches;
- the military leader, in different uniforms – marching, reviewing troops, sitting in planes and military vehicles.

Widely circulated stories of Mussolini's incredible capacity for work and his mastery of all aspects of government, almost entirely fictitious, backed up these images of the all-powerful leader.

National greatness

Italy's claim to be among the front rank of European powers was an important element in fascism's appeal from the start. In the 1920s, there were designs on Greek possessions, schemes that failed but were presented as Italian triumphs. At the same time, Mussolini struck the pose of being an important European statesman, dealing at least as an equal with the less vigorous, democratic leaders of Britain and France and best symbolised by his flamboyant arrival at the 1935 international Stresa Conference by speedboat.

By the late 1930s, however, Italy had embarked on serious military adventures and the propaganda effort promoting the nationalist expansionist nature of fascism became deafening. This was more than just a propaganda exercise. The state's resources were geared to war in Ethiopia and Spain, and Italy was moving into the embrace of Nazi Germany with its frankly expansionist policies. The stress was on Italy's military potential, its civilising mission in dark places in Africa, and its promotion of fascist values in other parts of Europe, building a Mediterranean empire worthy of the imperial grandeur of ancient Rome. From 1935, these expansionist foreign policy ambitions became the central preoccupation of the fascist state. Alongside, or rather subservient to them, were the repeated efforts to make the Italian people worthy of their imperial destiny, for that was the real point of the various economic 'battles' and bodies such as the semi-military fascist youth movements. In the late 1930s, Italy seemed at times to be a nation filled by men and boys in uniform. By this stage an important role for Italy on the international stage, preferably through military successes, had become the main, perhaps the only, purpose of the fascist state.

WAS ITALIAN FASCISM PART OF A WIDER EUROPEAN FASCISM?

Fascism is certainly best confined to describing right-wing movements in the 1920s and 1930s, but even with this considerable restriction it can easily mislead. The term originated immediately after the First World War in Italy but, as noted above, there was nothing simple and clear-cut about the movement even in its homeland. Its use when applied to events and individuals outside Italy, even in the inter-war period, can frequently obscure rather than assist understanding.

Fascism and Nazism
Common features
In general terms, both Italy and Germany were controlled by fascist regimes and they had common features:

- both were dictatorships based on the cult of the leader;
- dictators emerged, despite proposing radical changes within the state, as the result of support from right-wing conservative groups in the state who were then denied any share of political power;
- both were arguably totalitarian states in which individual lives were seen as subordinate to the purposes of the state;
- both used a mixture of repression and propaganda to remove dissent and exerted great influence over people's everyday lives;
- both became expansionist military regimes.

KEY THEME

The SS and the Gestapo The SS (Schutzstaffel) were the Nazi secret and security police, led by Heinrich Himmler. They took over the Gestapo, which originally operated only in the state of Prussia. Both bodies became notorious for their persecution of 'enemies of the state' and for their association with the German concentration camps.

Differences
The central difference between the two countries was that the Nazis came to power in 1933 committed to an obsessive racial agenda that gave the regime a clear purpose, which in turn drove it to radical solutions. In Germany, it led to an important role for the Nazi Party in directing Germany's internal affairs and to the creation of powerful paramilitary police agencies like the SS and the Gestapo. Mussolini had no such clear agenda and from the outset he was prepared to compromise with existing powerful bodies.

The new regime in Italy was far less radical and had much less impact on society than the shorter-lived regime in Germany. The reason for this may well have been because Hitler obtained power over a powerful centralised state which its citizens were accustomed to obey, whereas Mussolini came to office and was then dictator in a state that had enjoyed many years of inept government and where most citizens had lived their lives in their own locality, in blissful ignorance of events elsewhere in the country. In practice, Italy was much less powerful than Germany and soon became the junior partner in international matters. German military might was formidable, Italian often laughable.

Despite their radical claims neither power was particularly efficiently governed. Nazi government has been described as a chaos of conflicting authorities, and Italian fascist government characterised by compromise, lethargy and corruption. It is probably best to identify the German and Italian regimes as Nazi and fascist respectively rather than describe both as fascist and risk failing to establish the important differences between them.

The right in Spain

From the outset of the Spanish Civil War in 1936, Italian support was of immense help to **Franco**'s right-wing forces. Franco's nationalist movement had much in common with Mussolini's fascists. Both:

- were anti-socialist;
- were dependent on the goodwill of the Catholic Church in their respective countries;
- relied on the backing of conservative forces – the armed forces, great landowners, the middle classes, the conservative peasantry.

And yet the Spanish dictator's cause and his eventual triumph owed far more to Spanish history than to any fascist philosophy. He achieved power as an army officer through military victory in a vicious, prolonged war against his enemies of the left. Franco's nationalists were the embodiment of right-wing Spain, a country of deep class divisions and vested interests; it lacked a radical agenda and this certainly set it apart from the early radicalism of the Italian fascists. It may have had more in common with the fully established, compromised fascism of Italy in the 1930s.

With victory, Franco became an old-style conservative despot, committed to protecting the vested interests and the social values of those who had put him in power. In doing this he repressed potential enemies and stamped on criticism and individual liberties. In his first months in power, he carried out a terrible purge of those who had opposed him in the Civil War on a scale that never occurred and was not needed in Italy. Once in power he found it convenient to copy Mussolini's cult of personality, taking for example the title of *Caudillo* (leader).

CONCLUSIONS

Fascist ideology reached its most coherent expression in the notions of national greatness and the subordination of the interests and lives of all citizens to promoting that end. Increasingly, fascist Italy became a state committed to the necessity of waging a successful war in order to achieve national greatness. These are simple but powerful ideas, greatly stimulated

KEY PERSON

Francisco Franco 1892-1975 A Spanish general who waged a successful civil war against the left-wing government. After three years of bitter fighting (1936–9), he established a right-wing dictatorship based on one-party rule by the Falange (nationalists).

HEINEMANN ADVANCED HISTORY

by international crises and military triumphs. They neither required nor received the accolade of a supporting philosophy.

In the 1930s, fascist ideology narrowed into a series of justifications for the personal, highly centralised political dictatorship exercised by Mussolini. Increasingly from 1935, fascist energy and ideology were devoted to promoting the *Duce*'s ambitious foreign policy. This fatally narrowed the fascist vision. The fascist movement had from its origins always been stronger on action and clearer on who its enemies were than on formulating its own political philosophy. Its propaganda role for the Mussolini dictatorship denied it any chance of developing a clear set of ideas on how Italian society should develop. Even the attempt in 1938–9 to introduce a new rigour in the fascist state – with sweeping educational reforms, a new racist agenda and an enhanced political role for Mussolini – was a response to the nation's military role in international affairs. The new moves had no intellectual base in any developing fascist philosophy and their most striking feature – the promotion of racism – simply copied the most vile aspect of Nazi society.

SECTION 4

Was fascist Italy a totalitarian state?

INTRODUCTION

Both the communist and fascist states of the twentieth century were commonly defined as **totalitarian**. In the 1930s, this was usually to distinguish them clearly from democracies such as Britain and France and then, after the Second World War, to distinguish the Soviet Union from the western democracies, their opponents in the Cold War. Historians tended to avoid using the term, not least because there were so many variations between different forms of totalitarian state. In this section, the term is defined (see margin) and then applied to fascist Italy, simply to see what can be learned about the nature of that state and not for the purpose of comparing the Italian experience with that of other states.

In the aftermath of the Matteotti murder, it was Mussolini who first publicly used the term 'totalitarian' to describe his tough new policy towards opponents. He set it in the context of intending to destroy all opposition to his regime and ensure that in the future 'fascist' and 'Italian' would come to mean the same thing. His ideas of fascist values being embraced by all Italians and of every Italian subordinate to the state became the most enduring strand in fascist philosophy. The intention was to involve every Italian in the fascist cause of national greatness and not just create a fascist elite within the state. Fascism was to be a national, not a party movement. This required the state to control important areas of economic activity and the lives of individual citizens. These extensions of the role of the state into economic activity, social provision and social control can also be regarded as typical features of totalitarian states.

KEY POINTS

An answer to the question heading this section will need to consider the following:

- **The location of political power in the state.** In the late 1920s, Italy became a one-party state in which Mussolini acquired dictatorial powers. Opposition was illegal and the media were state-owned or subject to rigorous censorship.

KEY TERM

Totalitarian 'A political term relating to a form of government permitting no rival loyalties or parties, usually demanding total submission of the individual to the requirements of the state' (*Oxford Reference Dictionary*, 1986).

- **State control of the economy.** The fascists made much of the role of the corporate state, but did this amount to totalitarian control of economic activity?
- **State direction of individual lives.** The state set up many institutions to encourage citizens to be loyal to the fascist ideal and made many provisions for their social welfare, but did fascism succeed in winning the undivided loyalty of the Italian people?
- **The practical limits of totalitarian control.** These were imposed by inefficiencies and corruption within the political system and by the fact that Italy had never been a strongly centralised state. The continuing existence of independent institutions, notably the Catholic Church and the monarchy, was an even bigger obstacle to total fascist control.

HISTORICAL INTERPRETATIONS

Post-Second World War writing on Mussolini's Italy stresses the powerful and repressive nature of the regime. M. Gallo, in *Mussolini's Italy* (1973), considers the regime to be 'thoroughly fascist' and to have profoundly impregnated everyday life so that 'special supervision was the fate ... of all Italians'. However, historians studying totalitarian states in 1930s Europe and setting fascist Italy alongside Nazi Germany and Stalin's Soviet Union have usually concluded that Mussolini's regime was the least totalitarian of the three. In *Modern Italy* (1996), Martin Clark surveys the attempts of the Italian fascist regime to control the lives of its citizens and is unimpressed by its efforts. The best recent examination of Italian totalitarianism is by Philip Morgan, *Italian Fascism 1919–45* (1995). In a chapter entitled 'The construction of the "Totalitarian" State 1925–29', the emphasis on the word 'totalitarian' indicates his reservations about applying the term uncritically.

HOW DID THE FASCISTS SET OUT TO CREATE A TOTALITARIAN POLITICAL STRUCTURE?

The late 1920s were the key period in creating the structure of this new totalitarian state. The first task in the pursuit of total state control of Italian life was to ensure fascist control of the political machine. This meant eliminating the opposition political parties, which was done with surprising ease.

- The opposition deputies who withdrew from the Chamber in the Aventine Secession of 1924 were physically prevented from re-entering.
- Opposition newspapers were closed down or bought by fascist supporters.

- In 1926, the police were authorised to banish undesirables to remote country areas; opposition party members were the chief victims of these extensively used powers.
- By the end of 1926, laws had been passed closing down both the opposition parties and the non-fascist trades unions.

By these measures Mussolini eliminated all legal avenues for expressing dissent. Now fascist propaganda would go unchallenged.

The legal basis for totalitarian rule was established equally quickly.

- The **new office of 'head of government'** was created for Mussolini, who was no longer to be accountable to parliament but to the king alone.
- The Grand Council of the Fascist Party was given *state* responsibility of approving the lists of candidates in parliamentary elections and, in an apparent challenge to the monarchy, to nominate Mussolini's successor. To ensure Mussolini's total control over its deliberations it became his responsibility as head of government to summon the council.
- A Decree on Public Security (November 1926) gave the government-appointed provincial prefects the power to place under police supervision anyone even rumoured to be a danger to public order. Central control of the localities was further tightened by closing local councils, which were now to be governed by government appointees (the *podestà*). The pyramid of state authority now stretched directly down from Mussolini to the most remote and backward province.
- A Law for the Defence of the State (November 1926) meant that anyone accused of political crimes would be tried by the Special Tribunal, which it set up, and operated according to military law.
- The Fascist Party Statute (October 1926) ensured that the party did not have an independent existence outside Mussolini's authority by bringing the provincial sections of the party under the control of the central officers. Party posts of any importance were now to be filled by appointment from above instead of being elected. Mussolini also made it clear that the party in the provinces was subordinate to the control of the prefects who became the key figures in a pattern of state (rather than Fascist Party) control of local government and local life.
- The Rocco Law of 1926 required all labour relations to be controlled by the fascist syndicates and corporations, and a Ministry of Corporations was set up to develop and supervise this new structure. It also had the potential to transform and control the entire Italian economy.

With the rapid introduction of these measures Mussolini ended any hope of independent political challenge to his regime and went a long way towards being able to control the lives of the Italian people. In theory, by 1928 fascist Italy seemed close to meeting the criteria for a totalitarian regime as defined above.

New office of 'head of government'
Mussolini was given the power on a permanent basis to issue laws by decree and also to supervise what business was placed before parliament.

BY WHAT MEANS DID THE FASCIST STATE TRY TO CONTROL PEOPLE'S LIVES?

As Mussolini moved towards becoming a dictator he encouraged the development of totalitarianism, both in his speeches and by encouraging the philosopher Gentile to formulate a fascist totalitarian ideology. With his political control of the state assured by 1928 he was in a position to put into practice his idea of harnessing the Italian people to his vision of Italian greatness. The challenge was to persuade or force them to accept this ideal and to subordinate their private lives to the demands of the state. If he succeeded then Italy would be a truly totalitarian state.

Corporate state

In economic terms many of the urban working classes were easily vulnerable to pressure from the state. Their independent trades unions had been closed down and they became dependent on labour organisations set up by the fascists. The plans, drawn up by Rocco, for labour relations to be administered by syndicates of workers and employer corporations, but with a significant number of state representatives in both types of body, provided a route for wider control of the economy by the state. The new structure developed slowly, but by 1934 it was widely established across the economy. Italy was increasingly referred to as a corporate state. Government intervention in the economy in the early 1930s was much admired overseas as in distinct contrast with the failure of democratic nations to resolve the economic problems caused by the worldwide economic depression.

Propaganda

Outside the workplace it was more difficult to control and direct the citizens' lives but much was still done to draw the Italian people into the embrace of the state. Above all, they were subjected to an endless barrage of state propaganda in newspapers, on the state-run radio network and at the cinema. It was almost impossible to acquire an independent view on political issues, domestic or foreign. The thrust everywhere was to glorify the fascist regime and to celebrate Italian greatness and, in its control of the presentation of public affairs at every level, the regime perhaps came closest to controlling the minds of its citizens. For example, it provided free radios to schools and communal radios to villages. One important aspect of propaganda was to promote the cult of the *Duce* (see A2 Section 5) and another was to glorify Italian military achievements. In both respects the unsophisticated, often illiterate, native Italian society helped. The Italian people were the first to be subjected to mass twentieth-century propaganda. Whatever their private views on the credibility of some claims the propaganda offensive ensured the general public acceptance of the regime until the late 1930s.

Press censorship

As well as creating a large press office to control newspaper content and comment, Mussolini personally took an almost obsessive interest in what appeard in the daily newspapers. He and the press office communicated with newspaper editors on an almost daily basis, not just on the nature of editorial comment but on the type of stories to be given prominence, any deed or word of the *Duce*, and those to be suppressed, any form of bad news even down to the trivialities of road accidents. It therefore proved possible, almost up to the collapse of the regime, to hide from the Italian people the growing deterioration in the military situation in the Second World War.

Leisure and education

The imaginative widespread provision for leisure, the encouragement of sport and physical fitness, together with the glorification of some real sporting achievements and the provision of cheap holidays, through the OND, all encouraged Italians to embrace the regime. Pressure on the education system and the provision of suitable fascist textbooks as well as the numerous fascist-sponsored youth clubs and women's organisations worked to the same end. Whether or not it added up to a totalitarian ideal is considered in the next part of this section.

HOW TOTALITARIAN WAS FASCIST ITALY IN PRACTICE?

Politics

The theory of totalitarianism was quite simple: the political structure to implement the idea appeared to be in place as early as 1928. The success of the enterprise is, however, open to challenge. Martin Clark, in *Modern Italy* (1996), has commented that the claim to be a totalitarian state was 'laughable' but has, at the same time, insisted that fascist Italy was in important respects quite different from the preceding Liberal State. A thoroughgoing authoritarian regime was established before 1930 and survived unchallenged for over ten years, with profound consequences for the Italian state and the lives of its citizens.

The left-wing enemies of fascism had been trounced and their parties abolished, as had other parties of the centre; those of the right had chosen to merge with the Fascist Party or had disbanded. Some opposition leaders had chosen to go into exile abroad but their efforts to organise contacts with their fellows who had remained in Italy were totally ineffective so that formal political opposition to the regime, with the possible exception of a tiny communist underground, was at an end before 1930 and did not resurface until Italy faced total defeat in war in 1942.

Fascist control of the media was total: Italians received the news and opinions that the regime wanted them to receive and in a form agreeable to the regime. Such media control was used by state and Fascist Party officials to bombard the populace with endless propaganda to achieve the objective of securing the support of the mass of the people for actions of the regime. Some of these became less popular from 1936 but only began to be seriously questioned in public when the fortunes of war only too clearly swung against Italy and its allies.

The economy

The attempts to exercise state direction of the economy through the institutions of the **corporate state** proved less successful, being constantly evaded by the larger employers who preferred to intrigue with individual civil servants or government ministers in order to direct the country's economic policies into paths they thought favourable to their own company's interests. At a lower level and despite creating a bureaucratic web of petty regulations, licences and committees, the corporate system worked ineffectively and often stifled economic activity. If the aim of totalitarianism was to produce an economically efficient nation directed towards national greatness through victory in war, then it failed miserably.

Outside the central planning and directed activity of the corporate state many small businesses, especially countless little shops, survived and often prospered. Small light-engineering firms in particular remained largely unregulated but proved to be major economic success stories. Even by 1940, some 50 per cent of industrial workers in the northern towns remained outside the syndicates. In rural Italy too, especially in the south, small peasants were unaffected by state planning and pursued their livelihoods much as they had always done, uninterrupted by Mussolini's totalitarian visions.

The *Dopolavoro*

These activities involved more people actively than did the syndicates. Membership was much higher among the middle classes – perhaps over 80 per cent among salaried state employees – than among workers in the industrial cities of the north where fewer than 50 per cent had any contact with the social facilities provided. In rural areas, especially in the poorer south of the country, the peasants and their children were usually not involved in either the *Dopolavoro* or youth clubs.

The clubs and their leisure activities did, however, draw great numbers of people closer to the regime than was ever the case in democratic countries. When engaged in *Dopolavoro* activities citizens were under the eye and indeed the supervision of party officials and subject to pro-fascist propaganda. While great numbers were involved in enjoying the social facilities of the *Dopolavoro* they would not be involved in undesirable political activity. With these social provisions the fascist regime was certainly able to organise the lives of many of its citizens to an extent impossible in more liberal countries. To this extent people's lives were less private than they would have been. Many were happy simply to enjoy the new social and welfare opportunities. Few seemed to object.

Other social controls

A similar mixed verdict is possible on the state's other attempts at social engineering to subordinate its citizens to its fascist objectives. The most effective organisations were those directed at men, notably the **Fascist Militia**, which with uniforms, parades and much military swagger kept its members out of disorderly mischief-making and made them feel involved in something important.

Organisations for women, like the Rural Housewives League, were never as fully developed or certain of their role. Fascists believed a woman's place was in the home and this was not totally compatible with organised public activity. The emphasis was on conservative family values as the bedrock of the regime and, above all, on a family's duty to provide the regime with large numbers of children who would ensure the future greatness of the Italian state. This objective was vigorously promoted by generous tax concessions, preferred promotion at work for fathers, home loans on favourable terms, grants at the birth of children and a ban on any reference to birth control practices. It was a massive effort at social engineering.

If the success of fascist totalitarianism is judged by the Battle for Births then it must be judged to have failed. Even a punitive tax on men who remained **bachelors** failed to bring down the average age at marriage, which remained, at over 28 for men and 25 for women, slightly higher in the 1930s than it had been when the fascists first achieved office in the early 1920s. The extensive propaganda and the incentives failed, with only 10 per cent of women of child-bearing age giving birth in any one year, in sharp contrast to almost 15 per cent who had done so before the First World War. Equally unsuccessful was the state's attempt to keep women in the home by restricting their job opportunities, for this led to more women staying at secondary schools and entering universities.

Ruralism

Fascism also stressed the virtues of rural life and a strong peasant economy, both as the basis for social stability and in building up a reservoir of men available for the military. In one of its most powerful messages, fascist propaganda made a systematic attempt to emphasise the attractions of rural life. Efforts to stop migration from country to town were also enforced by licensing systems and encouraged by propaganda. It was all to no avail and the urban flood continued unabated. The failure of the sustained campaign to emphasise the importance of rural values and rural life is a clear indicator of the limits of totalitarianism. Uneducated peasants were prepared to ignore all the legal obstacles and

Fascist Militia It contributed significantly to fascism's purposeful military image both at home and abroad.

Bachelors Almost 10 per cent of Italian men remained unmarried and this in a country where, thanks to the ravages of the First World War, women made up well over 50 per cent of the population.

all the state propaganda in order to find a better life among the urban proletariat.

Education and social control

The nation's youth were the fascists' best long-term hope for securing a docile and loyal population committed to their ideals of service to the fascist state as the greatest purpose in life. Education provision at primary and secondary level certainly improved under the fascists, and both the streaming of pupils and a newly introduced system of state examinations at secondary level raised standards and encouraged more pupils to stay at school at the secondary level. The curriculum emphasised suitable fascist subjects: ancient and Italian **history**, Latin and philosophy, all received more attention. Fascist symbols, activities and propaganda were everywhere; there was great pressure on teachers at all levels, including the universities, to conform to fascist ideals and to join the Fascist Party. Although schools provided by the Catholic Church continued to flourish it was only at the price of avoiding any suspicion of opposition to the regime. For approximately ten years, Italy's young people were brought up and educated in a fascist system. Most of them accepted what they were taught as normal.

The regime was in any case quite popular with, or quietly accepted by, many parents and, until 1940, it appeared to have many positive achievements to its credit. Fascist education did not produce zealous commitment to fascist ideals, but equally there was no significant dissent or opposition to what was provided. The Italian education system did not at any level become a hotbed of resistance to the regime; the vast majority of teachers and pupils showed at least enough outward support for Mussolini and for the fascist dream in order to be left in peace to secure an education that would fit them for satisfactory jobs in the fascist economy. It was not heroic but it was eminently sensible.

Church and state

In the early 1930s, fascist determination to capture the support of the nation's youth prompted an attack on the youth clubs run by the Catholic Church. The Church resisted but its clubs were required to limit themselves to religious objectives and lost much of their attraction when their sporting facilities and teams were closed down. The Church survived, however, and retained the allegiance of the vast majority of Italians. This survival on its own seriously undermines any claim that Italy under Mussolini was a totalitarian state. The survival of the Catholic Church's privileges and independence rested on the deal struck between Mussolini and the Church in the Lateran Pacts of 1929. These were the price Mussolini was obliged to pay to secure the support or at least the acceptance of the Catholic population for his dictatorial regime. The survival of an independent Catholic Church meant that, for many people,

The teaching of history This was based on one or two officially approved textbooks, which stressed Italy's past achievements as a nation. Its central purpose was to persuade young people to commit their lives to building a new Italy worthy of its historical past but also inspired by the cult of the *Duce* and practising true fascist virtues.

a significant part of their lives – one based on church attendance, confession and family piety – was unaffected by the demands of the regime. In this respect, the totalitarian ideal of 'fascist' and 'Italian' having the same meaning was not achieved.

The monarchy

The Lateran Pacts were not the only compromise Mussolini made. In 1922, he accepted office as the king's prime minister and, despite all the irregular increases in his personal power within the state, even as head of government, he could still be dismissed by Victor Emmanuel. The king failed to act against Mussolini at the height of the Matteotti crisis and after that did not attempt to interfere in fascist control of the state. At a personal level, the two men got on less well together as time passed: Victor Emmanuel was irked by Mussolini's title of 'head of government' and by the powers given to the Fascist Grand Council to settle the succession to the throne. Theoretically more dangerous was his having, in 1940, to surrender the monarch's role as head of the armed forces to Mussolini in the event of war. In practice, by formally handing this over to the *Duce*, Victor Emmanuel retained his royal prerogative as head of state. For his part, Mussolini became more vain as time passed and increasingly resented the fact that, particularly on the formal ceremonial occasions he enjoyed so much, unlike Hitler, he was not the head of state.

The military

Until 1940, the armed forces owed their allegiance to the monarchy not immediately to Mussolini. Even if the king himself could usually be ignored, they could not. Mussolini had to pursue policies that were acceptable to the military leaders and he was fortunate that, until defeat in war became inevitable, their interests and ambitions usually coincided. Mussolini, however, never had the will or the energy to dominate his generals as Hitler and Stalin did their military. In late 1939 and early 1940, with a European war raging around them, military leaders were outraged that the military supplies they desperately needed were instead being sold off to foreign buyers. This nicely illustrates how even the most totalitarian of regimes can make irrational decisions which detract from their true purpose.

The traditional elites

The limits of totalitarian control were also set by Mussolini employing the traditional institutions of the state and the traditional local and national elites to enforce his dictatorship. This made compromise with them, and acceptance of Victor Emmanuel's role, inevitable. Mussolini's state showed many of the features of totalitarianism but, in the last analysis, rested on the continuing tacit support of the powerful groups and interests that had been content to allow the fascist takeover of the state in the 1920s. This in turn limited any prospect of Italy experiencing a radical social revolution on fascist lines. It meant that fascist Italy cannot really be described as a totalitarian state unless the term is so seriously qualified as to raise doubts about its value in describing Mussolini's empire.

CONCLUSIONS

The abrupt end of the regime underlines the same message – that Mussolini never really had total control of the state and its resources. Hitler, a more truly totalitarian ruler, dragged Germany to total military defeat and yet survived as the country's leader until almost the last day of the Second World War. When, in 1943, Italy faced even the prospect of military defeat, Mussolini was first challenged in the Fascist Grand Council, then dismissed by the king, and finally arrested and imprisoned. With his dismissal the fascist regime vanished and the traditional forms of government resumed, with the king appointing Marshal Badoglio as prime minister to head a non-fascist government.

SECTION 5

What was Mussolini's role in the fascist state?

INTRODUCTION

Mussolini's role was central at key moments in the creation of the fascist state, notably:

- developing fascism as a popular movement from 1919;
- the complex bluffing that made him prime minister in 1922;
- establishing his dictatorship in 1925–6.

This section examines Mussolini's role as leader – *Duce* – of fascist Italy during the 1930s.

KEY POINTS

In assessing Mussolini's role in the fully formed fascist state in the 1930s the following points need to be considered.

- **His political role in the government of Italy.** Mussolini's dictatorial powers were secured in 1925–6. He was the central influence on all aspects of government policy – domestic and foreign, important and trivial – throughout the 1930s. At any one time he was head of several ministries, including all the armed forces and the Ministry of the Interior, with power over the police.
- **The cult of the *Duce*.** Fascist propaganda worked hard to create the image of Mussolini as the great leader, endowed with super-human stamina, intelligence and energy, capable of intuitive decisions and decisive action in a great number of different fields.
- **His ambitions for Italy.** These centred first on an important role for Italy in the wider world. His conduct of foreign policy is analysed in more detail in A2 Section 7. But Italians had to be worthy of international greatness and much of Mussolini's energy in domestic policy was devoted to achieving this.
- **His personal qualities.** He had a considerable reputation as an orator and journalist, which stood him in good stead in times of crisis. He lacked the patience to be an effective government minister and also the essential ability to delegate minor matters to subordinates.

HISTORICAL INTERPRETATIONS

Students are fortunate that one of the most accessible biographies of any major twentieth-century figure has been written about Mussolini. Published in 1981, Denis Mack-Smith's *Mussolini* is still widely available in public and school libraries. A paperback version (1982) is still in print. Chapter 8 on Mussolini as leader is an entertaining read but is also packed with perceptive comments both on the private man and on his role as *Duce*. R. Collier, in *Duce: The Rise and Fall of Benito Mussolini* (1971), stresses his subject's huge popularity in the period before 1936 and argues that the cult of the *Duce* arose spontaneously but that Mussolini became corrupted by his own publicity, then worked harder than anyone else to fan the flames of the cult. An analysis of the role of the *Duce* as a cult figure and an example for Italians to follow can be found in an essay by Gori Gigloria in J.A. Mangan (ed.) *Superman Supreme* (2000). It contains a number of interesting photographs of Mussolini as well as an analysis of the aims of fascist propaganda. A book still readily available in public libraries is the historian Sir Charles Petrie's *Mussolini* (1931), which – admiring the *Duce*'s personality and politics – gives a valuable insight into contemporary foreign views of the Italian leader.

WHAT PART DID MUSSOLINI PLAY IN THE GOVERNMENT OF ITALY?

Personal role

Even as the strong state emerged in the late 1920s the most remarkable feature of its central government was the great number of ministries that Mussolini personally occupied. In practice, this often meant that civil servants within the ministries did the important work on policy. However, Mussolini was reluctant to delegate decision-making. He liked to exert his powers and demonstrate his authority, relying on his intuition, on which he set great store, as the best basis for decision-making. It therefore became easier for administrators to put off issues until the *Duce* had made his own decisions, often at quite trivial levels. He was a poor manager and worse as a planner: he quickly became too bored to supervise and consolidate the many initiatives on which he embarked.

It was particularly unfortunate that civil servants soon got into the habit of seeking the *Duce*'s agreement by his signature, or even his initial, on a key document, then using this to promote their own preferred policies. This worked quite effectively in the short term because Mussolini enjoyed making quick decisions; it fitted in with his dramatic image of himself as the decisive leader. But he had neither the time nor the patience to ensure continuity in decision-making and, in the longer term, this caused great confusion and led to loss of direction. He had little or no skill in encouraging ideas from his ministers or civil servants and avoided discussing important issues, preferring to act decisively rather than reveal his own inadequacy. Largely because Mussolini became indispensable in too many areas, fascist Italy was not effectively governed – a serious weakness in an over-centralised state.

Lack of trust

Mussolini's other personal weaknesses also had a far greater impact than they would have done in a more decentralised system. He came to distrust his leading officials as possible rivals so that the more able of them – men like Rocco and Turati – were dismissed and replaced by less able men like Starace, the flattering new party secretary. Mussolini failed to seek advice from his council of ministers, which became merely a sounding board for his own, hastily constructed, opinions.

In the 1930s, despite being indispensable, Mussolini became a very isolated figure: he had no 'candid friends' to challenge his perceptions of reality and only a series of mistresses to provide him with the distraction of social company. Although he continued to put in many hours on political matters he was no intellectual and, as his fund of ideas for the future direction of fascism soon dried up, he increasingly worked at or read about routine political matters with no real sense of purpose. He had become bored with many aspects of his role as *Duce* and yet was determined to retain his hold on dictatorial power. For the Italian state this was a recipe for disaster.

HOW DID OFFICIAL PROPAGANDA PRESENT THE *DUCE* TO THE ITALIAN PEOPLE?

Mussolini devoted much attention to ensuring that the Italian people saw him in a suitable light.

- Other areas of government activity were often neglected or received only fitful attention, but it is significant that government and **personal propaganda** were always close to his heart.
- Even before the dictatorship emerged in 1925, a prime minister's press office dealt with both the Italian and international press and, from 1926, the state-controlled news agency controlled the flow of news items, working broadly on the principle that editors were forbidden to publish bad news – even down to the level of traffic accidents.
- One enduring myth was that Mussolini, the great orator, spoke to the crowds even on the greatest public occasions quite spontaneously and from the heart, but in reality he usually took great care to see that such occasions were closely stage-managed and his speeches carefully

KEY THEME

Personal propaganda
Mussolini spent many hours each day reading newspapers, paying particular attention to press-cuttings that dealt with his own image and achievements, and making sure he was on good terms with both Italian and foreign journalists.

prepared. Privately, he affected to despise the crowds whom he addressed so effectively but he was still careful to make sure that he created the right image with them.

In the late 1920s, it was Fascist Party organisations such as the women's and youth leagues and the *Dopolavoro* that played an important role in promoting positive views of Mussolini. From the early 1930s, however, as newspapers and journalists became much more tightly controlled, the government press office began systematically to promote the cult of the *Duce*. Both propaganda and control of the media were more systematically organised in 1934 when Mussolini's son-in-law, Galeazzo Ciano (later foreign minister), took control of the press office and in the next two years quadrupled the numbers of its staff. After 1935, Italian propaganda became focused on justifying and **glorifying the nation's military adventures**, and here too the image of the uniformed *Duce* was to the fore.

In the late 1930s, the propaganda emphasis moved to the more difficult task of winning the hearts and minds of the Italian people to the closer ties with Nazi Germany. Images of Mussolini playing host to, and the equal of, Hitler, dominated cinema newsreels when the German leader paid a state visit to Italy.

WHAT WAS THE SIGNIFICANCE OF THE CULT OF THE *DUCE*?

The public face of Mussolini – endlessly promoted by the propaganda apparatus of both state and party – was intended to provide for the Italian people the essential message of the fascist experiment. The regime set out to promote a vision of the Italian people as 'an elite race of supermen' and used images of Mussolini, some far removed from reality, in order to do this. The *Duce* was not just the political leader of the Italian state. Perhaps more importantly he was presented to the Italian people as the symbol of all fascist virtues. In this role he is vastly more interesting to historians than as a political leader of limited ability and, in the end, quite limited vision.

Authoritarian regimes on pre-1914 lines had rarely concerned themselves with the management of public opinion, but fascism was raised up by harnessing mass public feeling and worked constantly to retain mass support. The myths developed around Mussolini, from as early as 1926, were an important aspect of fascist stage management and indeed are as important for historical understanding of the nature of fascism as the reality of his governing role. Even the effort of creating the myths took on its own political importance, for the endless personalised propaganda effort served to alter the nature of Italian fascism, turning it into idolatry

KEY THEME

Glorifying the nation's military adventures The 1935 declaration of war on Ethiopia was, for example, turned into a carnival with Mussolini at his most dramatic giving the news from a balcony to a vast hysterically enthusiastic crowd in Rome's central square. The event was also broadcast across the nation by radio.

Mussolini, the
military leader.

of the strong leader and denying it any other purpose. As a result, during the 1930s, fascism – having lost its radical edge and any revolutionary purpose – was transformed into Mussolinism.

WHAT DID MUSSOLINI WANT FOR ITALY?

Promotion of the *Duce* to the Italian people was set in a wider context of their fascist destiny as a new master race. Above all, there were the repeated efforts to relate fascist Italy to its Roman imperial past; even here Mussolini had a role to play, seeing himself as a latter-day emperor. New public holidays were established to commemorate important fascist landmarks or to celebrate recent military triumphs or the glories of ancient Rome. The ceremonies, parades and sporting contests that accompanied these new holidays were rarely complete without a long and theatrical speech from the *Duce*, preferably set against a background of ancient Roman statuary. A recent vivid description of Mussolini as orator depicts him with 'hands on hips, legs wide apart, jaw contracted, eyes rolling, the orator Mussolini spoke to the crowd in a deep stentorian voice', adding that it was usual to picture him from below 'to lengthen his rather stumpy figure' (Gori Gigloria in J.A. Mangan (ed.) *Superman Supreme*, 2000).

It is at this point that the myths begin to conflict with the reality of what we know about Mussolini the man. Writings about Mussolini invariably stressed his virtues and his strengths.

- Among the most enduring images was that of **Mussolini as a heroic military man** whereas his military career in the First World War, though much enjoyed, was brief and unheroic. Indeed, as war and the threat of war came closer in the late 1930s, Mussolini traded on this vision of himself and seemed to spend his life in military uniform.
- Another myth arose from frequent newspaper references to his tireless energy, often working through the night in the cause of the Italian people.
- He was presented as **a man of the people**;
- His **physical prowess** was captured in numerous photographs of him on horseback, fencing, skiing or playing tennis.

Mussolini was presented as a master in all these varied activities and state censorship ensured that nobody could question his prowess.

- No references were allowed to any illnesses or to his having to wear glasses, or indeed to his birthdays, which marked his passing years and might undermine the cult of ever-youthful vigour.

KEY THEMES

Mussolini as a heroic military man His claim that 'A minute on the battlefield is worth a lifetime of peace' became a much-quoted fascist slogan.

A man of the people Mussolini often appeared bare-chested alongside peasants, getting in the harvest in the Battle for Grain; visiting schools and hospital maternity wards to encourage the Battle for Births; or as modern technological man, preferably in a racing car or flying a plane.

Physical prowess A surprising number of images show Mussolini bare-chested or dressed for display on the beach, despite his lack of height and a gently spreading waistline; the embodiment of male virility – a true new Italian.

Mussolini on the slopes, on a toboggan.

- Throughout the 1930s, his press office bombarded newspapers and radio stations with positive information about both his political and his leisure activities.
- Pictures of the *Duce* in military or sporting mode were an important part of the regular propaganda diet provided by cinema newsreels.
- The admiring comments of foreign leaders received prominent coverage in Italian newspapers.

Self-delusion

The sheer scale of the propaganda effort devoted to the cult of the *Duce* makes him the first of the twentieth-century dictators to manipulate news and images to impress the masses of his followers. Others, like Hitler and Franco, self-consciously copied many of his techniques and tried to emulate his success. The adulation and the deliberate way in which it was encouraged and manipulated give some indication of the *Duce*'s colossal vanity. His isolation from candid advice has already been noted and it was then only a short step before he began to believe the stream of messages put out by his propaganda machine. By 1940, he came to believe that he was about to lead Italy in war towards a dominant position in southern Europe and the Mediterranean region, and also that the Italian people, re-created on fascist lines, were capable of winning that prize through military victory. Within two years it was clear that this dream was a nonsense. Mussolini became the most notable victim of his own skilfully promoted cults of the infallible leader and the Italian super race.

Support of Italian people

It is difficult to estimate to what extent the Italian people 'accepted' or 'were taken in' by these visions of a heroic *Duce* as a tireless example of the fascist Italian superman whom they were expected to follow and emulate. There was no open questioning of the propaganda claims but, from 1936, some people must quietly have had doubts even if these did not come to the fore until things started to go seriously wrong after 1940. On the other hand, fascist propaganda and total control of the media and the education system were able for more than a decade to make the most of the many 'triumphs' for which Mussolini could be given the credit. The slogan 'Mussolini is always right' chalked on so many walls in the mid-1930s – the years of internal stability and easy foreign triumphs – suggest that some at least were totally convinced by the state propaganda that attributed all of the regime's successes to him. This, of course, left him cruelly exposed when triumph turned to disaster.

AN ASSESSMENT OF MUSSOLINI

Time and historians have not been kind to Mussolini.

- The personality cult so energetically promoted in his years in power made claims for his many virtues that are patently absurd.
- His physical appearance and his high-blown oratory now make him seem a figure very easy to mock.
- His dreams of imperial glory based on fascist domestic virtues were all too easily blown aside in crushing military defeats, which exposed the emptiness of his claims to have created a new and powerful Italy.
- At the end he was a lonely and defeated figure; in death he was treated with contempt.

The destruction of his reputation has been so complete that it is now difficult to see why he was able to retain power and indeed the affections or acceptance of many of the Italian people for so long. His rise to power, even to the role of dictator, can be understood when set in the context of Italian history from 1914 to the late 1920s, but his survival and evident popularity in the 1930s are less easily accessible to historical explanation.

Personal qualities

Is it possible that historians have relied too much on hindsight in their verdicts of Mussolini's personal qualities and so have underestimated him? Such issues are important but are probably the responsibility of biographers rather than general historians. After coming to power Mussolini continued to lead a frugal and quite isolated private life, avoiding both social occasions and meeting strangers. This isolation grew worse after the death in 1931 of his younger brother, Arnaldo, the first promoter of the cult of the *Duce*. Mack-Smith (*Mussolini*, 1982) argues that Mussolini's isolation was based on contempt for his fellow men, which made him on occasion cruel in his treatment of political enemies and disdainful of supporters who fell out of favour, though he acknowledges that 'Mussolini was less cruel than many, perhaps than most, dictators'.

Failing to see the best in his fellows also made Mussolini a poor selector of men whom he could trust and very poor at delegating public business. Eventually, he cultivated aloofness as a necessary part of the role of *Duce*. His need to act out this role came to dominate both his private and his public life. His biographer sees the actor in his desire to appear inscrutable and impulsively unpredictable, as well as in his love of action and activity, even violence. Perhaps his least attractive feature was his colossal certainty that on every issue he was instinctively right. Even this may have been a pose, masking personal insecurity and even, as Mack-Smith stresses, timidity, for close contemporaries including his wife saw him 'as much less virile than his legend'.

CONCLUSIONS

Mack-Smith's biography stresses his subject's many failings and weaknesses. The *Duce*, whatever the propaganda, was no superman. His hold over Italy has to be explained in terms of the country's troubled past and its dreams of future greatness, both of which Mussolini and his propagandists exploited superbly. Perhaps in the end it was his ability as an actor, bringing the stage to life, that was the key to the *Duce*'s hold on the Italian imagination, a hold that nostalgically lingered on in Italian right-wing circles more than half a century after his humiliating end. A common Italian response, when asked for an opinion about Mussolini, is that until he moved into Hitler's orbit he had done much good for Italy. Even this may be seen as a generous verdict and few Italians would go as far as the *Duce*'s grandson, Guido, who, in 2001, claimed that 'Mussolini was right 95 per cent of the time'.

SECTION 6

Analysing fascist Italy: central issues

INTRODUCTION

As the first modern experiment in dictatorial rule, fascist Italy attracted a great deal of contemporary attention from foreign observers, much of it admiring in tone. In contrast, historians writing after the end of the Second World War – and inevitably influenced by its outcome – have tended to note the many weaknesses and imperfections in the fascist regime. For them there were many significant gaps between fascist theory and propaganda on the one hand and fascist practical achievements on the other. This section looks at issues in the domestic history of fascist Italy, concentrating particularly on the 1930s

KEY POINTS

Inevitably this section is based on an arbitrary selection of the issues examined by historians studying fascist Italy. The key issues that are crucial in understanding the nature of Mussolini's fascism are as follows.

- **The corporate state**. The underlying theory of the corporate state, its origins of corporatism, achievements and limitations.
- **The efficiency and the achievements of the fascist economy**. This is a chronological analysis stretching from the free-market economics of the period 1922–5 through the world depression of the early 1930s to the quest for self-sufficiency in the 1930s and on to the Second World War. There are also sections on Italian living standards and on industrial growth in the fascist period.
- **The support enjoyed by the regime**. This section concentrates on the period from the early 1930s economic depression through to Italy entering the Second World War in 1940.
- **Fascist oppression**. The main issues here are the activities of the fascist police force, the ways in which opponents of the regime were treated and the adoption late in the day of policies of racial discrimination.

HISTORICAL INTERPRETATIONS

The most accessible analysis of fascist society and the fascist economy is in Martin Clark's *Modern Italy* (1996), Chapters 12 and 13, which contain his argument that fascism was the child of war and in practice was essentially a military regime. It is right therefore to judge both society and the economy in military terms. The true test of fascist Italy was its fitness for war. Philip Morgan, in *Italian Fascism 1919–45* (1995), also sees the purpose of the state as being to equip Italy for war and stresses the essential links between Mussolini's foreign policy and totalitarian domestic policies relating to both the economy and society. The books by J. Pollard and John Whittam, cited in the Bibliography, have valuable recent analysis of fascist social and economic policies. Historical interest in the economy under fascism has centred on policy, notably the corporate state, rather than performance. This may well be because Italian economic statistics for the period are notoriously inadequate, but there is a useful introductory chapter in Russell King's *The Industrial Geography of Italy* (1985) and a less easily followed chapter in the *Fontana Economic History of Europe*, Vol 6 (1973), edited by Carlo Cipolla.

The question of the popularity of the regime and of how far the Italian people consented to fascist rule has been a contentious one. Early Italian historians, notably G. Salvemini in *The Origins of Fascism in Italy* (1928) and other works, stressed the fascist use of force and the oppressive nature of the regime. M. Gallo and Denis Mack-Smith are both pessimistic on the subject of fascist oppression and stress the pressures put on the Italian people to conform. Gallo cites the high level of police activity 'every night rounding up' people still on the streets after dark and sees repression as the 'keynote of the state'. In 1977, Renzo de Felice caused a storm, in Italy at least, in *Fascism: An Informal Introduction to its Theory and Practice,* asserting that, until 1936, the regime commanded general consent and that this fact was the key to the regime's survival. British historians, notably R. Collier, in *Duce: The Rise and Fall of Benito Mussolini* (1971), had already acknowledged Mussolini's personal popularity, at least until 1936. Essays by British historians edited by D. Forgacs and published in 1986 (see Bibliography) also tend to paint fascist Italy in a less repressive light than the works by earlier writers.

WAS THE CORPORATE STATE JUST A MIRAGE?

As noted in A2 Section 3, arguably the most original fascist political innovation was the creation and development of the corporate state.

The theory of the corporate state

The central theory of the corporate state was that the economy – or more precisely the production of goods and services – would be organised by corporations in which both employers and workers would be represented. Firms would remain in private hands but would be regulated by the corporations in order to ensure that production was directed in the national interest. The corporations were to be state bodies and so included state and Fascist Party officials among the membership precisely in order to ensure that the interests of the state were paramount. The corporations would bring about good labour relations, provide rational plans for production, stimulate enterprise and generally encourage the production of wealth in a setting free from traditional class conflicts between labour and management. In the light of Italy's troubled industrial relations after the First World War it was an enticing prospect.

The origins

The idea of **co-operation in production** had its origins in nineteenth-century writing where it attracted the support of some socialist trades unions and also Catholic writers who were inspired by a rosy vision of the co-operative production methods of the medieval guilds, where worker and master toiled side by side. The origin of the Italian corporations can be quite precisely dated to the years 1925–6 when, in the constitutional turmoil in the aftermath of the Matteotti crisis, the failure of the fascist trades unions (syndicates) to command mass industrial worker support became clear. The fascist government mediated a settlement between these syndicates and the largest employers' organisation (*Confindustria*), which agreed to recognise only the fascist syndicates in future negotiations. In return, the syndicates accepted that they would exert no control in managing the factories where authority would remain in the hands of the owners. But, because they had no representation within the factories, the syndicates were unable to monitor the behaviour of the employers in regard to agreements that had, in theory, been accepted. It was not simply that the fascist syndicates were denied any say in economic policy, which they were, but that the new system also constituted a major loss of previously hard-won workers' rights.

The corporate structure

As noted in AS Chapter 5, the important founding legislation was the work of Alfredo Rocco in the late 1920s. He established an economic administration based on the production of wealth. In each area of the economy separate syndicates of workers and employers were gradually set up and met together in corporations, which – in theory at least – controlled their sector of the national economy. The separate nature of the syndicates represented a considerable dilution of original syndicalist ideas and confirmed the exclusion of the syndicates from any role within the workplace that had been agreed with *Confindustria* in 1926. It meant that the corporations became consultative bodies, largely over labour issues, and not the direct managers of industrial undertakings.

This dilution, or distortion, of syndicalist theory was inevitable, given the compromises Mussolini had to make with capitalist forces in Italy in order to build up the fascist movement. Under Rocco, however, syndicalist ideas were adapted to give the state, rather than the workers, the key economic role. In practice, government nominees dominated the corporations and the corporate state became an avenue for state control of the economy rather than a daring innovation in co-operative production and control. All this fitted in well with fascist ideas on the overriding importance of the state and the subordination of citizens to the purposes of the state. This subordination to the interests of the state marked an important moment in Italy's post-1925 drift towards totalitarianism.

Corporatism in operation

The agreement on the role of the fascist syndicates broke the power of the Catholic and socialist trades unions and left the fascist syndicates as the sole protectors of the workers. In 1926, the terms of the agreement were included in the **laws regulating labour relations** throughout the country, which were devised by Alfredo Rocco and which became the founding documents of the corporate state.

In the early stages of the corporate system there were some encouraging signs that the new structure was being taken seriously by the government. In July 1926, a new Ministry of Corporations was established with its first minister, until 1929, Mussolini himself. This was merely one of the many ministries of which Mussolini was, in name at least, the head. His deputy and, after 1929, the minister was one of the most able of fascist administrators, Giuseppe Bottai, who was determined to make the new structure central to the Italian economy. There was, however, a fatal flaw in the corporate structure. The Rocco Law regulated the power of the workers' syndicates but merely allowed, rather than compelled, the employers to form their corporations. These bodies grew up piecemeal over the next eight years and in that period the only function of the corporate system was for the syndicates and the state-appointed officers to discuss labour rights and payments. This restricted pattern of activity was never broken.

The workers' syndicates were also **deliberately fragmented** and unsurprisingly these soon proved incapable of defending the interests of their members, particularly in the difficult economic conditions brought on first by the revaluation of the lira, then the onset in the early 1930s of the worldwide trade depression. The employers in the meantime retained their independence and power. In this period, the Ministry of Corporations was an empty title hiding the reality that the corporations did not in practice exist. Bottai had worried the employers by producing a high-sounding **Charter of Labour**, but in practice this never came to anything except on paper.

Gradually, and in piecemeal fashion, corporations appeared in the majority of industries. In 1930, the National Council of Corporations

Laws regulating labour relations
These laws, devised by Rocco, declared that only state-recognised bodies could negotiate labour relations and in each area of production there would be a single such body recognised. Throughout their existence the corporations then became subordinate to the economic interests of the big industrialists. Government appointees on the corporations almost always acted in the employer's interest.

Deliberate fragmentation
The workers' syndicates were separated into six distinct parts, industry by industry instead of in one large confederation.

Charter of Labour
This charter supposedly defined workers' rights.

was set up with seven sections across the economy and it seemed that it was intended that this body should have a national planning and co-ordinating role. In 1934, the final structure of 22 corporations across the economy was in existence and Mussolini was able to talk grandly of this new, essentially Italian, **Middle Way** between communism and unregulated capitalism.

Flaws in the corporate system

The corporate ideal was flawed when put into practice.

KEY TERM

The Middle Way
In practice, this was an ideal way of strengthening the control of the fascist regime over both the economy and the workforce. Mussolini spoke to the Italian people and to admiring foreigners as though the new economic system, the Middle Way, actually existed and worked efficiently, though in fact this was not the case.

- At the highest level, too many economic decisions remained outside the scope of the corporations. The Ministry of Economics worked throughout to limit the powers and responsibilities of the corporations and even Bottai was unable to prevent this. The great employers were happy to work outside the restrictions on their freedom that corporatism implied. Initiatives, reorganising or expanding major industries, usually with the aid of state money, were undertaken by the Instituto per la Ricostruzione Industriale (IRI) and without reference to the corporations. During the early 1930s depression, the banking system and many great manufacturing firms came under state supervision and sometimes control but this, a massive extension of the role of the state in economic matters, was done quite outside the corporate system and through negotiations between owners and state officials.
- The National Council of Corporations restricted the independence of the separate corporations but in turn had its own range of business defined and severely controlled by Mussolini as the head of government. The economy was placed on a more warlike footing from 1935, and its own powers of co-ordination and planning were ignored as the government, dealing directly with the producers of military and other essential supplies, took key decisions.
- The tendency for the state to ignore the corporations became even more marked in the late 1930s when the economic priority became self-sufficiency (autarky). As state contracts, subsidies and directives took on greater economic significance, so state officials preferred to deal directly with the big industrialists. At the level of national policy the corporations became simply spectators of the new direction taken by the economy.
- The corporate system became a vast and unwieldy bureaucracy in which large numbers of middle-class Italian men found comfortable jobs of a routine form-filling nature. They operated at the level of middle management, well away from macro-economic decision-making. Issuing licences and permits became a way of life. Far from rationalising production and encouraging enterprise this corporate bureaucracy became a brake on economic development and an additional obstacle to be overcome by entrepreneurs.

- Denied access to meaningful economic decision-making, the corporations remained largely involved, as they were at their inception, in matters related to labour relations and to wages. In this role the bias in favour of the employers, which was evident in the early days, remained. The real success of the corporate state was in providing employers with a docile labour force whose standards of living, and therefore the employers' labour costs, were forced down steadily. This was done quite deliberately as an act of state policy, for the notion that the state representatives, who grew more numerous, were there as independent arbiters between worker and employer remained a fiction to the end.

Significance of the corporate state

The **corporate state** was a useful propaganda device for the fascist regime both internally and internationally. Italian propaganda, echoing Mussolini, presented it as a unique middle way between the failed anarchy of capitalism and the oppressive command economy favoured by the communists. It gave the fascist experiment a distinctive identity, even an ideology to set against that of communism. In practice, it was never the partnership of workers and owners that the government claimed it to be, and the most important economic decisions were made without reference to it. It was more than a mirage because, eventually, a corporate structure did emerge but its range of business was always limited and controlled by the government. Its real significance was as an effective tool for the centralising fascist state to control the working classes. It could not even have done this effectively had it not operated in a strongly authoritarian state where means of opposing the government were stifled.

In a more open society the corporate state's inefficiencies would soon have been exposed. Under the pressures of total war the corporate system crumbled away. Despite all the plaudits and all the admiring attention, the corporate state contributed nothing of lasting importance to either political theory or to economic management. Belatedly, in 1939, it was decided that the corporations should become the basis for elections to the Chamber of Deputies – a producers' parliament. The fact that no elections were held during the regime's remaining years provides a neat verdict on the essential emptiness of the corporate dream.

HOW EFFICIENT WAS THE FASCIST ECONOMY?

Any verdict here is in danger of being undermined by the absence of reliable statistics of economic performance for the inter-war period and by the danger of treating too seriously the regime's propaganda claims. Italy's catastrophic military record in the Second World War, despite preparation for war having been the state's first priority throughout much

KEY THEME

The corporate state As it developed in the early 1930s, the idea attracted much attention and admiration among foreign observers, many of whom saw it as providing an impressive response to the problems brought on by the world economic depression.

of the 1930s, certainly suggests serious economic weaknesses. On the other hand, the fascist record has to be set against the low level of economic development achieved by the end of the 1914–18 war when compared with countries such as Britain and France. Economic growth before 1914 was distinctly patchy and the fascists inherited an unbalanced economy with an industrial north enjoying higher standards of living and investment than the struggling agrarian south of the country. Equally, the fascist regime cannot be held responsible for the debilitating effects of the world trade depression of the early 1930s.

The political priorities of fascism did, however, have three serious economic consequences.

- The desire to see Italy as a great nation had an impact long before military adventures became important. In particular, it encouraged the decision, based on little more than Mussolini's personal whim, to revalue the currency and to retain that revaluation through the years of world depression which, by over-pricing Italian exports, did adversely affect the economy.
- The drive to promote self-sufficiency (autarky) in the 1930s distorted both the agrarian and industrial sectors of the economy.
- The ballooning national debt of the late 1930s came about as a result of the military involvement first in Ethiopia and then in Spain, and was increased by the need to expand Italy's military capacity as it moved closer to alliance with Nazi Germany.

Inefficiency arising from the workings of the system of corporations, squarely a fascist responsibility, has been discussed in the previous section.

HOW IMPRESSIVE WAS THE FASCIST ECONOMIC ACHIEVEMENT?

Economic recovery of the 1922–5 period
This continued at a slower rate until 1927.

- It was based on better labour relations (so fewer strikes) and on liberal trade arrangements that allowed Italy to share in the post-war growth of international trade and encouraged investment in industry.
- Settlement of Italy's war debts to the USA led to a boom in US investment in Italy.
- By 1925, unemployment was down to half a million, a quarter of its 1920 level, and industrial output was 40 per cent higher.
- In the optimistic economic climate, hundreds of small new industrial firms were started and the state invested heavily in improvements to the railway system.

The boom owed much to international conditions and, with rising inflation, was beginning to look threatened after 1925.

Weathering the depression

Here the fascist record was, at best, a mixed one.

- The state, well ahead of other capitalist countries, boosted the economy and helped fight the growing unemployment by increasing spending on public works projects, doubling investment on road-building in the worst years and increasing welfare payments to families with children.
- Continuing the deflationary policies, which had started with the revaluation of the lira, had the opposite effect by depressing wages and therefore purchasing power so that fewer goods were bought.
- On the other hand, **the state helped the banking system** to survive the monetary crisis that accompanied the trade depression.
- The fascist regime also encouraged industrial firms to amalgamate in order to survive, though this swiftly led in the heavy engineering industries to the emergence of uncompetitive price-fixing cartels.

As a result of state economic intervention, although officially registered unemployment figures went up from 100,000 in 1926 to over 1 million by 1933, the Italian unemployment situation was never as bad as in France and Britain. Comparisons are dangerous, though, because the bald Italian figures hide the fact that the depression forced a temporary end to migration from country to town and this in turn encouraged even more overmanning of inefficient farms, which remained a serious weakness until after the end of the Second World War.

The drive for autarky

There were impressive successes in the drive for self-sufficiency (autarky) that became the dominant economic policy of the 1930s.

- Thanks to the Battle for Grain the country became self-sufficient in that basic foodstuff with annual production of wheat increasing across the decade from 4.8 to 7.6 million tonnes.
- New crops such as cotton were introduced.
- Industries like chemicals, iron, steel, heavy engineering and shipbuilding greatly expanded.
- Particular attention was paid to oil and gas exploration, and the oil refining industry was much expanded.

However, it has often been pointed out that the expansion of grain production came at the expense of other agricultural products for whose production Italy was more naturally suited and that grain was often grown, owing to the artificial market that government subsidies created, on quite unsuitable land. All this badly distorted Italian agriculture and,

KEY THEME

State help with the banking system By creating first the IMI (Instituto Mobiliare Italiano) and then the eventually better-known IRI (Instituto per la Ricostruzione Industriale), to rescue banks facing collapse when their long-term loans to industry could not be repaid, the state effectively limited the effects of the spread of the depression across other areas of the economy and also sowed the seeds of future recovery. This contrasted sharply with the dire situation in Austria and Germany in the years 1929–33.

in particular, worsened one of the country's most serious economic problems – namely the acute poverty of the south of the country, which was largely unsuitable for grain production. Equally, there was no sustained effort to develop the economies of Italy's African colonies, either as markets or as sources for raw materials, and of course the vast oil reserves in Libya remained undetected.

The policy of autarky was pursued for political rather than economic reasons, relating to Mussolini's foreign-policy ambitions. It badly distorted the Italian economy by discouraging production of consumer goods at the expense of living standards and denied investment to the non-military sections of the engineering industry. But it was bound to fail, for in key areas Italy could never be self-sufficient in raw materials such as iron or in coal or oil – all essential for creating a strong military or for fighting a war.

The war economy

In 1939, Mussolini realised that, despite all his efforts and ambitions, Italy was not in a position to enter Hitler's war against Britain and France. In 1940, he was tempted to enter the conflict, not because of any improvement in the country's economic or military capacity, but by the prospect of easy gains on the back of overwhelming German military successes. The Italian economy in 1940 has been described by the economic geographer Russell King, in *The Industrial Geography of Italy* (1985) as one 'woefully unprepared for war'. He notes, for example, that Italian steel production was one-third that of either of Mussolini's new enemies, Britain and France, and that, in 1938 – the last full year of European peace – Italy manufactured 52,000 cars in contrast to the 300,000 produced in each of Britain and France. More serious still for the country's long-term prospects was the uncomfortable fact that 60 per cent of its imports were foodstuffs, which had to come by sea past British Gibraltar or through the British-controlled Suez Canal. The quest for economic self-sufficiency to provide a base for international grandeur had failed and so cruelly delivered Italy into the hands of its wartime enemies. The strains imposed on the Italian economy by the Second World War are discussed on pages 132–4.

Living standards under fascism

During the early 1930s depression, because both wages and prices fell the living standards of those who managed to remain in work probably dropped only marginally. Those who became unemployed suffered more because the benefit system supporting them was very rudimentary. With economic recovery, the implementation of the policy of autarky and increased military spending from 1935, prices began to rise but **wage rates** failed to keep pace with this rise, so that at the end of the decade the purchasing power of wages in industry was below what it had been in

KEY TERM

Wage rates These were varied for two main reasons.

- They were much lower in the south of the country, reflecting the fascist failure to tackle the deep-seated economic weaknesses of that region. Only in the bleakest days of the industrial depression did significant numbers of men stop trying to escape to the industrial towns of the north.
- There were gender variations, with women's wages being 'exceptionally low' and 'less than half the male rates' (King, 1985). Fascists may not have been too concerned at such a differential, for the official fascist view was that a woman's place was in the home bringing up her children.

1920. It had, indeed, fallen to pre-1914 levels. This was the price large numbers of Italians had to pay for Mussolini's foreign-policy dreams.

As Italy came out of the depression, welfare changes eased the bleak lot of many workers a little, but at the expense of leaving them more dependent on the state and its agencies.

- Any account of living standards needs, of course, to bear in mind the leisure and welfare services provided by the *Dopolavoro*.
- As part of the Battle for Births, family allowances were first given to industrial workers in 1934.
- Free medical care was provided for the urban poor in the same year.
- The practice of giving workers a Christmas bonus began in 1938.

By the 1930s, Mussolini would, in any case, have asserted that fascism was not about living standards but about national greatness. His socialist days were long behind him and in private he argued that economic privation would harden the Italian people for the greater struggles ahead.

Industrial growth

Although important areas of the Italian economy did develop during the fascist period this was often not as a direct result of fascist policies. Heavy industry, the roads and railways and the electricity industry were the exceptions, for all benefited greatly from government direction and finances. The relatively rapid economic growth in the manufacture of cars, motorcycles and home appliances, however, owed little to government policy and simply paralleled development elsewhere in the capitalist world. Fascist Italy never began to bridge the gap between its own industrial capacity and that of other developed European nations much less that of the USA. The fascist regime inherited an undeveloped industrial economy and, partly because of the depression but more because of a pursuit – for non-economic reasons – of self-sufficiency and military expansion, industrial development remained limited. The war effort was crippled by accute shortages of power and raw materials (see AS Section 8). Italy became an advanced industrial and trading nation only with the economic revolution of the 1950s and early 1960s, and then not under an authoritarian centralising regime but under a democratic political regime adopting market-led economic policies.

Agriculture

The well-publicised battles for grain and for land have been examined in AS Chapter 5. Both produced much favourable publicity for the regime, but the achievements were essentially flawed. The Battle for Grain was a central part of the drive for autarky, but it distorted the agrarian economy and yet still left Italy dependent on imports of many foodstuffs and raw materials. The Battle for Land, despite some over-publicised reclamation schemes, lost most of its impetus in the late 1930s. Italian agriculture remained far less efficient than unregulated production in France and was not modernised, especially in terms of overmanning and under-mechanisation, until after the downfall of the fascist regime. Food shortages and rationing during the war provide a telling comment on the failure of the drive for autarky and in particular the Battle for Grain.

HOW POPULAR WAS THE REGIME BEFORE 1940?

There are several reasons why this question is difficult to answer.

- From 1925, the fascists kept tight control of the radio and newspapers, and prevented public expression of any hostility to the regime.
- Reports of the secret police, who kept a close watch on any possible critics of the regime and compiled many reports about them, cannot be relied on, for they are contaminated by private grudges and by the need for the police to justify their salaries.
- Any opposition to the government was repressed and driven underground or into exile abroad, and has therefore left little or no evidence of its existence and activities.
- The Ministry of Press and Propaganda developed great expertise in manufacturing and manipulating both news and opinion through a variety of skilful propaganda techniques.
- The cult of the infallible *Duce* was promoted so relentlessly that the private opinions of the Italian people about their leader have been drowned out.

Support for the regime

The behaviour of the regime suggests that there was some opposition in some quarters. If this had not been the case then why all the efforts to manipulate and censor opinion? The continued activity of both the Fascist Militia, the numerous secret police, and the bodyguards who always surrounded Mussolini on public occasions and provided him with a succession of stage-managed enthusiastic receptions at least suggest that his and the government's popularity could not be taken for granted. Unfortunately, foreign observers living in Italy are an unreliable guide to popular opinion about the fascists, if only because they are so divided in their estimates. In *Mussolini* (1982), Dennis Mack-Smith cites extremes in the foreign estimates of support for the regime, 'some thinking that fascism was secretly detested by the vast majority of Italians, others believing almost the opposite; one guess was that 80 per cent of Italians would back him in a free vote'. Criticism of the regime remained muted and private. It could find no public voice so that the historian is reduced to haphazard speculation.

- There are the euphoric public demonstrations in 1935–6 at the news of successive military victories in Ethiopia, which propaganda may have exaggerated but can scarcely have invented.
- It was a time of economic recovery, the benefits of the *Dopolavoro* were evident, internal anarchy was at an end, sporting triumphs abounded and imperial greatness seemed to beckon.
- As the years passed, more and more young people came through the fascist-controlled education system and youth movements; they had known no alternative to fascism.

All this must have ensured some degree of either warm support or at least tacit acceptance for the regime. It has been argued that there was at most a public acceptance of fascism that hid private cynicism, which it would have been foolish to reveal. The total failure of even leading fascists to support Mussolini at the moment of his dismissal from office in 1943 has been cited as evidence of the hollow nature of the 'support' for his regime. That situation came after a series of disastrous military reverses and in the midst of immense wartime suffering, and it may well not be applicable to the quality or quantity of support for fascism at the time of the triumphs of the mid-1930s.

THE FASCIST REGIME AND THE CATHOLIC CHURCH

General acceptance of the fascist regime was made much easier by Mussolini's negotiation of the 1929 Lateran Pacts, which ended the unhappy tensions that had always existed between the Church and earlier liberal regimes.

In 1922 some in the Church had been ready to welcome Mussolini as a protector of Christian values faced with the onslaught of godless communism. After 1922 Mussolini worked hard to win the Church's goodwill, living down his own atheist past and making concessions to the Church in the important field of education.

The Church authorities had rightly remained suspicious of the fascists, whose central emphasis on the need for individuals to commit themselves to the service of the state was quite incompatible with the Christian message. But the Church did recognise that it had much to gain in terms of influence in Italian society by ending the unhappy relations with successive Italian governments. After 1926 it was clear to Pope Pius XI and his key political adviser, Cardinal Gaspari, that Mussolini had established firm control over the country. The time had come, he felt, to negotiate an agreement – and this led to the Lateran Pacts of 1929 (page 90–1).

The Lateran Pacts ended any possibility of the Catholic Church leading an official or, indeed, underground political movement opposed to the fascist regime. In view of the Church's immense influence among the Italian people this was a great asset to Mussolini, though the continued existence of the Church as a powerful, independent institution severely dented any ambitions he had to make fascist Italy a truly totalitarian state. However, it did ensure the everyday acceptance of the regime by the Catholic faithful and therefore played a large part in ensuring their consent for fascist policies.

Opposition
There were hints at more public opposition.

- In the early 1930s, the effects of the depression encouraged several localised and short-lived strikes and demonstrations, suggesting the Italian left still had some life, though the oppressive tactics of the regime saw an end to this activity as economic recovery began.
- Italian left-wing intellectuals managed to produce several limited circulation and short-lived opposition papers, but the number of anti-fascist activists remained small and their efforts ineffective.
- Although acceptance of the regime had been greatly helped by the state's 1929 agreement with the Catholic Church, even here there were limits to the degree of official acceptance of fascist rule. These were reached in 1937 with the beginning of official propaganda against Italian Jews, which became a full racist assault in 1938–9. The Catholic hierarchy then issued a formal and quite unprecedented condemnation of the regime's actions.

The late 1930s
In practice, many Italians probably remained non-fascists, loyal still to the Church and their families, outwardly accepting the fascist regime but certainly not prepared to defend it in a crisis or even undergo the rigours of war in its support. After 1936, the regime became less popular.

- Fascist idealism, creating a new Italy, had become tainted by corruption and self-interest.
- The zealous fascists of 1922 had grown older; many of them had been purged and driven from public life.
- In office since 1922, the fascists had failed to develop a second generation of leaders with the inevitable result that, despite the continuing cult of youth and physical vigour, the fascist leadership began to look distinctly unfit and ageing. Even Mussolini's waistline began to look more impressive than his bare chest.
- The regime also began to make mistakes – persecuting Jews, requiring state officials to wear uniforms and the army to adopt the faintly ludicrous goose-step march, endlessly imposing the fascist salute and,

above all, increasing military expenditure, so squeezing living standards, and moving closer to a warlike alliance with Germany.

HOW OPPRESSIVE WAS THE FASCIST REGIME?

Fascism intruded into people's private lives in ways that no liberal government did. This was an inevitable consequence of its closing down independent institutions and replacing them with agencies approved by the government. Mussolini's government also had the mission of creating a new and better Italian people, obedient to the needs of the state. This too required the direction and manipulation of people's lives. All this was arguably oppressive and perhaps totalitarian (see A2 Section 4) but here 'oppressive' is defined more narrowly in order to examine what happened to those who opposed or questioned the regime or were in some way seen by the regime as 'undesirable'.

The police
One great difference between fascist Italy and states such as Britain and France was the level of police activity. Despite Mussolini providing a new name, *OVRA*, for the secret (or security) police, this remained a shadowy organisation within the much larger and elaborately organised police force. It was certainly very active in identifying possible dissidents, then mounting large-scale surveillance operations of them and their contacts. Even members of the Fascist Party were frequently subjected to this invasion of privacy, often as a result of private grudges being worked out between individual party members or at the whim of the deeply suspicious *Duce*. The head of the police, Arturo Bocchini, reported regularly to Mussolini and the sheer numbers of Italian police inevitably meant a closer level of scrutiny of the lives of ordinary citizens than had been the case in pre-fascist Italy. On the other hand, security did remain the responsibility of the state and was not in the hands of zealots from the Fascist Party, thus avoiding many of the excesses perpetrated in Nazi Germany.

Punishments
The punishments inflicted on 'undesirables' were not savage compared to those of other twentieth-century dictatorships.

- There were very few death sentences passed by the courts. More serious offenders were usually placed in penal settlements on one of Italy's islands where life was harsh rather than savagely punitive, although some prisoners were subjected to interrogation that involved torture.
- Lesser offenders, following a pre-fascist tradition, the *Confino*, were banished to specifically named isolated villages, which they were not allowed to leave (see Carlo Levi's compelling novel about life in 'the south', *Christ Stopped at Eboli*, 1982).

> ## KEY TERM
>
> **OVRA** Set up in 1926, *OVRA* was a police force responsible to the fascist leadership. However, it was placed under the control of the leader of the traditional police, Arturo Bocchini.

- As the Fascist Party became more respectable and the local *squadristi* leaders were tamed, so the rough and ready meting out of informal punishments, beatings or forced drinking of great quantities of castor oil, became less common simply because they were less necessary.

In short, the regime's oppression was at a petty level that could often be evaded by quiet acceptance and obedience. For much of the period of fascist rule there was no systematic brutality on the scale practised by the Nazis in Germany or by Stalin's Soviet Union.

Racial persecution

Unlike the Nazis, Italian fascists did not, before 1937, identify a lesser race of state enemies who had first to be brutally cowed into submission, then outlawed from society. Italian Jews were few and continued for many years to live undisturbed in Mussolini's Italy. The **persecution of Jews in Italy** began only in 1938 and was a direct result of the closer ties with Hitler's Germany. The *Duce* felt that he had to show solidarity with his ally.

After 1940, events took on a more sinister tone. Even then Italy's Jews were not systematically pursued: by 1945 perhaps 10,000 out of the 75,000 who remained in the country in 1940 had been killed. This appalling example of racial persecution needs to be set against the deaths of perhaps 60,000 out of 70,000 Jews in Austria or in German-occupied Greece or Yugoslavia. The Italian regime came to racist brutality slowly and with limited zeal. To Italy's credit there were also many who opposed the racist policies and took enormous risks to help Jews avoid their intended fate. The introduction of racist policies lost the fascist regime much support and brought the Catholic Church into open opposition to the state for the first time since the Lateran Pacts of 1929.

CONCLUSIONS

The corporate state was always more important politically and in terms of state propaganda than for anything it achieved economically. Economic policy and the efficiency of the fascist economy can often be analysed separately from corporate ideas and structures, but even then it is important to separate fascist propaganda claims from the more limited actual economic performance.

Judgements on how popular and oppressive the fascist regime was are inevitably inter-related. In both respects the situation changed significantly after 1936 as Mussolini attempted to impose a more strictly fascist regime on the country while at the same time embarking on more perilous foreign policy initiatives.

KEY THEME

Persecution of Jews in Italy from 1938–40 Some 5000 Jews left the country; others lost their jobs, particularly in education; Jewish businesses were closed down; mixed marriages forbidden; and Jewish children were removed from state schools.

SECTION 7

Analysing Italian foreign policy, 1935–40

INTRODUCTION

There is an outline account of Italian foreign policy from Mussolini becoming prime minister in 1922 to Italy entering the Second World war in 1940 in AS Chapter 7. It first examines foreign policy in what has been described as 'the quiet period' through to the 1935 Stresa Conferenc, then provides a factual account of the more adventurous policy pursued after 1935. The rest of this section is based on that AS account.

From 1935 to 1940 Europe moved with breathtaking speed from apparent international stability to the outbreak of the Second World War in 1939. The few weeks from spring 1940 onwards saw the German military domination of continental western Europe.

KEY POINTS

Analysis of Italian foreign policy in this crowded period needs to include examination of the following.

- **The Stresa Front.** In 1935, Mussolini's played an important part in achieving stability by helping to create the anti-German Stresa Front. This followed his blocking of German ambitions to take over Austria in 1934.
- **The Ethiopian war, 1935–6.** Intended to create an Italian empire in Africa. Victory was achieved only at the expense of condemnation by the League of Nations and strained relations with Britain and France.
- **The Spanish Civil War, 1936–9.** Here, Italy and Germany provided substantial help to the right-wing forces. This further strained relations with Britain and France, and drew Italy closer to Germany.
- **The Pact of Steel, 1939.** This was the full-blown military alliance with Germany, which developed from the cool relations of 1935 to taking Italy into the Second World War on the German side in 1940.
- **The start of the Second World War.** Italy's dilemma on whether or not to join in 1939 and its, eventually fatal, resolution in 1940.

HISTORICAL INTERPRETATIONS

One of the most significant of recent analyses of Italian foreign policy in the 1930s is by Philip Morgan in *Italian Fascism* (1995) where, in two chapters, he examines the important interaction between domestic and foreign policies. The most useful full account of Italy's imperial ventures in Africa is in *Mussolini's Roman Empire* (1976), by Denis Mack-Smith. The same writer's *Mussolini* (1982) examines foreign policy from 1935 to 1940 in four equally readable chapters. One great strength of this account is the way in which Mussolini's dwindling options in foreign policy are clearly pointed out. Any history student would benefit greatly from taking the time to read selectively in these two works by Mack-Smith. The writings of the Italian historian Renzo de Felice (*Fascism*, 1977) on Mussolini's conduct of foreign policy have proved controversial. He argues that, in 1939, Mussolini was still trying to find a role as a mediator between Germany and its enemies and that, even in 1940, he was only reluctantly pushed into the war by Italian public opinion. Few accept this analysis but Richard Lamb's *Mussolini and the British* (1997), examining relations between Mussolini and the British government, argues that, in August and September 1939, Mussolini genuinely strove to prevent the outbreak of the Second World War and was rebuffed by the British, just as he had been when trying to restore good relations after the Ethiopian war. Lamb's is a major piece of revisionist writing on the conduct of both Italian and British foreign policy in a critical decade. Morgan (see above) has argued persuasively that de Felice was wrong to portray Mussolini as 'a normal player on the international stage in the late 1930s' when in fact he was committed to the German alliance as the best means of promoting fascism's international aspirations. Until and unless opinion among historians is swayed by Lamb's view or a compromise emerges, then this remains the generally accepted view of Mussolini's role.

WHAT FACTORS INFLUENCED FASCIST FOREIGN POLICY?

Three main factors influencing the conduct of Italian foreign policy were:

- traditional national interests, including the maintenance of a secure northern frontier, the pursuit of an empire in Africa, maintaining a significant presence in the Mediterranean, a desire to expand Italian influence into the Balkans;
- Mussolini's central role in all matters of foreign policy;
- fascist theory on the nature and purpose of the state.

National interests
These were pursued in a haphazard fashion.

- The traditional protection offered to Austria was abandoned in order to further the German connection. After permitting the Anschluss, the security of Italy's frontier with the enlarged Germany depended on continued good relations with Hitler.
- On the other hand, Italy's historical interest in north-east Africa was pursued with a new energy that led to the Ethiopian war. Turning the Mediterranean into an Italian lake provided an effective piece of propaganda, and may well have been one reason for interfering in the Spanish Civil War, but neither the navy nor the air force were ready to make it a reality, nor was any strategic planning devoted to the problem of the powerful British naval presence at Suez, Malta and Gibraltar.

Mussolini's role

Foreign policy was important for fascists. Their central philosophy related to making the nation great and their domestic policies, especially those related to the military and the economy, were in this respect always subordinate to the requirements of their foreign policy. An important qualification to any analysis of fascist foreign policy is that, even more than domestic policy, it was subject to the erratic whims of the *Duce*. Here as elsewhere he was sometimes a master at taking advantage of opportunities provided by others, or by circumstances, but decidedly weak at constructing rational plans devised to achieve sensible objectives.

Mussolini's isolation from criticism, or even alternative opinion, made him prone to miscalculation and more inclined to believe his own propaganda and to accept at face value the claims put out as to his superior personal qualities and indeed his infallibility. In fact, he was far too easily flattered in international matters by the attention Hitler paid him, and was too happy making dramatic gestures and taking action for its own sake, to be at all adept at the careful diplomacy required for the conduct of foreign policy in a period of mounting tension. There is, however, no doubt that he was the key figure in devising and conducting Italian policy. For many years he held the post of foreign minister and then, in the late 1930s, his son-in-law Ciano was merely a figurehead as foreign minister, carrying out the *Duce's* orders. His undisputed control of foreign policy matters is nicely illustrated by his embarking on the risky war in Ethiopia against the advice of his civil servants and his generals, and in the face of the king's grave doubts about its wisdom.

Fascist theory

Fascism provided Mussolini with a set of values that, however inconsistently, he sought to further in his conduct of foreign policy. Above all, fascism valued strength, in men and in nations. It embraced the cult of action rather than thought. Twinned with the idea of national greatness, the outcome was likely to be aggression and eventually almost certain war. Many aspects of domestic policy – autarky, rearmament, the

Battle for Births, the cult of the great leader – were intended to prepare Italy and the Italian people for an adventurous, risky and violent foreign policy. Martin Clark (in *Modern Italy*, 1996) has described fascist Italy as a bellicose society, a society looking for war: Mussolini's conduct of foreign policy was not solely based on personal whims but also reflected that fascist priority. Foreign policy objectives arose from the nature of fascist society.

WHY WAS IMPERIAL EXPANSION SO IMPORTANT TO MUSSOLINI?

In his socialist phase before 1914, Mussolini was a pacifist and opposed the wresting of Libya from Turkish control. He later changed his mind and came to support Italy's entry into the First World War and, from 1922, his government pursued a ruthless policy of suppression of local rebellions in Libya. Many of the fascists who joined the movement after 1922, notably the bloc entry by the nationalists, were old-fashioned right-wing imperialists and this altered fascist views on foreign policy. Even the early fascists had emphasised the need to assert Italy's international interests; the 'betrayal' of the country by its allies in the Versailles Peace Treaty of 1919 was an important theme in fascism's early days.

Italian greatness

In the 1930s, with the regime fully in control at home, fascist theory, Mussolini's vanity and domestic propaganda all called for an international adventure that would underline Italian greatness. In Europe, French and British sensitivities about preserving the boundaries agreed at the Paris Peace Conference meant that Mussolini's freedom of action was limited. Even attacks on weaker Balkans neighbours were likely to draw in the major powers, for neither Britain nor France would be prepared to see their own predominance in the Mediterranean area threatened. There was also a strong feeling in the Italian foreign ministry that expansion should instead occur in Africa. It was not feasible to expand Italy's hard-won gains in Libya, pinned as they were between French-controlled Tunisia and British-dominated Egypt, but the independent kingdom of Ethiopia in north-east Africa presented a better prospect. The Italian colonies Eritrea and Somaliland provided bases from which to mount a war of conquest against Ethiopia – the last independent African state – and there was a general European acceptance that the region, poor and undeveloped as it was, fell within Italy's sphere of influence.

Establishing an Italian presence in Africa would also strengthen one of the increasingly important aspects of fascist propaganda, which, in the 1930s, sought to stress the links between fascist Italy and the glories of the ancient Roman Empire. An important part of this myth was the emphasis placed on the cult of the *Duce* as the great leader, which was regularly set in an imperial context, with Mussolini likened to the great Roman leaders of the past. The image Italian propaganda created of Mussolini – always right, a man of action leading Italy to greatness – had to be sustained by international triumphs. Mussolini's own vanity and belief in his own propaganda led him in the same direction.

WHY DID ITALY'S CONQUEST OF ETHIOPIA AFFECT EUROPEAN INTERNATIONAL RELATIONS?

Mussolini expected that there might be international protests about the Italian attack on Ethiopia, but he convinced himself that there would be no long-term effects on Italy's international standing. In particular, he believed that, while the British and French might feel compelled to protest publicly at the attack, they would privately accept the Italian occupation of the country. He had several reasons for believing this.

- The other European powers accepted that the region (the Horn of Africa) fell within the Italian zone of influence in Africa.
- The killing of Italian soldiers on Ethiopia's border and the deplorable anarchy, including mass slavery, within the country could be used to justify the Italian action as a civilising mission, as many Catholic Church leaders in his own country were content to describe it.
- The other major nations of Europe had more serious matters with which to concern themselves, notably the new aggressive tone coming from the Nazi regime in Germany, still potentially the most powerful European state.
- At the Stresa Conference in 1935, where Britain, France and Italy presented a joint front against German attempts to alter international agreements made at Versailles, Mussolini understood that France and Britain, themselves with vast African empires, informally accepted Italy's right to take action against Ethiopia.

Sanctions by Britain and France

Mussolini may well have deluded himself about British and French attitudes but these two countries were, in any case, not free simply to look the other way while the Italian attack proceeded. Ethiopia was a member of the League of Nations and, as such, had the right to appeal to it for protection. Britain and France were the two leading members of the 50-strong League and would have to take some action on its behalf or see the organisation crumble.

Mussolini also seriously underestimated the impact public opinion could have on the actions of the democracies. It was, for example, anti-Italian public opinion in Britain that prevented the government there trying to sponsor a compromise deal that would have given Mussolini half of

Ethiopia and left Haile Selassie as ruler of the rest. For these two reasons, the British and French governments felt compelled to try to protect Ethiopia and resorted to economic sanctions against the Italian aggressor in order to force it to abandon its attack.

Move to alliance with Germany

The fact that the two governments appeared to act reluctantly, and certainly ineffectively, was irrelevant to the outcome. Sanctions first united the previously hesitant Italian people behind their government and then drove a wedge between Italy and these two leading members of the League of Nations. Mussolini never forgave Britain and France for what he saw as their hypocritical opposition to Italy acquiring an African empire. Sanctions also forced Italy to look elsewhere for war supplies and raw materials. Germany's willingness to help was the beginning of the closer links between the two countries that dominated international relations in the course of the next five years.

Italy's switch – from co-operating with Britain and France over European matters to moving into the orbit of Nazi Germany – constituted the most important single diplomatic event of the 1930s. Although it was triggered by Italy's attack on Ethiopia, and consolidated by joint Italian–German action in the Spanish Civil War, it reflected the fact that Mussolini had always resented French dominance in the Mediterranean region. After 1935, he increasingly felt free to break away from French domination of his foreign policy. It was the loss of much British goodwill that was Italy's more serious loss; most historians have taken the view that Mussolini saw this as more than compensated for by Italy's growing attachment to a powerful Germany (but see page 213 for a recent challenge to this view).

WHY WAS ITALY DRAWN INTO THE GERMAN ALLIANCE FROM 1935 TO 1939?

The closer relations between Italy and Germany were the most important diplomatic development of these years; its various stages are listed in AS Chapter 7. The initial momentum came as a consequence of the Ethiopian war and also related to Mussolini's personal domination of all aspects of Italian foreign policy The Ethiopian adventure meant that Italy made enemies of France and Britain. Relations with France had frequently been strained and the significant change was that Britain's attitude to fascist Italy now became distinctly more suspicious. Until this point, Mussolini had had a good press and influential admirers in Britain but the attack on Ethiopia and the defiance of the League undermined this. He did not fully recognise this change in Britain's position and, confident in Italian strength, was probably not unduly concerned by it.

Mussolini's ambitions

With Italy's empire in Africa secured, Mussolini now consciously took Italy into closer alliance with Nazi Germany, a revolution in terms of foreign policy but one that made a great deal of sense in terms of the *Duce's* continuing dream of making Italy the dominant power in the Mediterranean area. This could only be achieved at the expense of France and, except in Mussolini's wilder military fantasies, could not be achieved by Italy acting alone. German power and German ambitions, tying up French resources on its northern frontier, became central to Italian ambitions. Hitler was quick to flatter Mussolini into becoming an equal partner in an enterprise that would in theory leave Germany dominant in northern and eastern Europe and Italy free to pursue its ambitions in the south. Italy drew closer to Germany because of Mussolini's ambitions for Italian greatness which, because of his unquestioned domination of foreign policy, became Italian government policy. Although in the broad sweep of those ambitions the German alliance made much sense the detailed planning to implement them was never undertaken.

Mussolini's lack of reality

There was no consequent attempt to reassess Italy's strategic role in this new diplomatic situation. In particular, the significance of British naval domination of the Mediterranean from its bases at Gibraltar, Malta and Suez was never acknowledged – almost certainly because Mussolini had accepted totally the advice of his admirals that, in the event of war, the Italian navy would easily drive the British out of the Mediterranean and turn it into an Italian lake. In practice, the switch of alliance placed mainland Italy at the mercy of the British navy. Only sweeping German victories early in any war could alter that. Mussolini did not appreciate this and none of his ministers or foreign office staff were in a position to make him do so. If he thought about the possibility of Italy being involved in a European war it was to reflect on the national and personal glory that such a dramatic outcome would involve. It was automatically assumed that, in any war between the fascist nations and the feeble democracies, Italy would swiftly emerge victorious. As a result, little or no thought was given to how the war should be fought and supplied.

These strategic miscalculations rested on a flawed political analysis of Britain's likely role. Mussolini was badly served by the Italian embassy in London, which got into the habit of feeding him views and information that he would find acceptable. In particular, he never appreciated how much the mood in Britain changed after the Munich sell-out of Czechoslovakia. He met British prime minister Neville Chamberlain at Munich and later entertained him on an official visit to Rome but formed a poor opinion of him as an essentially weak man. In the late 1930s, he developed a searing contempt for the democracies and simply assumed that they would never stand firm against the fascist powers.

One reason why Italy accepted the onerous commitments of the Pact of Steel was that the military realities were never faced. The seriousness of Hitler's intentions was deliberately hidden from Mussolini who, in 1939, was scarcely informed of German plans to occupy the rest of Czechoslovakia and to attack Poland, much less for Germany to sign a controversial military pact with the Soviet Union. Mussolini assumed that fascist powers would not be involved in a major European war before 1943 and that victory would swiftly follow. He also deluded himself that he still had an independent role to play, mediating between the other powers (now read again page 213). Italy drifted into the German alliance at the whim of Mussolini who underestimated German intentions and over-valued Italy's military capacity.

It is to Mussolini's credit that, in September 1939, he allowed reality to intrude and was persuaded not to get involved in Hitler's war. However, the scale of the German advance by June 1940 made him realise that, if he stood aside any longer, Italy could lose its best chance of becoming the major power in southern Europe.

HOW WERE ITALIAN FOREIGN AND DOMESTIC POLICIES RELATED?

Italian foreign policy from 1935 was aggressive, expansionist, ready to risk military action: all in order to make Italy a great nation. All this was part of the appeal of fascism from the start and was, arguably, its dominant strand by the time Mussolini achieved dictatorial powers in the late 1920s. His conduct of foreign policy in the 1930s was a direct extension of what fascists had advocated since the early days of the movement. It had its inspiration as far back as D'Annunzio's seizure of Fiume, cutting through the cowardice and the hesitations of liberal politicians in order to protect and enhance the nation's overriding interests.

The central purpose of fascist policies within Italy, however ineffectively pursued, was to prepare the nation for its international role – to prepare the Italian people for national greatness.

- The cults of the *Duce* as the all-powerful leader and of Italy as the successor to the Roman Empire, both central to fascist propaganda, created a climate in which the Italian people were ready to accept their international destiny as a great nation.
- The stage-managed reception of foreign-policy triumphs and the presence everywhere of men in uniform achieved a similar psychological effect.

- Fascist social policies, particularly those promoting physical fitness and military values like loyalty and discipline, were intended to create a nation of men fit to fight for Italy.
- The Battle for Births was directly promoted as necessary for military and imperial purposes.
- Economic policies, protecting heavy industry as the basis for military might, and all the policies unrealistically geared towards making Italy self-sufficient in food and raw materials, were intended to create an economy ready for war.
- The closer ties with Germany in turn led to growing oppression at home, including the introduction of racist policies attacking the Jews.

The foreign policies of the other great inter-war dictatorships, the Soviet Union and Nazi Germany, often stemmed from their pursuit of particular domestic policies. This was not the case with Italy where foreign policy goals dictated much of government domestic policy. The tragedy was that the foreign policy objectives were ill considered and the domestic policies operated largely at the level of propaganda.

HOW SUCCESSFUL WAS MUSSOLINI'S FOREIGN POLICY?

Judged by his own criteria, how effectively did Mussolini perform with regard to foreign policy? A simplified series of verdicts, covering the major foreign policy issues, might read as follows.

Austria
His early robust defence of Italy's northern frontier was surrendered to secure closer relations with Germany. In practice, this did not lead to any direct attack on Italian interests but concern about what an all-powerful Germany might do to take over the German-speaking areas of Italy was one factor (among many) that committed Mussolini to entering the Second World War in 1940.

The Ethiopian war
This was arguably a major triumph. He went ahead to victory despite the doubts of his advisers and correctly calculated that international pressure would not prevent a successful outcome. However, the new empire in Africa was not a success, except in propaganda terms, for the country was a source of expense and tied up military resources. Its conquest also led to the breach with Britain and France, limiting Italy's foreign policy options and driving it towards alliance with Germany. Having exaggerated the difficulties faced in Ethiopia, Mussolini from this point on deluded himself about Italy's ability to wage war and about the fighting qualities of the Italian armed forces. There was a direct line between the grossly exaggerated triumph in Ethiopia and the humiliating military disasters of the Second World War.

The Spanish Civil War

Italian intervention was based on a sensible wish to have a friendly right-wing regime at the western end of the Mediterranean rather than a communist one. The extent of the commitment was a mistake because, when added to the continuing occupation of Ethiopia, it proved a strain on the Italian economy and its military. Germany didn't become so heavily involved and was happy to see Italy entangled there, thus unable to take too close an interest in German policies. The outcome of the Spanish Civil War was very disappointing: the new fascist regime installed in Spain did nothing to advance Italy's Mediterranean ambitions by providing naval bases and refused to become involved in the Second World War.

Relations with Germany

Mussolini allowed himself to be flattered by Hitler and was too easily impressed by German military might. He soon became the junior partner in the alliance, ignored at crucial moments by Hitler. Closer relations with Germany lost Mussolini much popularity at home and closed down Italy's foreign policy options. The hastily constructed Pact of Steel was his biggest mistake and Italy was wise to ignore its commitments under the pact in September 1939. The German connection ended in disaster and, arguably, continued neutrality would have served Italy best. However, given France's military situation in June 1940 and Mussolini's foreign policy objectives, it is difficult to criticise his decision to enter the war at that point. In *Fascism: An Informal Introduction* (1977), the Italian historian Renzo de Felice argues that, even in 1940, Mussolini was hesitant about entering the war but was pushed into it by the weight of Italian public opinion impressed by German military victories. No other historians have taken this line. More typical is Martin Clark (*Modern Italy*, 1996): 'Mussolini finally decided to join the war ... This time there were no enthusiastic crowds shouting for war, as in June 1915; but there was none shouting for peace either. The king, Ciano, and the leading generals were all worried by the prospects, but they were all helpless once Germany seemed victorious.' For Clark it was Mussolini's war.

Relations with France

Mussolini's dreams of Italian greatness meant that French interests around the Mediterranean would have to be confronted. It is difficult to challenge this assessment but Mussolini's anti-French bombast and wild territorial claims simply helped to unite the divided French nation in opposition to Italian pretensions. His tactics were inept.

Relations with Britain

Mussolini's attack on Ethiopia lost him much of the goodwill that he had enjoyed in important right-wing British circles. This was probably inevitable, but he seriously underestimated the more determined mood that came about in Britain after Munich. This led to fatal miscalculations as to how Britain would respond to threats from Germany and then, in

1940, to an equally serious if understandable miscalculation as to the relative military capacity of the two countries.

The domestic impact

Italians were at first distinctly lukewarm about the Ethiopian war but, by its end and thanks only partly to effective propaganda, the *Duce* was at the peak of his popularity. The closer ties with Germany and their effect on internal policy as well as the growing threat of involvement in another European war quickly changed the public mood, which, from the proclamation of the Axis in 1936, became more critical of the regime.

The 1939–40 dilemma

In September 1939, Mussolini was reluctant to stay out of the war, but allowed himself to be persuaded by his ministers and his generals that Italy was not able to take part. He was also annoyed by Hitler's failure to keep him informed on German policy, including the attack on Poland. The decision was almost certainly in Italy's best interest and, when it was reversed in June 1940, conditions were much more favourable for easy Italian gains. Eventually, Mussolini miscalculated the final outcome of the war but, noting the military situation in June 1940, that is perhaps not surprising. Even at that point, however, Mussolini seriously underestimated Britain's capacity to maintain a military presence in the Mediterranean, despite appalling problems elsewhere. He was also wildly optimistic about Italy's ability to counter British naval power in the event of war. It was, for example, this optimism based on the belief that the war would be a short one, which allowed him to set aside the inconvenient fact that a major part of the Italian army was trapped in Ethiopia, well away from the main theatre of war.

Defeat in war

A rational assessment of the military situation in Europe in June 1940 would have had to conclude that Mussolini had entered the war just in time to share in the winning side's spoils of victory. Equally, for him to have kept Italy neutral at that point would have been to deny all that the fascist regime stood for. Once involved in the war, Italian military weaknesses were soon exposed and, equally, during the war Mussolini was responsible for major strategic mistakes, notably an inept attack on Greece and the despatch of large numbers of Italian troops to the Russian front. These matters are considered in AS Chapter 8.

CONCLUSIONS

Mussolini's views on foreign policy rested too much on fascist theories of what constituted national greatness and exaggerated Italy's capacity to achieve this. In his conduct of foreign policy he spent too little time on strategic planning, preferring to leave too much to his over-valued intuition. He knew too little about international matters and failed to remedy his ignorance, preferring to rely on his own propaganda. Three of his miscalculations stand out.

- From the end of the Ethiopian campaign, Mussolini exaggerated ideas of Italy's military capacity.
- He persisted too blindly in the notion of having to confront France.
- He underestimated Britain's eventual willingness and capacity to stand up to Hitler.

A2 ASSESSMENT

INTRODUCTION

A2 examination essays will rely on the same range of information as the AS essays and you will need to make use of the material in the AS part of this book in constructing your answers. It will also be useful to remind yourself of the advice on AS essay writing and examination techniques given at the end of the AS part.

A2 essays are likely to be more open-ended than those at AS level. You will be given more opportunity to present your own opinions on the causes and the consequences of major events. This implies that you will also have to make decisions about what arguments and historical information are relevant in constructing your answer. This was, of course, necessary at AS level and you will simply be carrying forward and developing the skills that stood you in good stead at that level.

To obtain high marks in A2 examination essays you will be expected to do the following.

- Analyse throughout the essay. You will need to plan a line of argument before you start to write the essay. This is not easily done because of the very limited time allowed in examinations. It is essential that you study the wording of A2 essays and that you practice drawing up essay plans, based on historical argument, long before the examination.
- Write and plan in paragraphs. Let each paragraph develop one major point of your analysis. Try to state what that point is at the start of the paragraph. Then use the rest of the paragraph to back it up with historical evidence. You are not using the evidence to tell a story but to support an analytical point. There is a clear difference between a narrative answer (telling the story) and an analytical one (putting forward a reasoned argument in response to the question). In terms of exam grades the difference is that between a minimum pass grade and, depending on the quality of analysis, the very highest grade available. You cannot do well in history examinations at A2 level unless you respond directly to the question presented. If you are doing this effectively you will just not have time to describe or narrate what happened.

The great advantage of having a paragraph structure for your essay is that, at the beginning of each paragraph you can ask yourself whether you are still analysing (and therefore directly answering the question set) or whether you have begun to break off into describing what happened.

Start each paragraph with words that will lead on to analysis, for example:
- The most important reason is …
- Another key point is …
- One should argue that …
- Essentially … .

Beware of starting paragraphs in ways that could quickly lead to a narrative style of writing, for example:
- In 1922 …
- This was followed by …
- Before one can answer this question it is necessary to know … .

- **Back up your argument by using well-selected evidence.** The evidence you select must be relevant to the point you are trying to make. You do not need, and will not have time, to elaborate at length and may well have to assume that the examiner knows its importance to your argument. At the very least hang on to the idea that the evidence offered should not swamp your argument – or you will be back to writing a purely narrative answer.
- **Make a clear and consistent attempt to reach a judgement.** You must argue throughout the essay. By all means pull your argument together in a final conclusion, but do not let that be the only argument you offer at the end of a descriptive essay. Try to make sure that you write something directly relevant to answering the question in each paragraph.
- **Show evidence of independent thought.** At this level and in the time you have available you do not have to provide original ideas, but do try to show that you have read this and other history books and can adapt the ideas you have met to the terms of the question that the examiners have posed.
- **Use your language skills.** It is essential that you write in paragraphs and that you are grammatically accurate. Get into the habit of structuring your essays in such a way that each new point of your argument means a new paragraph. Take pride in having an extensive vocabulary, particularly of terms frequently used by historians, and use historical terms correctly to strengthen your argument.

ESSAY QUESTIONS

Question 1

How far do you agree that 'prior to 1940, the fascist regime in Italy had little impact on the daily lives of the Italian people'?

Reading

Before answering this question you should read AS Chapter 6 (pages 84–96) and the relevant parts of A2 Sections 4 and 6 in this book.

How to answer this question

This question is not about Mussolini and state politics but about the lives of ordinary Italians. The most straightforward way to answer it is to form a preliminary judgement as to the line you wish to take. This makes planning your essay much easier. Few of us, in exam conditions, are capable of writing an essay that presents points on each side and then, like the writer of detective stories, reveals the truth at the end. It is much easier to develop a theme from the start. You could still indicate your reservations at the end of the essay.

With this essay one approach would be to say that although at first sight there is some truth in this claim it is far from satisfactory. You could then have one paragraph establishing how unaffected life was in some ways. Religion is one obvious continuity; daily working life in town and country another; the public authorities who ran the communities in which Italians lived were little changed – e.g. the police force was the same; the same landed aristocracy controlled the south of the country.

But then in several paragraphs *argue* that in other important ways life was sharply affected. These could be as follows.

- **Political**: the presence of the Fascist Militia and the Fascist Party everywhere; the need to join if you were ambitious; the lure of being in uniform and parading; the loss of freedom; state control of information; the fate of those who still spoke out against the regime.
- **Economic**: the fascist syndicates replacing socialist unions but failing to protect workers' standards of living; the fall in living standards was a major effect of fascism with its policy of autarky pushing up prices and heavy military expenditure.
- **Social**: fascist impact on education and on the young via youth clubs; effects of fascism on women, women's place in the home, women's organisations.
- **After 1936**: the more determined attempts to create a fascist society after 1936; the start of racist persecutions; even civilians in uniforms; military celebrations; and constant propaganda.

If your judgement is that life was significantly different under fascism, then you can build up a case (as opposed simply to describing) on these lines. Some of you may well think that I am over-stating the case and want to stress instead the failure of the regime to alter people's lives – the Battle for Births is an excellent example; the failure to stop migration from country to town is another. Most of us could work out an argument that the regime would have liked to have done much more to create committed fascists of all Italians but was let down by inconsistent policies and government inefficiency.

Debate
Take the essay title on page 225 and debate the issues, formally or informally, that it raises. Make a group list of the things in the 'daily lives of Italian people' under fascism that could be made relevant in your answer. Do not imagine you could ever work them all into an examination essay, so select the most useful ones for that purpose. Now go on to consider what your debate on Question 1 has provided to help with an answer to the commonly set examination Question 2 that follows.

Question 2

> How valid is it to describe Italy in the 1930s as 'a totalitarian state'?

Reading
Before attempting this question read A2 Section 4, pages 178–87 and especially study the definition of 'totalitarian' provided there. According to this definition, totalitarian governments:

- permit no rival loyalties or parties;
- demand total submission of individual citizens to the requirements of the state.

How to answer this question
A simple but effective approach would be to state these two different totalitarian concepts and take each in turn in the context of Italy in the 1930s.

A reading of AS Chapter 3, pages 41–61 and A2 Section 4 might suggest that, before the end of the 1920s, Mussolini had indeed created a political structure that very largely met the first of these definitions and also give you useful evidence to back up this opinion. The survival of the monarchy and the loyalty of the armed forces to it do however need to be noted. You might well feel less certain about how far the second definition applies to 1930s Italy. One way forward would be to argue that this was what Mussolini wanted – a state in which all Italians became true fascists – and point to some of the ways in which he attempted to bring this about. In the end, though, it might be sensible to explain how Mussolini's dream never became reality, even with the more radical policies pursued after 1936. Then give reasons why this was the case:

- Mussolini's weaknesses as leader;
- the continued survival of the Catholic Church;
- the Italian tradition of weak government and inefficient administration.

Question 3

For what reasons and by what stages did Italy move from enmity to military alliance with Nazi Germany?

Reading
Before answering this question you should read the relevant parts of AS Chapter 7 and A2 Section 7.

How to answer this question
This is a two-part question and identifying the stages chronologically could be a sensible way to start:

- hostility between the two countries because of Austria and at the Stresa Conference;
- 1935–6: the Ethiopian war led to coolness with France and Britain over sanctions, whereas Germany provided supplies;
- 1936–9: in the Spanish Civil War Italy and Germany fought on the same side;
- 1937: Italy joined the Anti-Comintern Pact; Mussolini's idea of 'the Axis';
- 1939: the Pact of Steel.

In explaining why the change occurred it will be important to stress Mussolini's personal control of foreign policy. His whims make up a powerful reason. Imperial ambitions (Ethiopia), the desire to expand fascism (Spain), the desire to turn the Mediterranean into an Italian lake, his growing fascination with Hitler and with German military might, linked to his desire for military glory, are all relevant. It is a vast question and will need careful planning. You should consider linking the stages to Mussolini's changing foreign policy ambitions rather than just producing a chronological list.

Question 4

How far do you agree that in the 1930s Italy was a country preparing for war?

How to answer this question
The important point about this essay is that you must precisely indicate 'how far' you agree.

Your answer might take this form.

- 'In some ways this claim seems convincing … ' Then give evidence that supports this view: the policy of autarky; uniforms everywhere; propaganda and vast crowds for all the victories claimed in Ethiopia and Spain; Mussolini's warlike speeches; his closer relations with Germany, especially the Pact of Steel – all getting the country psychologically ready for war.

- 'But in practical terms this claim is arguably absurd … ' Then point out the failure to address known military weaknesses leading to Italy not being able to join Hitler in 1939: no joint military planning with Germany; no strategic plans on how to fight a possible war; constant changes in the direction of policy (for example, in the Balkans Yugoslavia was seen as the enemy and yet Mussolini first attacked Albania and then Greece (1940)); no international spy network built up to keep an eye on future enemies or to collect information on public opinion in other countries. The people were not warlike: at first the Ethiopian war was unpopular; the economy was never put on a war footing; neither autarky nor the Battle for Births, both intended to make Italy strong in war, were ever successfully pursued. The preparation was almost entirely words.

- (Conclusion) 'If it was a society preparing for war then it was all very inefficiently done. Too much depended on Mussolini's whims for any continuity of policy. Even after Munich and the Pact of Steel he believed he could act as mediator between Germany and the other powers. In any case if there was a war he was convinced that, thanks to fascist superiority, it would be a very short one – so Italian preparations were laughable. Overall there is very little to agree with in this claim.'

This may strike many students as too strong an attack on the proposition but it does provide a direct answer to 'How far do you agree … ? Whatever verdict you reach, make sure that you answer the question as directly as this.

BIBLIOGRAPHY

The books listed in the first section are those considered to be particularly valuable to, or have been written specifically for, students working at AS and A2 levels. Books in the further reading section are probably better used selectively on particular topics of interest. Ambitious students at both levels are urged to make use of them in this way.

AS AND A2 BOOKS

M. Blinkhorn *Mussolini and Fascist Italy*, 2nd edn (Routledge, 1994)
M. Clark *Modern Italy 1871–1995* (Longman, 1996)
P. Morgan *Italian Fascism 1919–45* (Macmillan, 1995)
R. Pearce *Fascism and Nazism* (Hodder & Stoughton, 1997)
M. Robson *Italy: Liberalism and Fascism 1870–1945* (Hodder & Stoughton, 2000)
J. Whittam *Fascist Italy* (Manchester UP, 1995)

FURTHER READING

M. Blinkhorn *Fascism and the Right in Europe 1919–45* (Longman, 2000)
M. Blinkhorn (ed.) *Fascists and Conservatives: The Radical Right and the Establishment in Twentieth-century Europe* (Unwin Hyman, 1990)
C. Cipolla (see R. Ricossa)
R. Collier *Duce: The Rise and Fall of Benito Mussolini* (Collins, 1971)
R. Eatwell *Fascism: A History* (Arrow Books, 1996)
R. de Felice *Fascism: An Informal Introduction to its Theory and Practice* (Transaction Books, New Brunswick USA, 1977)
D. Forgacs *Rethinking Italian Fascism* (Lawrence & Wishart, 1986)
M. Gallo *Mussolini's Italy* (Macmillan,1973)
G. Gori *Model of Masculinity: Mussolini, the New Italian of the Fascist Era* in J.A. Mangan (ed.) *Superman Supreme: Fascist Body as Political* (Frank Cass, 2000)
H. Hearder *Italy: A Short History* (Cambridge UP, 1990)
E. Hobsbawm *Age of Extremes* (Michael Joseph, 1994)
R. King *The Industrial Geography of Italy* (Croom Helm, 1985)
M. Knox *Mussolini Unleashed 1939–41* (Cambridge UP, 1982)
R. Lamb *Mussolini and the British* (John Murray, 1997)
A. Lyttelton *The Seizure of Power: Fascism in Italy 1919–29* (Weidenfeld & Nicolson, 1973)

D. Mack-Smith *Italy: A Modern History* (Longman, 1969)

D. Mack-Smith *Mussolini's Roman Empire,* (Longman, 1976)

D. Mack-Smith *Mussolini* (Weidenfeld & Nicolson, 1982)

D. Mack-Smith *Italy and its Monarchy* (Yale UP, 1989)

P. McCarthy *Italy Since 1945* (Oxford UP, 2000)

C. Petrie *Mussolini* (Holme Press, 1931)

S.G. Payne *A History of Fascism 1914–45* (UCL Press, 1995)

J. Pollard *The Fascist Experience in Italy* (Routledge, 1998)

R. Ricossa *Italy 1920–70,* in C. Cipolla (ed.) *The Fontana Economic History of Europe, vol. 6, Contemporary Economies part 1* (Fontana, 1973)

G. Salvemini *The Origins of Fascism in Italy,* first published 1942 (Harper & Row, 1973)

G. Salvemini *The Fascist Dictatorship in Italy,* first published 1928 (Jonathan Cape, 1928)

C. Seton-Watson *Italy from Liberalism to Fascism* (Methuen, 1967)

E.R. Tannenbaum *Fascism in Italy: Society and Culture 1922–45* (Allen Lane, 1973)

D. Williamson *Mussolini: From Socialist to Fascist* (Hodder & Stoughton, 1997)

E. Wiskemann *Fascism in Italy* (Macmillan, 1972)

SOURCE BOOKS

R. Griffin (ed.) *Fascism* (Oxford UP, 1995)

S.W. Halperin *Mussolini and Italian Fascism* (Harper Torch, 1964)

W. Laqueur (ed.) *Fascism: A Reader's Guide* (Penguin, 1979)

FICTION

G. Bassani *The Garden of the Finzi-Continis* (Quartet Books, 1978)

C. Levi *Christ Stopped at Eboli,* written in 1944 (Penguin, 1982)

ARTICLES

The two most useful history periodicals for A level students are *Modern History Review*, which has regular brief articles on examination topics, and *History Today*, which has occasional articles containing relevant valuable historical background material. It is well worth working through back copies to find relevant articles. Recent copies have included:

S. Hood 'Partisan Memories (Italy 1943–4)', *History Today* August 2001

R. Parrish 'Mussolini's Rise to Power', *Modern History Review* April 2000

A. Young 'Mussolini: An Unprincipled Politician?', *Modern History Review* April 2000

WEBSITES

Calling up 'Mussolini' by any of the standard search engines produces an embarrassingly large number of references. Some are clearly irrelevant – for example, the film *Tea with Mussolini* – and others disappointingly thin. The vast majority of articles are undated and the qualifications of the authors are often in doubt. It sometimes seems as though every second American college student has decided to put thoughts on fascism or Mussolini on the Internet. Other sites exist to draw attention to recently published books or to history courses on offer around the world. It is worth persisting, for a time anyway, for the act of searching for information often makes what you do find more useful than if it had been fed to you.

Useful Internet tips
- Use the Internet at an early stage in your studies when all information will be relatively new to you.
- Do not expect many articles at an appropriate A level standard or length, but be grateful for isolated comments that you can use in written work.
- Go to Google Advanced Search – Image Search, which will provide over 2000 images of Mussolini (most of them of the right Mussolini). It is a wonderful way to start your study and also to remind yourself later that you are examining the life of a man who actually existed.
- Do not spend more time online than the information you are finding justifies. In terms of specific AS and A2 work you may well be better off selectively reading parts of books cited in the Bibliography.

INDEX

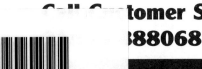